The Fabulous Flemings of Kathmandu

By Grace Nies Fletcher

In My Father's House
Preacher's Kids
No Marriage in Heaven
I Was Born Tomorrow
The Whole World's in His Hand
The Fabulous Flemings of Kathmandu

the
FABULOUS FLEMINGS
of
Kathmandu

THE STORY OF TWO DOCTORS IN NEPAL

by Grace Nies Fletcher

E. P. DUTTON & CO., INC., NEW YORK
1964

Published simultaneously in Canada by
Clarke, Irwin & Company Limited, Toronto and Vancouver

Library of Congress Catalog Card Number: 64-11095

Contents

Contents

List of Illustrations

The Fabulous Flemings of Kathmandu

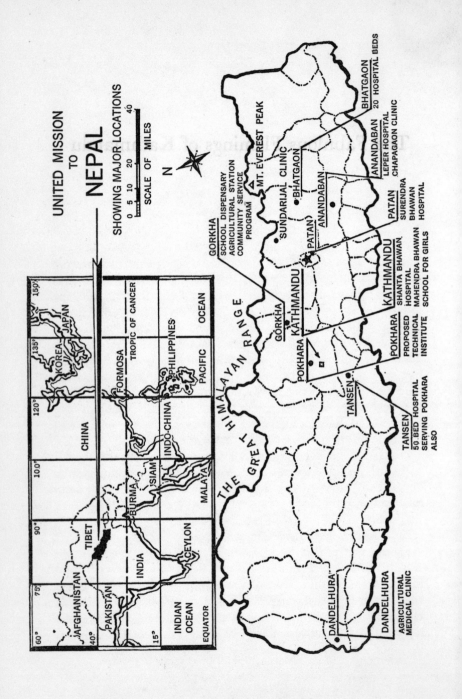

UNITED MISSION
TO
NEPAL

SHOWING MAJOR LOCATIONS

SCALE OF MILES
0 5 10 20 40

N

GORKHA
SCHOOL DISPENSARY
AGRICULTURAL STATION
COMMUNITY SERVICE
PROGRAM

MT. EVEREST PEAK

SUNDARIJAL CLINIC

BHATGAON
20 HOSPITAL BEDS

ANANDABAN
LEPER HOSPITAL
CHAPAGAON CLINIC

PATAN
SURENDRA
BHAWAN
HOSPITAL

KATHMANDU
SHANTA BHAWAN
HOSPITAL
MAHENDRA BHAWAN
SCHOOL FOR GIRLS

POKHARA
PROPOSED
TECHNICAL
INSTITUTE

TANSEN
50 BED HOSPITAL
SERVING POKHARA
ALSO

DANDELHURA
AGRICULTURAL
MEDICAL CLINIC

THE GREAT HIMALAYAN RANGE

GORKHA KATHMANDU BHATGAON
POKHARA PATAN ANANDABAN
TANSEN
DANDELHURA

AFGHANISTAN TIBET CHINA KOREA JAPAN
PAKISTAN 150°
75° 90° 100° 120° 135°
TROPIC OF CANCER
INDIA BURMA SIAM FORMOSA
INDO-CHINA PHILIPPINES
15° MALAYA PACIFIC
CEYLON OCEAN
INDIAN OCEAN
40° EQUATOR
60°

Chapter One

The Silent Samaritans Meet the King

This must be a nightmare! Terror swept over me in breathtaking icy waves as I clawed my way up out of the well of fever and pain into the strange, dimly lit room going round and round; first, the brown marble floor tilting slowly, then the green distempered concrete walls closing in menacingly upon the hard bed where I lay, unable to move my heavy body. Somewhere in the distance a faucet was dripping, dripping, hitting my aching head with hammer strokes, like a medieval torture chamber. I heard voices murmuring something about fever a hundred and three, a blood count of nearly nineteen thousand; there must be a bad infection somewhere. Then, as pain became a sharp sword in my side, I slid down again into the deep well of fear and loneliness.

"I'm cold!" I shouted but my voice came out a thin whimper.

"She has four blankets, a heating pad, and a hot-water bottle, Dr. Bethel," another voice protested. "And I put on her wool bathrobe and sweater!"

"I'm *still* cold!"

"The fever is inside you, Child."

I stared up, startled, into the steady, compassionate, wise brown eyes of Dr. Bethel Fleming, standing there beside my bed, regal in her crown of thick white hair. So this was no dream; I had crossed the Himalayas after all: I really was in Shanta Bhawan Hospital, the House of Peace, in fabulous Kathmandu! I had come to Nepal to find out how these two pioneer doctors, Dr. Bob and

Dr. Bethel Fleming, were living an everyday miracle. Could one actually run a 200-bed modern hospital in 1963 by faith? Why had this Hindu-Buddhist country welcomed these quiet Christians whose only sermons were preached not in words but in deeds, by treating patients on the operating table or in a leper clinic? Last year these Silent Samaritans had given medical aid to 100,000 Nepalese! Started only seven years ago, Shanta Bhawan Hospital alone averaged 250 outpatients a day. I had come to discover their secret of how the West and the East, Christian and Hindu, in mutual respect, could learn from each other.

"But I didn't plan to land here in bed as a patient!" I panted in short gasps, ruefully to Dr. Bethel. "Am I really very sick? What's wrong with me?"

"I don't know yet. Don't worry. The Lord's Plan for you may be different than your own. But you're too ill to be left alone tonight. We must find you a *sati*."

"A . . . a *what?*"

A *sati*, Dr. Bethel explained, was a relative or companion-friend of one's own caste or creed who prepared the patient's meals, because if a Hindu were given rice or water by a Christian, the Hindu would be defiled. A Tibetan Buddhist monk needed special fare, too. The *sati* cooked, ran errands, called the nurse when necessary, usually slept by or under the patient's bed.

"But I don't want anyone sleeping under my bed!" I panicked. When I'm really ill, all I want is to crawl under some dark hedge of forgetfulness, certainly not to have some stranger crouched by my bedside, watching my every breath!

"Very well. The men's ward is right next door. If you want the ward nurse you can ring that bell." Dr. Bethel was too wise to argue with hysteria. When I shivered uncontrollably, she drew up the rose-sprinkled nylon cover she'd taken from her own bed, tucked it comfortably up under my teeth-chattering chin. "That's better. This time of year the wind blows straight down from Chandragiri, from the Mountains of the Moon." Magic words— the Mountains of the Moon! But a long way from my home, and out there beyond, in the icy dark, towered the mighty snows where lived the mysterious "lords of the sky" who were not my gods. And only a few hundred miles away lay more human danger. Mt. Everest, the tallest mountain in the world, had one slope in Nepal and the other in Tibet where lurked the Chinese Red Army. I was 9,000 miles from Boston, Massachusetts, sick and scared. Dr. Bethel read my mind for she said gently, "The Lord is here too, you know. Why don't you surrender your pain to Him and go to sleep?"

And then she was gone. It had been a long time since anyone had spoken to me about the Lord as if He were a member of the family with whom you could talk over your troubles! Not since I'd been a child in my father's house where my preacher dad had invited the Lord to share and bless our breakfast of mush and honey. A parishioner kept bees, so paid his church tithe in honey for the parsonage family. And when you said grace, you would add a silent P.S. for the Lord to help you with your arithmetic that morning at school. A new agonizing sword pierced my body, set the Shanta Bhawan hospital bed rattling. How did I "surrender" an unbearable pain that shook me like a terrier a rat? If I—"passed on" was a lukewarm cliché but "dying" was such a cold word—would Dr. Bethel send what was left of me back to my children in New York?

My son and his wife had been right, as usual. I shouldn't have come to Nepal in the middle of a war, whether hot or cold, between India and China. Things are rather upside-down in our family: my children in their twenties are always pointing out what isn't safe "for a woman of your age" (what a horrible phrase that is!) while I am the perennial adolescent yearning to try the unknown, to "express myself."

"Don't you realize that Nepal is only a very small bite that Big Dragon up north may decide to chew up at any moment?" My son had tried to sound patient as he spelled out the facts of life to his parent. He begged, "At least take a short-wave radio with you so you'll know if the Reds decide to advance again. Remember, you're *American* and that's a bad word in Peking!"

I sniffed. "What good would a radio do? All the Chinese I

know is *chop suey* (if that *is* Chinese). Do you think any Red general is going to broadcast, 'O.K., Mrs. Fletcher, here I come'?"

So here I was, sick, alone, and scared to death. Suddenly I had an overwhelming need and grabbed for the bell on my bed.

"Memsahib wish?"

I stared at the little brown man who popped in my door. What was this ragged Nepali stranger doing in my bedroom in the middle of the night? His soiled khaki greatcoat collar was turned up around his ears against the mountain cold and the woolen scarf wound around his head left only his eyes, nose, and mouth visible, like a Nepalese dance mask. I gasped, "I want the Sister, quick!"

"*Me* Sister. Me Balmakunda. Dr. Bethel say, bell ring, Balmakunda come quick. Memsahib wish?"

Dr. Bethel might at least have warned me the night nurse was a man! I blurted, desperately, "I want the bedpan, please!"

"Me Sister" was back with what I needed almost at once. But politeness is always a must in Nepal. First, he put the pan carefully down on the floor, folded his hands under his chin to beam, "*Namaste!* I bow to you." Before I'd recovered from the shock of a bedpan with greetings, he'd discreetly disappeared. When I rang again, he shot back into the room. What next? Was I supposed to beam, "*Namaste*, hail and farewell" before he'd finish the job? Balmakunda let out so loud a yell I almost fell out of bed and an even smaller brown man, barefoot on the icy marble floor, pattered in, disappeared with the pan into the bathroom, which consisted of only a maddeningly dripping cold-water faucet and an Eastern-style toilet, a hole in the concrete floor. Of course! Balmakunda was too high-caste a Hindu to do a sweeper's job! Suddenly I began to chuckle; laughter welled up from deep down inside me, warm and satisfying.

Balmakunda, startled, came to lay a gentle brown hand on my hot forehead. He promised, "Do not fear, Memsahib, I am here."

And so was the Lord whose word was as sweet and real as honey. Perhaps, as Dr. Bethel had said, His Plan for me to know Nepal and Shanta Bhawan was wiser than my own; perhaps I'd learn more about these fabulous silent pioneers, Dr. Bob and Dr.

Bethel Fleming, inside the hospital than outside, peering in. Fear and strangeness slid out of my hot body into Balmakunda's cool friendly hand. This was the real Kathmandu, the mysterious lovely friendly country I'd come to find, a Nepal so close to the good earth that all things were natural, courteous, genuine, a gold thread of simplicity in a tangled world. This was the House of Peace where trust was as tall as the mountains. I said silently, "Good night, Lord. It's your job now." Almost at once I slid off into a deep healing sleep.

This is the fantastic story of two space-age missionaries, Dr. Robert and Dr. Bethel Fleming, who trekked happily together over the high Himalayas and slid down a mountain of mud to bring modern medicine to the fabled Valley of Kathmandu. They found Nepal's nine million people fighting a losing battle with almost every known disease from cholera to worms. There were only a handful of qualified doctors and five trained nurses. In this Hindu-Buddhist country it is against the law to change another man's religion, so the Shanta Bhawan Hospital couldn't even be labeled "Christian." Yet last year these Silent Samaritans, who live their creed in deeds, not words, treated 100,000 patients.

Strangely "Dr. Bob," as he is affectionately known in Kathmandu, isn't even a physician; he took his doctorate in education and is an ornithologist who knows more about the birds of the Himalayas than any other living scientist; he has collected some 700 species for the Chicago Natural History Museum.

Dr. Bethel has been a doctor of medicine for over thirty years, mostly practicing in India. Since 1956 when she started this now 200-bed hospital in Kathmandu, Shanta Bhawan has included among its clientele patients as diverse as the Queen Mother of the Royal Family of Nepal; the Russian ambassador; Nepalese farmers and street cleaners; Tibetan refugee weavers of yak wool with their holy Buddhist priests; lepers banished to the streets by their frightened families; American Peace Corps boys and girls as

well as Embassy and USAID officials; mountain climbers from
Europe, Asia, or the Americas who had frozen their feet or contracted pneumonia; harlots whose noses had to be sewn back on
after being cut off as punishment for their crime of cohabiting
with a man of other than their own caste. All nations, creeds, and
castes are alike welcome, for Shanta Bhawan means its title of
"Palace of Peace."

Getting permission from the government to start a Christian
medical mission in Nepal, however, had not been easy; it took the
Flemings five years to achieve official sanction to heal and bring
hope to the sick of Kathmandu.

"We came to Nepal on the wings of a bird," Dr. Bob explains
with his warm smile that speaks friendship in any language. When
he first ventured into Nepal to collect game birds in 1949,
Kathmandu was as much a forbidden city as Lhasa, and as tightly
closed to foreign travelers. Not only does the northern slope of
Sagarmarth, as the Nepalese call Everest, lie in Tibet, but the
two countries, neighbors for thousands of years, have much in
common, ethnically and psychologically.

Nepal is still today an independent monarchy, a little-known
land of deep lush valleys, crowned by the highest mountains in
the world. The country looks on the map like a 500-mile-long
cucumber, only a little larger in extent than the State of New
York, yet it has great strategic importance for the balance of
power, politically. Across its 100-mile width the two giants, China
on the north and India on the south, glare at each other as if each
might easily take a bite out of that brave little country.

Anything fantastic can happen in Nepal and frequently does.
One of its chief exports to the West is yak tails, used to make
Santa Claus beards; its principal internal source of hard cash
comes from the pensions of former Gurkha soldiers, some of the
bravest, most loyal little fighting men in the world, whose tradition is that, once taken out in battle, their short, wickedly curved
sword, the kurkri, cannot honorably be sheathed until its blade is
bloodied. To get more foreign currency, the Nepalese government
rents out the Himalayas. Climbing rights are purchased by moun-

tain expeditions from all over the world, men who dare brave the wrath of "the lords of the sky" to reach the summits of Makalu, Lhotse, Annapurna—or especially that of Everest, which stands over five miles high (so lofty that its peak often resembles a huge black jagged tooth against the sky because its pinnacle towers so far above the snow and storms raging below).

Dr. Bob, who climbed the Himalayas as a different kind of scientist, is a deceptively mild-looking little man with an impish twinkle that starts in his eyes and lights up his lined pleasant face; but he has a tough wiry body that can take off up a mountain at the chirp of a bird. His voice is the slow pleasant drawl of the school master; only the gleam in his bright blue eyes and the jaunty tilt of his flowered cotton Nepali cap over one ear clues you in that this is a man completely unafraid of any creature that crawls, walks, or flies. To get a good specimen of impeyan pheasant, he will cheerfully scale a precipice or swim a river in flood; he considers any mountain under 8,000 feet a hill and calls climbing it a picnic, because he takes along his lunch. Tigers roaring or wolves stalking around his tent at night are merely occupational hazards.

"We Christians waited two thousand years to get into Nepal," Dr. Bob is fond of saying. "Then when the Lord was ready, he sent a bird to show us the way." The miracle happened while Dr. Bob was teaching science in Woodstock High School in Mussoorie India. The Rana hierarchy, headed by the Maharajah, still controlled Nepal tightly, keeping its frontiers closed; even King Tribhuvan, shut up in his ice-cream-colored palace in Kathmandu, was allowed out only when the Ranas permitted. It didn't seem likely they'd welcome an American scientist wandering about their private mountains. But Dr. Bob had a restless, strangely compulsive urge to try anyway.

"I knew that Dr. Ripley of Yale had gotten permission to cross into this mysterious country where, in 1947, he had discovered the spiny babbler, a species that had not been seen alive for over a hundred years," Dr. Bob Fleming recalls. "I was on fire to go bird-hunting in Nepal, too! I didn't really think I had much chance of crossing the closed border but I wrote anyway to the United States Embassy in India to see if they could get me permission. To my amazement, almost at once I got permission to conduct an ornithological expedition in Nepal for six months! I had never heard of the Orient working this fast in all the twenty-five years I'd spent teaching in India.

"You can call it coincidence if you like; but as Dr. Bethel and I look back, the Lord's good Plan for us to work with sick bodies and eager minds in Nepal is plain. My request had 'just happened' to land on the desk of Roy Bisbee, the son of a Methodist Missionary, who had been a former student of mine in Woodstock School. He walked across the street to the Nepalese Embassy and 'just happened' to find a man in charge who was intensely interested in Himalayan birds, so he said 'Yes' to a fellow ornithologist. I had 'just happened' to have developed a good pair of mountaineering lungs by climbing about in India for years. So I was ready for the Nepalese Himalayas."

Dr. Bethel Fleming did not go into Nepal with her husband on this first trip; but she made his expedition possible by taking charge of the 400-bed hospital in Fatehgarh, India, so that its Chief of Staff, their friend Dr. Carl Taylor, could go with Dr. Bob. Dr. Bethel knew her husband: he would be ecstatically chasing any bird he wanted over a Himalaya without regard for limb or life and that there wouldn't be a drugstore on every street corner. As a matter of fact, it turned out there weren't even any streets: merely mountain paths; steps carved in cliffs 1,000 feet high; rivers with currents so swift the Western scientists and their Nepalese porters had to hold hands to keep from being swept away before they reached the far bank. The only medicines available were the few Dr. Bob's ornithological expedition had been able to bring along on the backs of their porters.

The story of his early visit to Tansen, Nepal, is best told in Dr. Bob's own words. He himself is as restless, as alert as any bird, perching first on the edge of his chair, then when he gets excited, walking rapidly up and down, his face alight, words pouring out as naturally as a lark sings and soars. He will never grow old because he still has that childlike sense of wonder at the intricate beauty of the universe, at both small and large miracles, the glory of the mountains and the sleepy chirp of a bird at twilight.

"The speed with which I received permission to enter Nepal took me by surprise," he admits. "It presented a problem; as superintendent of the high school, how could I just walk out in the middle of the semester? Fortunately Woodstock realized this was an extraordinary chance for their science department to get some firsthand information, so they agreed to let me go that October. I wrote excitedly to the Chicago Museum, where Dr. H. Boardman Conover, the curator who had first encouraged my study of game birds and birds of prey, arranged to finance my trip. Now all I had to do was to collect my companions for the expedition and have some cards printed with 'Chicago Natural History Museum Expedition' . . . very official. We had an exasperating series of delays before we could actually take off. We planned to go far into the mountains, up toward Dhaulagiri and Annapurna following the Kali Gandak River Valley. But the Presbyterian Board didn't make up its mind to let Dr. Carl Taylor go until October 15th and we were supposed to start for the border of Nepal on the 27th. Our check from America to buy supplies in India for the trek did not arrive; the check had been missent to Bombay, but even that turned out to be fortunate, for during the time the money was sitting there, exchange rates went way up and we were able to buy many more supplies! Harold Bergsma, one of my Woodstock students who had gone home on a trip to Grand Rapids, Michigan, was supposed to bring the American equipment back with him, but Harold did not arrive until two days before the expedition was slated to start. That same evening we set off impatiently for Lucknow to order our store of food and other necessities sent on to the Nepalese border."

Dr. Bob, Dr. Taylor, Harold Bergsma, and Rev. T. R. Bergsaka from the Norwegian Mission traveled by the Oudh and Tirhat Railway to Nautanwa, six miles from the Nepal border. There they bogged down again. It was raining and none of the food had arrived from Lucknow. The second day it went on pouring rain and no food; third day the same. Dr. Bob told Harold, "You'll have to go back to Lucknow to get the stuff moving." The boy hopped on the train which was just pulling out of the station when Bob noticed a pile of boxes on the platform. "Hey, Harold, get off! The food's here!" he yelled. Bob had to run after the train, yank off the bewildered boy. They piled the food onto a dilapidated truck, drove over the border to Butwal. There, on the northern edge of the *terai* where tigers, wolves, and other wild animals still stalk, it was too dangerous to travel after dark, so they had to make camp for the night where the road ended. The party walked the rest of the ninety miles to Tansen, accompanied by their porters and curious villagers collected along the way, most of whom had never seen a Westerner before.

"The very first night when we put up our tents in a forest we were delighted to discover a new species of green pigeon which we named for our sponsor . . . Dr. Conover. *Teron pompadora conoveri*," Dr. Bob reports. "The bird was green on breast and abdomen, gray on back and wings, yellow at the throat with just a tinge of orange on the breast. The next day a snake made the mistake of slithering across my path. I caught it, bottled it in alcohol; when we sent it back to Chicago it took the authorities two years to identify that reptile. Everything was new, mysterious, and thrilling. We felt like Adam exploring the garden of Eden. But climbing was slow, for we had to mount steps cut in the cliffs, up 4,500 feet to the city of Tansen, the capital of Western Nepal. To its several thousand inhabitants who flocked around excitedly we were as inexplicable a sight as the snake had been to us!

"We pitched our tents on the parade grounds at Tansen where the fruit bats in the trees made such a racket it was hard to hear each other talk. His Excellency the Governor, General Rudra Shumshere Jung Bahadur Rana, graciously granted us an audience:

We were met at the palace door by a son of His Excellency, Colonel Ishwar Shumshere Jung Bahadur Rana, who spoke English and was most interested in bird collecting. When His Excellency arrived he greeted us in Hindustani. I opened the interview, but India-born Dr. Taylor carried on with the language. We made a small presentation gift of the book *Look at America,* and in return His Excellency pointed to the skin of a rare Himalayan bear on the floor of the reception room and said he would like to give it to Chicago Natural History Museum. His Excellency also provided the party with a police official and two assistants to accompany us. The cordial reception and the generosity of His Excellency were characteristic of all the officials we met.*

"The very first thing, just outside Tansen, what should we see the next day but a spiny babbler, the rare bird Dr. Ripley of Yale had discovered, two years before." Dr. Bob's eyes flash after all these years as he relives those early days. "In as many miles we saw and heard seven of these supposedly scarce birds. I have seen hundreds since in Nepal but none that gave me the thrill of that first one. The spiny babbler looks rather like a brown thresher, hides under the ferns on a hillside, but once you hear it, you can't mistake its distinctive call. It is also one of the best mimics of other birds I have ever heard, rather like a mockingbird or catbird in the States. These spiny babblers have become so common in Nepal that now I am collecting only nests and nestlings for the Museum.

"We followed the Kali Gandak River to within thirty miles of Tibet and collected 2,500 specimens, representing 490 species and subspecies. We used pack animals to carry our stuff, but the path was so narrow, when the animal turned a corner, the packs would bang frighteningly against the side of the cliff. If either the animals or we had slipped, we would have gone down 1,000 feet over the precipice, and only a few splinters of bone would have been left. Worse, the specimens would have been lost!"

At Tukche where they made a high-altitude camp at 12,000 feet, they saw fifty giant snow cocks in one day. Yet wild as the countryside might appear, the local official, "Burra Subha Sahib," assigned

* Austin L. Rand and Robert L. Fleming, Fieldiana, *Birds from Nepal,* Zoology, Vol. XLI, No. 1 (Chicago Natural History Museum, October 11, 1957).

these wandering ornithologists a comfortable stone house in which to stay and sent them down a seventeen-course dinner. Even though it was raining and the cliffs slippery and dangerous, they were too excited to stay in camp. They climbed up to 18,000 feet hunting new specimens. When the sun broke through, majestic beauty held them spellbound as they stared, awed, up at the mighty snows appearing from the mists, at the high peaks of Dhaulagiri and of the Annapurna range. Scorning to notice little men crawling precariously about their feet, the Himalayas stood aloof, regal, immovable, lost in time, to whom a million years were but a day that is gone. This was Nepal where few Westerners had ever explored before—the new Eden for Dr. Bob.

Dr. Carl Taylor was equally busy exploring another kind of mountain—the urgent needs of hundreds of very sick patients at Tansen. Rumor flies faster than radio waves. When the people of Tansen heard there was a trained doctor of medicine tenting on their village parade grounds, they rushed there in such crowds that Dr. Bob Fleming had to place his tin trunks, which held his bird specimens, in a circle around their tent to keep it from being pushed over. Dr. Taylor performed operations until his rubber gloves were in ribbons.

"You never saw so many desperately sick people, Bethel," Dr. Bob told his wife almost tearfully when he got back to the Woodstock School. "They had tuberculosis, leprosy, worms, goiters as big as Volkswagen rubber tires around their necks, tumors that must have been building up for years in swollen abdomens. . . . The children were heartbreaking. One baby had been burned over three quarters of his body and the wounds were suppurating into a mud poultice—"

"Next time, I'm going into Nepal with you, Bob," Dr. Bethel interrupted firmly. "We'll take in all the medicines the Mission Board will let us have and that we can carry."

"If there is a next time," Dr. Bob warned.

The very next year, 1950, the Rana government, which had kept Nepal tightly closed off from the rest of the world for a century, was overthrown, and King Tribhuvan came back from exile in India to become the real ruler upon his rightful throne in Kathmandu.

The first thing he did was to declare Nepal a member of the world of modern nations by opening up her borders to foreign aid and to visitors; he hoped sincerely to lead his country out from its sixteenth-century seclusion into the twentieth century of scientific progress.

Dr. Bob's glimpse of the terrible need for modern medicine in the Tansen area naturally made the Flemings eager to help. But when they wrote to the Nepalese government for permission to start a medical clinic in Tansen, their letter was not even answered. With oriental tact, the Nepalese hesitated to say "No," especially on paper, so the Flemings were neither accepted nor refused. A suspicion of outsiders that has gone on for several thousand years is not easily overcome, especially when the foreigners are missionaries of a different religion from Hindu-Buddhist Nepal. Yet nine million people with so few doctors with recognized medical degrees, with tuberculosis or malaria afflicting thousands, had urgent reason for wanting the best that modern medicine had to offer.

Government aid from outside countries had already been accepted by King Tribhuvan, and the USOM (United States Operations Mission) had been allowed to rent a large former Rana palace, Rabi Bhawan, for its headquarters. The head of this new Mission, Paul Rose, and his wife, Mary, happened to be good friends of the Flemings and urged them to come to Kathmandu for a visit.

"We have plenty of room here at Rabi Bhawan . . . accommodations for eight families and only us rattling around as yet," Mary Rose wrote to Dr. Bethel. "Why don't you come, get acquainted with some of the new government officials here? They are still very cautious, understandably, about the kind of foreigners they let in to stay. But if they got to know you and you them, you might like each other!"

The Flemings accepted the Roses' invitation on their next Christmas vacation from Woodstock School. But there was no travel agency to sell them a ticket for a commercial plane that flew in a few hours from New Delhi or Calcutta to Kathmandu, as airlines do today. Intrepid travelers had to *walk* over the Himalayas into the Valley of Kathmandu. Dr. Bob and Dr. Bethel took a train to the Indian border at Raxaul, then shifted to the narrow-gauge little railroad that runs only twenty-seven miles into Nepal before it ends at Amlekhganj. The coaches were so crowded that if the train stopped suddenly the passengers were in imminent danger of falling out the windows or off the roof. At the end of the track, the two Flemings crammed themselves, along with the rest of the passengers, laden with huge bundles of clothes and food, cans of kerosene, and loudly protesting chickens, into a rickety native bus which rattled precariously over a narrow road, through sixteen tunnels, then crossed a frighteningly swaying bridge to the end of the road at Bhimpedi, so named because the local god had left his footprint in the nearby holy spring.

Dr. Bob and Dr. Bethel then had to climb the rest of the precarious mountain paths to Kathmandu on their own two feet, with a bevy of porters carrying their belongings. They mounted up and up 2,000 feet and thankfully arrived at the Chisapani Garhi rest house by dark. Here, fantastic, in the wilderness of rock and mountain, the Guest House was equipped not only with running water but with electricity! After all, the wealthy Ranas had also needed a place to spend the night on their way home from London or Paris to their white palaces in Kathmandu. Equally astonishing was the popping up from nowhere of uniformed customs officials who checked the Flemings' baggage and inspected their permission to go to the capital city, holding the document gravely upside down, for less than 5 percent of the Nepalese could then read or write. But they knew an official-looking paper when they saw one.

"Up to now," Dr. Bethel recalls, "Bob and I hadn't really quite dared to believe we'd make it to that hidden mysterious city behind the Mountains of the Moon, but now it looked as if we were actually off for the fabled Valley made (according to legend) by a god who had cut with his sword a cleft in the mountains, letting a lake run out in two holy rivers."

It took the Flemings three weeks to complete the steep climb to Chandragiri Pass, 8,000 feet up, for the altitude bothered Dr. Bethel: she gasped so for breath that they had to stop to rest frequently. But they made the grade finally. As they flung themselves, panting, down on the grateful ground of the summit to rest, their Nepalese porters suddenly went wild, screaming and yelling at the top of their lungs. "My goodness, Bob, are we being attacked?" Bethel gasped. She was too tired to move; she'd die right there.

"They're only scaring away the evil spirits from the pass," Dr. Bob explained, watching the porters adding stones to the great pile that was a Buddhist chorten, a holy place. "So we can get through safely."

Dr. Bob and Dr. Bethel added their own propitiatory stones, but they might as well have skipped their offerings because the weather immediately got worse. It began to snow, and the melting slush made the precipitous mountain clay path a slippery sliding toboggan down to the valley below.

"We looked like mud pies when we got to the bottom, to Thankot where Mary Rose, bless her, was waiting for us at the end of the road in her American jeep," Dr. Bob recalls. "But we were proud we hadn't gone flat even once, just skidded in mud soup. Were we glad to see Mary Rose and that jeep! We tumbled inside, never even felt the potholes on the seven bumpy miles into Kathmandu. Rabi Bhawan and the Stars and Stripes flying over it surely looked good to us weary, filthy travelers. All we yearned for was a large bar of American soap!"

The Flemings, with the tactful aid of the Roses, soon got acquainted with the leading families of Kathmandu. General Rudra and his wife Ranee Shumshere and their large family had already become their firm allies in Tansen. Once a friend, a Nepalese is always loyal; it is the first step that is hard to take. Mary Rose took Dr. Bethel and Dr. Bob to Singha Durbar, the 1,500-room palace built as a home for a former Rana Maharajah which now held hundreds of King Tribhuvan's new government officials. There the two Dr. Flemings met the director of the government health services, Dr. Jit Singh Malla, and General Kaiser Shum-shere, defense minister in King Tribhuvan's cabinet, as well as the Prime Minister, M. P. Koirala, and other important Nepalese officials. Everyone was extremely polite but no one suggested it would be a good thing if the two Christian doctors moved to Nepal to open a medical clinic. Resigned but still the eager scientist, Dr. Bob went with Mr. Rose to the hills around the valley to collect more birds and ferns to fill the tin trunks he had brought along to hold additions to his collection. Two days before the Flemings were to leave for home in India, Dr. Bob set up in the north room of Rabi Bhawan a display of the birds and ferns they had discovered near Kathmandu and returned Nepalese hospitality by inviting a number of their new friends in for the evening. The Flemings also showed Kodachrome pictures they had taken of Dhaulagiri and the Annapurna massif (Annapurna is sometimes called The Blue Mountain, due to its majestic icy slopes) and "we generally had a jolly time together."

The Flemings were due to fly out of Kathmandu the next day on one of the U.S. government planes which were used to transport USOM personnel and supplies, but although Dr. Bob and Dr. Bethel arrived at Goucher airfield in plenty of time (*goucher* means "cow pasture," which it still was in that day) for some reason no American plane came soaring in over the mountain into the Kathmandu Valley. Back again at Rabi Bhawan, Mrs. Rose comforted the crestfallen Flemings, "Don't worry. The plane will come eventually; it took me three trips to the airport before I took off the last time. Maybe they had a dust storm at New Delhi. Or a cloud of mist came up, so the pilot couldn't take off for fear of bumping into a mountain." They were settling down for an indefinite wait when Bethel happened to glance out the window.

"Hurry, Bob!" she gasped. "Open the front door. We have guests!"

Guests with a capital G. Crown Prince Mahendra (now King of Nepal) was at the Rabi Bhawan door, accompanied by his two brothers, Prince Himalaya and Prince Bhasendra. "The royal family has never called on any foreigners before, to my knowledge!" Mrs. Rose whispered excitedly to Bethel. The princes explained that they had come to see Dr. Bob's collection of birds and ferns. To ease the stiffness of the unusual situation, Prince Himalaya announced, his black friendly eyes twinkling, "I have decided to enter my children in your Woodstock School."

"But you haven't any children!" Bethel reminded him. "Yet!"

In the laughter that followed, the ice was broken and Americans and Nepalese chattered away like old friends. They handled and commented upon the birds and ferns which Bob unpacked especially for them. (It had never occurred to him to invite the royal family to his talk!)

"The three princes stayed an hour and when they left we felt we had really been admitted into the generous heart of Nepal," Dr. Bob says. "Yet the royal visitors didn't say a word about our wanting to open a medical dispensary. So we hardly dared to hope, though we wanted even more desperately to return, now we knew the friendly people, saw with our own eyes how many sick there were who needed the medical help we could bring to Nepal."

"My heart ached," Dr. Bethel recalls, "especially for the little children who were lepers; others were obviously tubercular, limping along the city streets. We had the odd feeling we were no longer strangers, that we belonged there. We had never flown before, but as our plane took off the next day, and Bob and I clung, half fearfully, to the hard bucket seats, the Mountains of the Moon seemed to call to us, 'Come back, come home!' "

Perhaps their pleasant meeting with Crown Prince Mahendra had nothing to do with what happened later but at least he and the Flemings were not complete strangers when they met later, in 1956, after King Mahendra had been crowned with great pomp and ceremony to take over the throne vacated by his dead father, King Tribhuvan. This year had also brought great changes to the two Dr. Flemings, for they had been allowed officially to rent Shanta Bhawan, a former sixty-room Rana palace in Kathmandu, in which to develop the first modern, fully equipped hospital in Nepal. Their initial, most important job was to make the illiterate man in the street understand that these Western Christian doctors were there to help them get well, not to make dangerous magic with X-ray machines or electrocardiograms. It was also rumored in the bazaars that the new doctors even used knives in the operating rooms to let out the evil spirits from the sick man. Would not submitting to this be worse than the disease?

Until the 1950's most Nepalese (except for the wealthy Ranas who could afford to go to Calcutta or Europe to consult specialists) had treated an earache by driving a nail into a wooden god by the roadside and toothache prayers could be nailed into another god. Lepers, turned out into the streets by their frightened families, had to fend for themselves or die. True, there had been a government hospital of sorts in Kathmandu, but it was hardly antiseptic. One of the hospital attendants of those early days recalls vividly, "When I first worked there, the patients used to spit on the floor, on the walls, and even on the ceiling if they had that much spit. You couldn't really blame them; our country people are used to living on cow-dung floors with their water buffaloes and chickens as valuable members of the family. The hospital windows had no screens, so the birds flew in and out to snatch at tidbits and at mealtimes the pi-dogs from the street would rush up the front stairway of the hospital to finish off whatever the patients left on their plates. How those pi-dogs knew when it was mealtime, I'll never know!"

Conditions are entirely changed now, thanks to both Nepalese and United States government aid. Bir Government Hospital has an efficient, well-trained staff of excellent doctors and nurses expert in modern methods, but in 1956 it was Shanta Bhawan Hospital run by Dr. Bethel and Dr. Bob which pioneered by having the first modern operating room, the first X-ray machine, a modern laboratory routine, and by giving the first blood transfusions and intravenous feeding.

"It's terribly important that the first operation we perform here at Shanta Bhawan be a success," Dr. Bethel reminded Dr. Bob. As head of the medical staff she was both surgeon and general practitioner, while Dr. Bob took care of everything else, polite arguments with government officials, keeping the often makeshift equipment running till their prayers should be answered and they could get better machines, trying to explain to a patient who could not read why he must take only one pill a day for a week instead of devouring the whole bottleful at once.

Dr. Bethel is as different physically from her wiry, sparkling, witty husband as it is possible to be. If he is quick and gay as one of his own birds, she is a big poised woman, calm as a mountain, holding her silver-white head as regally erect as her strong shoulders under her physician's jacket which seldom shows a wrinkle, even if she has been up all night with a very sick patient, as frequently happens. Her slow smile that reflects her peace of mind makes fear ooze out the door when she comes into the ward, for her trust in the Great Physician is so complete, each patient, be he Nepalese or Western, rests more securely in his bed. Her face is lined with all the suffering and compassion in the world, but her clear brown eyes are unafraid, for both life and death are equally her friends. She lives in two worlds by faith and so is beyond fear. The only word to describe Dr. Bethel is "fabulous."

But in tolerance, courage, and belief in the essential goodness in every man as a son of God, whatever his creed or the color of his skin, the two Dr. Flemings are spiritual twins. They talk everything over with each other and together with their Lord. But sometimes His Plan for Nepal doesn't work out quite as they expect.

"I've picked a very minor operation for our first one," Dr. Bethel told Dr. Bob as she scrubbed up for the brand-new operating room at Shanta Bhawan. "That woman with the umbilical hernia will need only a mild anesthesia." They wheeled the patient in under the bright lights, Dr. Bethel breathed a short prayer before operating, as she always does, and advanced in her white gown to the operating table. What happened next nearly closed the doors of Shanta Bhawan Hospital before they were really fully opened. The tale is best told in Dr. Bethel's own words.

"We carefully gave the patient a local anesthetic, specifically, Novocain, so mild that it is used routinely even in dentists' offices," she recalls, her brown eyes darkening with remembered tension even now. "Unfortunately, as no one would possibly have foreseen, the patient had a violent allergy to this ordinary drug.

She died even before I could begin to operate, almost at once! The nurses and I stared at each other, appalled, over the operating table. What would the Nepalese say when the first patient we put on the operating table died?

"We soon found out. The Kathmandu newspaper came out with a vicious attack upon Shanta Bhawan and upon us personally, insisting that we tied patients to their beds, cut them up, did all sorts of terrible experiments with their dead bodies. The editors violently demanded an investigation! We braced ourselves, waiting; but for two weeks nothing happened except angry rumblings and dirty looks when we went downtown to shop. Should we answer the accusations which were, on the face of them, ridiculous? We decided the best way was to ignore them, to get on with our job, for we had already twenty very sick patients in the wards.

"I had just finished an appendectomy one morning when the door to the operating room burst open and a pop-eyed messenger gasped, 'The King is downstairs! He wants to talk to you!'

"So it had come, the turning point which would decide if we could stay in Kathmandu, do the work of healing we so passionately wanted to do, or whether ignorance and fear should defeat us before we had really begun. King Mahendra, whom we had known as the Crown Prince, was now His Majesty, ruler of all Nepal. Would he remember us? He was an intelligent, well-read monarch; there was still hope he would understand what had happened. I hurried downstairs in my white operating gown, not waiting to change, for one does not keep royalty waiting."

The King was not alone in the hospital lobby; Queen Ratna and a group of attendants and officials with grave faces clustered about His Majesty. Dr. Bethel begged silently, "O, Lord, tell me what to say and how to say it rightly!" Then the big calm doctor of medicine advanced in her white robe and crown of white hair to greet her royal guests, with the consciousness that she had done no wrong. Sincerely humble herself, yet tiger-brave to protect her patients, she knew she had done what she could. But would His Majesty agree? Bethel took the royal party directly to the operating room, showed the King the patient's record, explained that no one living could have foretold the fatal reaction to Novocain. She showed him every inch of the hospital: wards where twenty beds of pain-racked patients now filled a Rana salon where pictures of maharajas hunting on elephant-back still decorated the walls; laboratories, private rooms, X-ray, even the kitchen; she had nothing to hide.

But would His Majesty believe her? His eyes hidden behind his dark glasses told her nothing nor did his firm mouth in his impassive oriental face. After all, he was the absolute monarch and she was a stranger in a mysterious land, here only on sufferance. Moreover, he was head of the Hindu religion in Nepal, considered the reincarnation of the great god Vishnu, the Preserver. The word of this Hindu god-King would be final for the new Christian hospital. Bethel's heart was suddenly a pulse beating in her throat, thundering in her ears, as she waited for the King to speak.

"You are doing a fine job, Dr. Fleming," His Majesty said graciously. "We are glad you are here."

No more newspaper articles appeared. Had not the hospital been investigated by King Mahendra himself?

The subsequent growth of Shanta Bhawan Hospital to nearly 200 beds proved just the beginning of the United Medical Mission to Nepal. Starting only a few years ago with nothing but a small black bag of Dr. Bethel's own surgical instruments, limited medicines, and a pocketful of faith, this Christian mission now operates four large city hospitals as well as numerous clinics in cities and in mountain villages scattered all over the country. Some of these clinics are so far from any road that patients have to be carried in litters by their families over steep mountain paths for two weeks to reach the doctor. But they come, oh how they come for help! The medical staff, started by Dr. Bethel and Dr. Bob, now numbers over ninety doctors, trained nurses, and technicians coming from twelve different countries, including Japan, India, England, Canada, Scotland, the Scandinavian countries, Germany, and nearly every section of the United States. A training school for Nepalese nurses has already graduated three classes and grows larger each year. All this became possible because a wise Hindu King and a brave Christian doctor had faith in each other's integrity.

Chapter Two

The God Who Gargled

Dr. Bob and Dr. Bethel Fleming not only belong to that strange
new breed of Christian missionaries, the Silent Samaritans who
live their religion daily in the wards and clinics of Shanta Bhawan
instead of talking about it; they also respect a culture other than
their own. They render unto Caesar the things that are Caesar's.
The Nepalese form of religious freedom is to live and let live; you
may worship any god you choose as long as you do not interfere
with another's beliefs. Everyone in Kathmandu knows that Shanta
Bhawan serves the sick and wounded in the name of Jesus Christ.
Chapel services and Bible classes are held at the hospital for the
Christian workers there, but no Nepalese on the staff are required
to attend. The Flemings consider themselves as guests in Nepal
and, as such, respect and obey the law of the land.

The Nepalese mean what they say about proselytizing. One
Christian minister who came up from India (who had no connection at all with the Flemings nor with the United Mission) gave
baptism to eight Nepalese Christian converts in Tansen and all of
them landed in jail. The preacher went to prison for six years while
the baptized converts were jailed for only one year. Although after
six months King Mahendra pardoned the baptized Nepalese, by
ancient Hindu law they lost their family inheritance; and as they
emerged from the prison gates they were informed that they were
all now Hindus again . . . although they had been demoted to the
lowest caste. The offending Indian preacher is still in custody.

At first the Shanta Bhawan staff were not allowed to hang upon the hospital wall even a Christian Madonna at Christmas time. But so convinced of their law-abiding sincerity have the Nepalese authorities become that now it is permitted that each night a great luminous white Cross lights up the inner hospital quadrangle around which the patients' rooms are grouped. "Let your light so shine before men that they may see your good works and glorify your Father which is in Heaven." Thus Christianity sends down its silent roots into an alien soil and grows as naturally green and beautiful as a Nepalese rice field in the morning sun. The rice field has no need of words or sermons; it is food for the body and beauty for the eye and its value is self-evident.

Equally significant for the future of modern missions is the fact that the entire staff of doctors, nurses, technicians, and social workers are *all laymen*; there is not a priest or minister among them. Their creed is action. They try only to do what Christ might have done if He walked down the teeming sidewalks of Kathmandu where many of the passers-by have some form of tuber-culosis, leprosy, elephantiasis, perhaps even smallpox or some other dread disease; they heal the sick and broken bodies in His name. At Shanta Bhawan the Flemings also respect local customs. Since it is not permissible for a dead body to exit through the entrance for living patients, a new door was cut in the high hospital wall for the dead to be carried away, with proper ceremony.

Nepalese culture, unchanged for 2,000 years, is not easy for the foreigner to understand, as Dr. Bob Fleming early discovered. One reason he is still one of the best-liked men in Kathmandu is that, from the day he arrived, he has always admitted the right of the Nepalese to run their own business, and has insisted upon the fundamental freedom of each man, whatever his race or creed, to make his own decisions in his own way.

During the early days when the Flemings first started to convert the sixty-room palace of Shanta Bhawan into a workable modern hospital, they discovered that not enough water was available to serve the needs of the operating room and the ward patients, let alone those of the Western medical staff who preferred to bathe in water instead of anointing themselves with mustard oil, which most of the Nepalese prefer to soap. So Dr. Bob went to Singha Durbar, that great government palace, to ask for permission to pipe down water for Shanta Bhawan from a spring on a mountain behind the hospital.

"Sorry, this is impossible," he was told by a grave official. "The god, Chandesvari, gargles there at that spring every morning."

"Indeed?" murmured Dr. Bob. He went back to the hospital to think that problem over, but the next day he was back again at Singha Durbar to ask, "Would it be all right if we cemented the spring as a bowl for the god to gargle in? And piped only the overflow down to the hospital?"

"Certainly," the official beamed, delighted that the amenities had been satisfied and that each had what he wanted most.

Dr. Bethel has also insisted that Shanta Bhawan Hospital conform as much as is scientifically feasible to local Nepalese family life. One of her biggest problems was the varying diets and customs of several hundred patients. "Our first big hurdle in the hospital wards was feeding the Hindu whose food must be prepared by his own family or caste member or he becomes contaminated. Some of them cover their heads, go off alone in a corner of the ward before they will eat," she explains. "A Buddhist lama demands a different diet from an outcaste to whom any food is welcome so long as it stays down. When we first opened the wards with the help of the companion *satis*, they not only slept under the patients' beds, but kept their food, fuel, and clothes there, too. Frequently when I went into a ward at night to check on a very sick patient, I'd stumble over turnip tops!

"In the maternity wards we had difficulty keeping the mothers out of the babies' cribs. A mother would just sort of curl up protectively around her child. Once we lost a baby entirely, a patient upon whom I'd just operated; he simply disappeared. The nurse and I searched the whole ward frantically and finally found the mother had parked herself and the baby under the bed on the floor where she was more comfortable than on a soft mattress. But this was hardly antiseptic for a new post-operative!

"We solved some of the storage problems by building lockers for the patients' clothes . . . if we could get them off. The men would wear our hospital gowns without protest but the women were so modest they would put them on over their soiled saris. We built a long shed out by the front hospital green with charcoal stoves where each family could cook its own food in its own way. We got rid of the turnip tops but not entirely of the fear of contamination by Christian foreigners. This still makes for tragedy not only among the unlettered. I tried desperately to get one Rana lady who had three sons away in Europe studying in college to come to Shanta Bhawan for a much-needed operation. She refused; she preferred to die."

"She preferred her own heaven to breaking her religious beliefs, dear," Dr. Bob corrected his wife gently. They smiled at each other with the tolerant warmth of understanding, for faith to these two Christians is also a way of life, a path that leads naturally to another world where they will still work and love together.

Dr. Bethel believes that any patient should be allowed to die as well as live in accordance with his own religion. Good Hindus believe that if they die with their feet laved by the waters of the holy Bagmati River which flows along only a couple of miles from Shanta Bhawan Hospital, their sins are forgiven and at death their spirits will go directly to wherever good Hindus go. A great temple at Pashupatinath stands there beside the river with rooms where Hindus may wait comfortably for the final release from pain, so when Dr. Bethel decides a hospital patient's case is hopeless, she says quietly to his family, "It is time to take your brother to the River." Or she soothes, "He is better; you need not take him yet to the Bagmati." Sometimes nature fools her and the patient recovers down by the River, in which case he is brought back to Shanta Bhawan and everyone rejoices.

Another big job that Shanta Bhawan faced was building up a blood bank among people to whom transferring blood from one person to another is a sort of minor death. When blood was needed by a patient after a major operation, Dr. Bethel appealed to the family who had accompanied the sick man to the hospital.

"If he does not have new blood he will die," Dr. Bethel explained. "Will you not give him a pint? It will not hurt at all," she assured the patient's brother.

He shuffled his feet. "I—I have a toothache!"

The doctor turned to the patient's husky son. "How about you?"

Terror clouded his eyes as he stammered. "I—I just married me a new wife! I cannot!"

The patient's other son had a sore toe. Meanwhile the patient was dying. So Dr. Bethel offered her own arm and the frightened family watched while Christian blood mingled with Hindu and the patient's life was saved.

Tolerance for each other's customs is a vital requisite for any real understanding between East and West, especially in Nepal where a man's every act is conditioned by the sign of the zodiac, as related to the movements of the planets, under which he was born. The astrologer-priests control the smallest detail of the average man's daily living; they decide upon the auspicious day for a trip whether by airplane or yak, for marriage, for the right moment to begin the spring plowing down on the farm or for laying the foundations for a new house. No householder would dream of starting to build without first propitiating the *nag*, the resident land snake.

"You can tell an ordinary cobra from a holy *nag* because the cobra has a pointed tail but the *nag*'s tail is stubby," Dr. Bob Fleming explains.

One American employer had a Hindu clerk who was so very efficient that when one morning he came to work looking as if he'd been awake all night, then fell asleep at his desk, the employer said nothing. But each day the Hindu got worse and worse, staggering to his desk too bleary-eyed to be of any use, so finally the employer demanded, "What's wrong with you? You used to be my best man, but now you aren't worth a rupee!"

"It is the *nag*," the Hindu explained earnestly. "He has moved into our house. My wife has been very sick, so nights I have to get up to take care of her. I shake all over each night for fear I will step on the *nag*! He would surely resent it. When I get back to my bed, I am still shaking so I cannot sleep."

"Then why don't you get rid of the snake?"

"I cannot! If I put him out, someone in our house will surely die . . . my wife or my baby!" The clerk burst into tears.

Even the Nepalese who has been educated in Europe or the United States has a lingering uneasy respect for local taboos; if he meets a black snake on his way to board an airplane to fly to New Delhi, he is wise to go back home, to wait for another flight. But meeting a red snake is good luck to speed him on his journey.

"There are ways, of course, to fool the evil spirits," a well-known Nepalese anthropologist who has added much to the knowledge about the many races living in Nepal once explained to Dr. Bob. "If the only flight to where you must go proves to be on an in-auspicious Thursday, you may pack your suitcases on the auspicious Wednesday, put them outside your door. Obviously your journey has begun."

"Yet before he condemns the Nepalese as superstitious, should the Western skeptic not ask himself if this, like all knowledge, is not a matter of degree?" Dr. Robert Fleming argues. "What about our New York skyscrapers and hotels who do not have any thirteenth floor? What about knocking on wood and avoiding walking under a ladder? Even more astounding are our racial superstitions in the United States which are erupting in sit-downs in our city streets, with police dragging even ministers and priests to jail. Is it reasonable or scientific (the shibboleth of the twentieth century) to believe that a man's intelligence or social status depends upon the color of his skin? We call ourselves a Christian nation yet even at Our Lord's table a black or yellow man may not kneel beside his white brother in some of our American so-called Christian churches. In Nepal we are trying to get back to the early days when following Christ meant not a hundred different creeds but to love the Lord, thy God, with all thy heart and thy neighbor as thyself—whatever his color or social customs."

Another saving grace with which Dr. Bob greases the wheels of international understanding is his sense of humor. He confesses with a grin, "When the astrologers decide every year which day the spring begins, it's extraordinary how much warmer it always seems! I usually start off on a climb up to see the rhododendrons,

masses of glorious red and pink blossoms painting the whole side
of the mountain. Nothing in the world is more beautiful except
perhaps a sunset lighting to glory the high snows." He also insists
that all miracles are not in the Bible and some may even have
comical highlights. He chuckles about "one of our chaps from the
Tansen hospital who was walking back to Kathmandu. The wind
was blowing a gale and it was raining great guns as it can only in
the Himalayas, so as he walked along the narrow path beside the
thousand-foot precipice, the worker was holding his big black
umbrella open against the driving rain. Suddenly, to his horror,
a great gust of wind seized his big umbrella, blew it and him right
off the path out over the precipice! Fortunately, before he even
had time to pray, the wind shifted, blew him and his umbrella
right back onto the path and safety! So he lived to tell his story at
Shanta Bhawan."

Dr. Bob pauses dramatically, his blue eyes twinkling, for the
listener to picture how funny a man can look dangling from a large
black umbrella before he adds, gravely grateful, "But of course this
was one of our Christian workers who was following the Plan."

"What Plan?"

"Why, God's Plan for him and for Nepal, of course."

Faith is not necessarily funereal; it can make a man laugh as well
as cry. Prayer and laughter are as real a part of the Flemings' daily
life as breakfast, and if the Lord does not grant what they ask for,
they know it is because he has something better planned for them
and for Shanta Bhawan. After all, may not prayer be governed by
as yet undiscovered universal laws that, once conformed with,
result in miracles as great as the flight of Colonel Glenn who was
shot into space and then returned intact to his family? The rescue
of a man by a shift of wind, the unexplained recovery of a dying
man sent to the Bagmati River, the arrival of a long-prayed-for
additional X-ray machine from the States which was desperately
needed at the hospital—all these the Flemings accept as natural
phenomena, the fruit of faith. Their job is, like that of the students of the ionosphere, to try to discover the cosmic laws that
govern this wonderful universe which the Lord has created, and to

relate themselves to the law of the spirit. "You have to listen as well as ask, when you pray," Dr. Bob warns.

Actually there is nothing very new in this modern missionary approach; these workers in Nepal are merely going back to the early days of the church when each man, layman or apostle, was not an arguer about commas in a creed, but was first of all *a follower of Jesus Christ.*

Shanta Bhawan now operates its kitchen smoothly on a rather complicated system whereby the hospital feeds the Western staff and about a third of the in-patients, mostly those of the lower castes, while the families prepare the food for the rest of the patients. The nursing school, of which Balmakunda was one of the first graduates, now is starting its fourth class and demands not only four years of hospital training but an extra year of midwifery. The Nepalese trainees are all Hindus and Buddhists except for a few Christians who have come up voluntarily from India. The superintendent of the training school is a Menonite from the American Middle West, the head nurse is from Great Britain, and other trained nurses hail from Australia, Germany, India, Japan, Denmark, Canada, and the United States.

The real strength of this new kind of mission in Nepal lies not only in its silent sermons of good works but in the fact that, in spite of the twenty-four different creeds represented on the staff, each worker *is first of all simply a Christian.* Included among the many creeds are Lutherans, Methodists, Presbyterians, Quakers, Menonites, doctors sent by a group of Christian physicians in Tokyo, representatives of the Regions Beyond Missionary Union, which is a strong mission project but little known outside of England and Canada. Add to this variety of theological beliefs which could easily be a source of discord the further confusion that not even the workers doing the same job—nurses, technicians, or doctors—get the same salary; they are each paid by the sending church or organization which pays them whatever is their usual church wage. But once in Nepal, each worker accepts without question whatever job the United Mission has given him or her. At Shanta Bhawan, Dr. Bethel Fleming rules with a firm but gentle hand. "Dr. Bethel says—" is law even if her voice is as soft as the flower-decorated nylon comforter on her bed. Have you ever tried to tear nylon?

"Imagine any doctor running a big hospital with a staff that has been trained in twelve different countries!" marveled a member of the American Embassy staff who had been rolling bandages for the Shanta Bhawan at the weekly meeting to help the hospital. "Just to keep peace among her staff should be job enough for most executives. Add to this the foibles and folkways of Hindus, Buddhists, Tibetans, Europeans who fill the hospital beds and mob the clinics daily. . . . Glory, it gives you a new idea of what it means today just to be a Christian!"

"We are here to do the ancient job of brotherly healing in a 1964 way," Dr. Bethel explains quietly, "To give where it is needed most. The life expectancy of the average Nepalese today is still only thirty-five years—about what it was in the United States at the turn of the century. We are here because the Bible record doesn't read, 'a cup of cold water given to an Episcopalian or to a Hindu'. It says, 'a cup of cold water . . . in My Name.' "

But it is no secret to any patient in the hospital that Shanta Bhawan is run in the name of the Great Physician. A prayer is always given in the operating room before each patient is anesthetized. One morning Dr. Bethel noticed one patient facing a particularly difficult operation who was lying there on the operating table, smiling calmly. Standing beside him in her white gown, Doctor Bethel asked him, curious, "Have you no fear?" The Hindu replied, "I have faith in you and in your God to whom you talk."

Chapter Three

The New Pioneers

The two Dr. Flemings of Kathmandu are as different from the last-century popular image of a missionary as jet propulsion is from traveling by yak. How has this change come about from the missionary draping Mother Hubbards over the naked "poor heathen" on some spicy strand where "every prospect pleases and only man is vile," to the modern layman who considers himself merely one member in the international family of Christ? Who counts every man as worthy of respect and understanding; who lives his silent creed of mercy and healing so that all who wish may read; but who has no need of a pulpit for, like Paul, for him to live is Christ. Actually, this has always been true for all dedicated missionaries and it is due to yesterday's clear thinking that today's emphasis has shifted from preacher to layman. The peace of the world may well lie in the hands of these lay pioneers since, with nothing to gain for themselves, politically or financially, they are slowly wiping out the bitter memory of the arrogant white man, be he businessman, explorer, soldier, politician, or intolerant preacher imposing his culture in the name of religion upon black, yellow, or brown civilization, once too weak to talk back, now flexing their muscles of both body and spirit. Where did these modern Silent Samaritans come from and how did they get that way?

Dr. Bethel and Dr. Bob Fleming are both "preacher's kids" who grew up on the fringe of the Bible belt. Her father, the Rev.

Walter B. Harris, was a Presbyterian minister, while Bob's, the
Rev. Guy B. Fleming, was a Methodist. Both Bethel and Bob
absorbed as naturally as breathing the same sense of values, where
the needs of a neighbor (whether next door or in Timbuktu) were
paramount and money was something to be used to help, not to
hoard. To such simple faith, God was no far-off stern deity
throwing out thunderbolts of damnation but "the Lord," a warm
friend to be consulted and loved.

"My strength cometh from the Lord who made heaven and
earth," Bethel heard her father read at morning prayers, before she
could fully understand what the words meant; but she understood
the spirit of trust. Born in Elysburg, Pennsylvania, in 1901, Bethel
was the oldest living child in her family.

" 'Bethel' means 'temple of the living god,' " she explains. "The
Hebrew word is feminine. I was named for my mother's friend but
my father explained to me that they hoped I would keep my body
and mind a fit dwelling place for the Lord."

The Harris family originally came to New England from Scotland, but they early emigrated to Pennsylvania where Bethel's
grandfather was a man of substance. A justice of the peace in
Chester County, he was so much respected by the community that
he was called affectionately "Squire Harris." His son, Walter
(Bethel's father), did all the conventional things expected of a
gentleman's firstborn, graduated from Layfayette College and
from Princeton Theological Seminary. Yet the virus of adventure
was in his blood also. After his graduation, young Harris went to
preach in the mountains of Tennessee under the Presbyterian
Home Mission Board. But the climate did not suit him. He became
ill and was advised by his doctors to have a change of scenery for
his health. He chose Nebraska.

Pearl Graves, Bethel's mother, belonged to a "travelin' family"
of the restless era when "Go West, young man" was an imperative
for young people who wanted to get ahead. As a baby, Pearl was
taken by her parents from Binghamton, New York, to live in a
pioneer sod house in Superior, Nebraska. However, as the town
grew, her father became owner and publisher of the town news-

paper, built himself a proper home, and by the time young Harris arrived there as pastor, Mr. Graves was the leading elder in the Superior Presbyterian Church. What could be more natural than for the elder's daughter and the young minister to fall in love, to become engaged and married? As his health improved, Walter Harris yearned for his home state, so the young Harrises went back to serve the church in Elysburg where, after the tragic death of their first-born, the second baby, Bethel, was doubly welcome. Two years later Dorothy (gift of God) arrived to keep her sister company.

"We grew up in a comfortable old red brick parsonage on Lancaster Road on the way to Wilmington, where my family moved when I was four, to serve a large country parish," Bethel recalls nostalgically. "There was always a baby in our house for me to take care of and I loved it. But because I was the eldest, I saw most of my father. He had the theory that the country was the place to bring up children, that their feet should know the feel of 'the good earth,' so he planted a big garden where we children weeded and watered. He took me with him to the four weekly prayer meetings he held in his parish. His lovely white colonial church which seated 300 parishioners was crowded most Sundays, but the rest of the large parish was so strung out that a small chapel had to be built at the other end, and cottage meetings were held in houses for the farmers and their folks who couldn't get to more formal assemblies.

"I loved to go with him in the horse-and-buggy days, clumping along lazily through the placid countryside while Father talked about the peace that passes understanding as if it were a tangible gift to hold in your hand. I learned more from him than from any college book, for I learned that faith is the only creative way to live, that in quietness there is strength.

"I knew how to play only ten hymns on one of those little organs that gasped when you forgot to pump with your feet," Bethel chuckles. "So Father would tactfully announce a song I knew and I would launch forth with more vigor than accuracy. We took along a portable victrola and if the farmhouse didn't boast an organ, I would put on the hymn records and we'd sing along with Moody and Sankey." Thus Bethel learned to "make do" what what she had, that the spirit of worship was important, not the words. This knowledge was to comfort her years later when, a lonely Christian in a mysterious Hindu country, she sang the same hymns in Nepali.

Even as a child, Bethel knew what she wanted to be—a doctor of medicine. There was healing in her small fingers, a calmness in the face of emergency. She took her first-aid kit along with her to grammar school; when a classmate fell down in the playground or caught a finger in the school door Bethel was always ready to comfort him with a practical bandage or to reduce the swelling with ice water. She had four brothers as well as her sister to practice on in the parsonage. One brother, Laird, grew up to follow in his preacher father's footsteps. Another brother, Harold, is now a mechanical engineer; Donald, "Bethel's baby" whom she used to lug along to missionary meetings, is a scientist in the research laboratory at the U-boat base in New London. Vincent, the youngest Harris, died in 1962. All these, as children, Bethel helped to mother and to doctor, for to call in a physician meant cash and there was always too little of that available in a parsonage.

But it was her mother, Pearl Harris, who pushed back the horizons of young Bethel to include far places. Pearl had yearned as an adolescent to go to the mission field herself; but instead she had married, had found her home mission in caring for six children and her foreign service by keeping three missionary circles going at the same time in her husband's large parish. She took Bethel along with her to these meetings to keep the current baby quiet. Every visiting missionary who arrived in town came to dinner at the Harris parsonage, spicing the company fried chicken and hot biscuits with queer exciting foreign names. Thus it was that young Bethel heard about the Indian women with their mysterious dark eyes, who wore sparkling diamonds in their ears and noses but who died in childbirth because they would not let a male doctor come near them and there were few women doctors available. Bethel had long ago decided to study medicine; now she made up her mind that, once trained, she would go to India to help these women and their babies—a nice way to blend youthful love of adventure and a well-developed bump of idealism.

Getting a medical education on a preacher's salary, especially when one is a member of a large family, was not so easy. Even the carfare to go across the Delaware River to the Lambertville High School was hard to come by; the tuition for an out-of-town student like Bethel meant mending your clothes carefully and changing your good shoes when you got home to save them. But Walter Harris insisted that the best education was as much a necessity for his children as books on the parsonage shelves and prayer at breakfast to start the day right. The Good Lord would never let them go hungry as long as vegetables grew in their back garden and jars were available to can for winter; their minds must be fed too. Preachers' kids early learn to work for what they want, to carve discouragement into steps by which to climb to their goal. Bethel went to Wilson College in Chambersburg which gave free tuition to Presbyterian preachers' children, but even so she ran short of funds and had to take two years out to teach, so did not graduate until six years later, 1924. Bethel entered the Woman's Medical School in Philadelphia the following year, where she was awarded a $400 scholarship. But even this proved not enough to get along on; Bethel again had to drop her studies to earn money to go on, so that she did not graduate until 1931. Eleven years she had worked for the proud Doctor of Medicine degree she now held in her hand! But it was worth it. In a day when women doctors were still looked upon with some coldness if not suspicion, Bethel and one other girl were the first women interns to be admitted to the staff of the Williamsport, Pennsylvania, hospital.

"Was I proud of my new uniform!" Bethel chuckles. "It was starched so stiff I crackled as I walked through the wards with my head high and my stethoscope sticking importantly out of my pocket. But, alas, you know what pride goes before. . . . When I went into the lab I was so intent on being 'Dr. Harris' that I didn't notice a technician with a tray of specimens. We collided and

I went flat, sliding along the floor, with my new uniform a mess of dirt and some poor patient's blood. After that, I watched where my big feet went."

This brand-new woman doctor had not forgotten the waiting women in India. During her internship she applied to the Presbyterian mission board to be sent to that vast Asian continent. But it looked as if her dream were to remain unrealized. "The depression was on; few were being sent abroad to mission posts, and those who did go," Bethel explains, "had to be sent where they were most needed. The Board asked me to go to Africa. But I had yearned to go to India since I was a tiny girl! I had a big struggle with myself, but finally I was able to say, 'Thy will be done, Lord.' My letter telling the Board I would go to Africa was crossed by a telegram from New York saying, 'Emergency has arisen in India. Get ready to leave.'"

Remembering that longed-for message, Bethel's brown eyes grow darker with emotion even after all these years when she has become head of a great hospital in Nepal where hundreds of patients flow in and out of the wards and clinics. In spite of the crown of white braids around her head, the authority of her degree and experience, she keeps to the simple childlike faith she learned jogging along in the horse and buggy beside her preacher father. She explains, "I think the Lord wanted to teach me a lesson . . . that His will must be mine. If He wants you to do something, the way will open. Queer, isn't it, how you fight against the Plan? Then it turns out to be what you most wanted, after all. My years in India were a training school to understand Nepal, to practice living on a strength greater than my own." Her voice dies away until she is almost whispering to herself, "Underneath are the everlasting arms."

Bethel went out to Fatehgarh, India, in 1932, to a Presbyterian mission hospital run by the famous Dr. Adelaide Woodard. The emergency there had been that one of her women doctors had left to get married. "I hope you are not mixed up with any young man," Dr. Woodard asked Bethel anxiously, for to Dr. Adelaide the hospital was family and children.

Bethel assured her new chief that she was not even thinking of marrying.

"She was exactly my idea of what a doctor and a woman should be. I all but worshipped her," Bethel confesses. "Most older doctors on a hospital staff are apt to take the interesting cases for themselves, to leave the routine cases for the younger doctors. But Dr. Adelaide pushed me right along to get experience with all kinds of patients. She'd say, 'Now, Bethel, you're going to do this operation this morning.' I'd tremble inside, but because she believed in me, I came to believe in myself . . . and the operation was a success."

But even the energetic Dr. Adelaide couldn't buck nature; Bethel met Dr. Bob Fleming at language school at Landour, India, where she went to study Hindu in order to understand patients' needs more easily, without an interpreter. Already her thick hair was a glorious white, so Dr. Bob thought her even older than she was: he still regrets the wait before they fell in love and became engaged. "Just think of the time we wasted apart!" Dr. Bob mourns after a quarter of a century of marriage to Bethel. "Two years, when we might have been together!"

Dr. Woodard wept when Bethel hesitantly told her she was going home on furlough to marry Dr. Bob Fleming; the knot was to be tied by both their preacher fathers so it would be good and tight. "I thought you were married to India, to your profession!" the older doctor mourned.

"I am," Dr. Bethel protested, her arms around her friend. "I'm going to practice in the Community Hospital at Landour and be school physician at the Woodstock School where Bob teaches science."

But Dr. Woodard still wept; it was almost as if she had a prescience that in a few months she would die, and Dr. Bethel whom she had trained so carefully would not be there to carry on her beloved hospital. Dr. Bethel and Dr. Bob planned to set up housekeeping within view of the mighty Himalayas of India, which were later to draw them on to cross the border into Nepal.

Dr. Bob had arrived to teach in India against his will; he had

wanted to go to China but the Plan decreed otherwise. Bob's
father, the Rev. Guy B. Fleming, was pastor of the Methodist
Church in Ludington, Michigan, when his tiny son came squalling
into the world on March 22, 1905. Guy Fleming had started out
his career as a teacher, but had later decided to go into the min-
istry; Bob, his son, was to reverse the process, to decide that teaching from a school rostrum rather than a high pulpit was his métier.
Bob's mother, born Clara Thompson, had kindled her small son's
interest in China by pointing out to him proudly the Arch of the
Martyrs at Oberlin College in Ohio, bearing the names of her
great-uncle, Charles Price, his wife, Eva, and his daughter Flor-
ence, missionaries who had been killed in the Boxer Rebellion.
Young Clara had had dreams of following in her missionary
ancestors' footsteps, but instead she had married a minister, was
tied to America by the birth of her two sons, Robert and Joseph
Edgar, their sister, Helen, and a still younger child, Maynard
Harris, a family name.

"Bethel is a Harris, too," Dr. Bob points out with his gay little
chuckle that has smoothed out many a difficult situation; a smile
speaks the same language in Ludington, Michigan, and Kathmandu, Nepal. "Bethel and I like to think we are distantly
related . . . possibly through Adam."

Bob went to high school in Holland, Michigan, where the tulips
grow, and then to the Methodist Albion College. He had a good
scholastic record but just missed Phi Beta Kappa; later that august
scholastic society was to elect him an honorary member because
of his scientific contributions to the knowledge of birds of the
Himalayas. (Bethel comments that perhaps it's a little nicer to
earn your Phi Beta not by answering questions on examination
blue books, but by solving scientific problems in real life. Their
quiet pride in each other is a lovely thing, a light in their eyes
which, unlike the uncertain electricity in their Kathmandu home,
never dims.)

Young Bob was still restlessly trying to find himself, wondering
if he should be a teacher or a minister like his father. His heart
was in China, but when he went to Drew University for a year

of Far East study, no courses on China were available; instead he took a study of India, given by Oscar M. Buck, a teacher whose tales Bob found fascinating, especially the one about Professor Buck's mother whose farm had been part of the Gettysburg battle-field and who had sat on the platform to hear Lincoln give his famous speech. "Government by the people, of the people, and for the people . . ." Was this just for the young United States, Bob wondered, or for the entire world? If so, how could he be a vital part of the democratic process?

Trying to make up his mind, Bob went to a ministerial con-ference. "I felt smothered by all the theological shibboleths," he confesses. "Words like *oikumene* I had to go home to look up in the Greek dictionary. Why couldn't they just say 'the whole in-habitated world'? But when I went to a teachers' seminar at Ann Arbor, the good talk was like a spark to tinder. 'Science, the great and good world and how it got that way' is my field," he told himself. "A bird soars and sings and a man loves the same way in Detroit and Peking. And the same Christ loves them all, sparrows and men. I will ask to go to teach biology in China."

But the Mission Board wrote back, "We need you in India." Bob was so disappointed he didn't answer that letter or the next one. When the candidates' committee met in Chicago, he was summoned to meet them, but he went reluctantly. He was ushered into a large room where grave-faced people sat around a huge horseshoe; every eye focused on Bob, whose knees were shaking. One examiner asked him sternly, "What would you do on the mission field if you came up against a stone wall?"

"Why, why . . ." stammered Bob. "I'd stop!"

The group broke into such hilarious laughter that everyone at once became friendly. Bob came out, perspiring and still weak at the knees, to be told he'd better go home and pack; he was leaving in six weeks to teach science in the Woodstock School in Mussoorie, India.

"It was part of the Plan," Bob says gravely, sure his steps have been guided to Nepal. "I taught science which included biology and geography which naturally led to my interest in birds of India and then of Nepal, of all the flora and fauna of the Himalayas. I learned as much as my pupils, more, really; I learned that science does not have to be a dry collection of facts but can come alive. I encouraged my anthropology students to go down into the village bazaars, to find out at firsthand what Indians think and feel. This is common practice today but in those early days my method was criticized as 'too liberal, pampering the students.' I couldn't have been greener at teaching classes, and the first time I saw a mob of 150 small boys, my charges at the dormitory, converging upon me, I all but turned tail and ran. I was also expected to head up physical education, of which I knew exactly nothing. I solved that problem by asking one of the officers of the Black Watch, stationed nearby, to teach the kids field hockey. He loved it and so did the boys.

"I learned that a good biology teacher does more than fire a batch of boys and girls with a love of cutting up frogs or collecting butterflies. When I was young, I used to be acidly sarcastic in class, to mow down the transgressor. But as I grew older, I learned to detach the person from what he does, to evaluate his real motive. Some things that you wouldn't do yourself you can condone in someone else when you understand why he did it, the sort of environment in which he was reared. This does not apply only to students but to all Christians and non-Christians. It was a grand preparation for coming to a Hindu country where you find out that the real way to preach Christ is to love people as He did. The more you understand people, the more you love them; you can smile and not be upset when they do something that for you is wrong. Unless your inner self changes, and you yourself grow to meet new situations, unless you develop spiritually as well as physically, you might as well be dead. One never quite attains the perfect understanding of the other fellow, but he can go on trying."

Bob was supposed to teach only five years in Mussoorie before going home on furlough, but the depression had so lowered mission funds that he was asked to stay on another year, which he agreed to do.

"It was the luckiest year of my life because I met Bethel," he says simply. "We fell so much in love I didn't want to go home next year when I had to. We were so romantic we drove up to Agra, went up into the minaret of the Taj Mahal to say good-bye. Bethel, twisting her engagement ring on her finger, asked me dreamily what she could give me that I wanted most, and I told her 'a cobra.'"

It seemed an odd engagement present, but Bethel, who had worked eleven years for her degree, was not one to be stopped from giving her beloved what he wanted if she could manage it. She asked the district magistrate at Fatehgarh if he knew how she could obtain a nice cobra.

"That's easy," he told Bethel. "We have plenty in our own garden. I'll have our *mali* [gardener] collect one for you . . . if you're sure you must have one?"

"I must," Bethel assured him. "It's the very first thing Bob has asked me to do for him."

A few days later the magistrate, very much upset, rushed in to ask Bethel indignantly, "What kind of young man have you tied yourself up with, anyway, who sets his fiancée hunting cobras!"

"Did the *mali* get one?" Bethel asked eagerly.

"He most certainly did," reported the magistrate grimly. "I was busy in my office, so he put the snake in a basket near my open door. Suddenly I looked up, saw a big cobra slithering over my threshold! I was so startled, I jumped up so fast my glasses fell off, cracked to bits on the stone floor. I yelled for the *mali* and between us we killed the bloody thing." He glared at Bethel. "If your fiancé still wants a cobra, let him collect his own!"

Bob did exactly this at the Madras railroad station on his way back to the States to be married. He was carrying a big wicker basket full of his collection of Indian beetles and butterflies, together with his paraphernalia of chloroform and nets. Bob heard a boy calling in Hindi, "Cobra for sale. Only one rupee!" Bob bought the snake, transferred it from the boy's small basket to his own larger one, doused the excited snake in chloroform to soothe it, put a blanket over the top of the basket, and sat down on it to keep the basket from jumping about and attracting the attention of the customs officer.

"I've always thought sitting on a cobra was a rather dangerous way of calming a snake," Bethel says, laughing about the incident today; then her smile becomes a shiver. "Familiarity and lack of fear such as Bob's can be dangerous. One of our best friends, who had charge of snakes all his life for the Chicago Natural History Museum, was bitten on the day after he retired . . . and died. But Bob isn't afraid of anything that crawls or flies. The great outdoors is his natural habitat."

After their marriage knot had been tied securely by their two preacher fathers in 1936, the Flemings came back to honeymoon in Mussoorie where the tall mountains brood against the sky, to the school which Bob had now come to love, where he wrote the school song still sung by the students, including his own seventeen-year-old daughter, Sally Beth, who was a senior there this past year:

> Shadows fall across the valley
> At the close of day,
> As we sing together
> This is what we say . . .
> Up in the high Himalayan mountains
> That's where I belong. . . .

Already Nepal had begun to call to him, but Doctor Bob did not yet understand the words of dark magic by which that country of the lovely snows sings to her lovers. Many Indian and Nepalese young people came to the Flemings' hospitable home at Fern Oaks, so-called because of the many tall branching ferns that surround it. In his classes at Woodstock Bob taught the daughters of Mrs. Sarjini Naidu, first woman governor of the United Provinces and the nieces of Jawaharal Nehru, the daughters of Mrs. Vijaya Lakshi Pandit. Later the wealthy Ranas of Nepal recognized the high standards of the school by sending their children there. "The Rana children used to drop in for tea like members of the family," Bethel recalls. "When King Tribhuvan himself came to visit, we organized a welcome in which not only the Nepalese but the whole school took part. We had no idea that we would soon be petitioning this same king for permission to start a hospital in his country."

Dr. Bethel worked at the Landour Community Hospital right up to the day her son, young Bob, was born in the fall of the third year of her marriage. "She figured he wasn't due for two weeks, but I proved more accurate than science," Dr. Bob says with a grin. "I warned Bethel, 'It's a boy. He's coming two weeks early, like I did.' "

Bob was right. Bethel had been delivering babies for years, but when her own pains came, she wasn't sure they weren't false. Bob barely got her into the Indian carrying chair in time to bring her up to the delivery room; in fact, young Bob was so early making his appearance that there was no room for him in the hospital, and Bethel had to settle for staying in bed in "a sort of summer house." After a few weeks, she was able to leave the baby in the care of a trained Indian nurse, to carry on with her job as a physician. She remembered her promise to Dr. Adelaide that not even marrying was going to stop her from practicing medicine in India.

Sally Beth—full name: Sarah Elizabeth Harris—did not join the Fleming family until December 3, 1944. She was a war baby who "lived dangerously" from the very first yell; she took her first trip "home to the States" on the famous *Gripsholm*, along with her seven-year-old brother, her mother, her father—and thirty-one Indian snakes.

"The snow was four feet deep in Mussoorie when we left in 1945 and because of the war we couldn't get ship room for the family for months," Dr. Bob recalls. "There was an airstrip at Agra so we stopped there to help entertain the U.S. Air Corps boys. Taking them on trips to collect ferns, fauna, and reptiles helped to make them forget their homesickness because there was little for them to do in India between flights, except sweat. A rumor that there might be a ship leaving soon sent us rushing to Bombay, but there were a lot more important people than us to get back to the States, so we were marooned in Bombay with two restless, half-sick children from February 14th to July 6th. I myself got a virus infection caused by the Bombay dust and took to my bed; but someone loaned me an exciting book about the snakes of India so I got well at once, and went out to hunt for interesting snakes." He collected thirty-one "interesting" reptiles to take back to the States with him.

"Snake collecting isn't at all dangerous," Bob insists. "You just step on the snake lightly, seize it near the jaws, pick it up. I found a most unusual wart snake for my collection."

Once on board the *Gripsholm*, the homing Fleming family found that the snakes were a great help, Dr. Bob recalls. "Third class on the *Gripsholm*, where we were, was terribly crowded, but when people saw us coming aboard with our reptile baskets, they moved away fast, so we had plenty of elbow room.

"One day we lost a snake, which curled up in the shoe the man was taking from our cabin to repair. He yelled loudly, dropped the shoe, and disappeared; we never saw him again. The woman in the stateroom next to ours was terrified of snakes so we didn't tell her when another got loose. If that snake ever turned up in her cabin . . . When we retrieved the second reptile safely, Bethel said firmly, 'That's enough. I can't go through that agony again. Pickle the wanderer!' So we did.

"The *Gripsholm* docked in New York on August 3, 1945. The newsmen and photographers swarmed aboard, taking pictures of little Sally Beth, who was walking by then, and of Bethel; until I saw us through the reporter's eyes I didn't realize how bedraggled we all were! Bethel had on a washed-out, shapeless housedress and her bare scratched legs hadn't known stockings for months. The baby needed a haircut, had on a red dress cut down from a bigger child's; she looked so gay it didn't matter. But suddenly the war piled up on me; I was tired of being a refugee. 'Bethel,' I urged, 'let's get out of here, buy some decent clothes. You don't even own a hat!'

" 'But I don't like hats!' she protested.

"We had no trouble getting ourselves off the boat but the authorities at Jersey City didn't want our snakes. We had to pickle them all."

Unconsciously, the Flemings were already spelling out their family motto: Never worry. The Lord has a plan for your life, so whatever happens is for the best even if you don't see it that way at the time. Life is so richly exciting, getting to know snakes and birds, tigers, lepers, street cleaners and kings, why not enjoy every instant? Happiness is more Christian than gloom and makes more friends.

That the whole family was to follow a bird over the Himalayas to Nepal they did not yet dream. Yet an argument over a label on a stuffed pheasant was to kindle Bob Fleming's interest in ornithology until it became not only his life's passion but the key to open the door to far-off mysterious Kathmandu.

Chapter Four

Dr. Bob Meets the Kalij Pheasant

Ornithology is more than a science with Dr. Bob Fleming; it is an adventure into the world of wonder that the Lord should create any mechanism at once as intricately beautiful and useful as a bird. It was his preacher father who made young Bob think of the little creatures, barely a heart throb of soft feathers in the hand, as more than a wing and a song. When he took his small son with him on walks in the woods he would cry, "Hush! Listen!" When they heard the silver fluting of the hermit thrush rising amid the cathedral pines, the father stood radiant, his face lifted, to marvel to young Bob, "They're singing, 'Hallelujah!' "

Even in kindergarten Bob Fleming knew the names of most of the common birds because his teacher hung the Audubon prints upon the schoolroom walls, took the class outdoors in the Michigan woods to identify the originals. But most of the birds seemed merely a dark flutter against the sky, a swaying twig from which they had just taken off.

"I didn't take out citizenship in the far and beautiful country I was to explore until one day when I was so tired of books and studying, I seemed to be walking in a dream," Dr. Bob recalls. As superintendent of the Woodstock High School, he'd felt he needed a doctorate in education, so he had come back alone to the States, to the University of Chicago, to earn his coveted degree. He explains, "I had left Bethel behind to hold the family fort in India. I wanted to get back home as fast as possible, so I'd studied so constantly that I was all wound up tight as a spring. I decided to walk down to the Chicago Natural History Museum to unwind for a while. In one of the displays I noticed a Kalij pheasant with the label, 'This pheasant never studied by Caucasians because they are not allowed to go into Nepal.' Yet I was sure I'd seen a bird exactly like this in India. Crusty young upstart that I was, I rushed to the office of the curator to tell him his bird was wrongly labeled. Instead of being angry, the curator was pleased that anyone had interest enough to protest.

" 'If you look closely, you'll notice that the Indian Kalij pheasant has a white crest, while the Nepalese pheasant is black-crested,' he pointed out gently. Seeing my obvious chagrin he changed the subject asking, 'Have you ever read William Beebe's *Pheasants, Their Lives and Homes*?'

"He went to his office shelf, handed me the book; that night I read the volume through and was fascinated. I was so excited about what I had learned, the curator suggested, 'when you go back to India, why don't you send us some specimens for our collection? Mr. Field who started this museum left a fund to finance people collecting game birds and birds of prey.' I didn't know a thing about skinning or preparing birds, very little about ornithology, but youth never sees the difficulties, only the open door. I knew that Bethel would have to pay back $335 advanced by the Presbyterian Mission Board, because she hadn't completed her five-year contract at the Fatehgarh hospital but had married me instead. What nicer way to raise that money than to go together all over India during my vacations to collect birds?"

Bob bagged a new bird for the museum on his very first Indian ornithological expedition, and this encouraged him no end. "I soon learned how to skin a bird without its looking like a feather pillow." As early as 1938 he went to collect along the Ganges; almost every holiday for the Flemings turned into an exciting bird expedition. He and Bethel trekked through the Punjab where they found, besides the impeyan pheasant and other bird specimens, awe-inspiring cedar trees over 1,900 years old. "Did you know there are no such true cedars in the United States, darling?" Dr.

Bob asked his wife. He explained, "These trees in the Punjab are as old as the cedars of Lebanon! They may have been little seedlings when the Temple was built at Jerusalem. Make you feel awfully small, don't they? Almost as if you had no right to be here. I feel like walking on tiptoe, afraid to wake up the past." When the snow fell on the ancient trees the young Americans walked hand in hand through fairyland. Yet Dr. Bob was still the scientist collector. They found there the strange water ousels and, startled, watched them walk on the water to pick up insects, then disappear behind a waterfall.

Bob became Doctor Robert Fleming in 1937 and, back in India, he lost no time in starting young Bobby, his son, off on his scientific career. The following summer, 1938, the whole family spent bird collecting in Assam. "We took Bobby with us on this trip although he was only six months old and we pitched our tent in the jungle with a former headhunter for a cook." At first Dr. Bob had feared that taking the family along would slow him up, but he soon found that together there is added security. "I found it rather convenient to have a doctor along; wandering alone about the jungle can be dangerous. And Bobby made even a tent a home.

"We collected so many species of birds that the Chicago Museum was impressed. They wrote me, 'We'd like five of that last species of pheasants if you can get them.' Goodness, there were hundreds available!" So Bob with a gun over his shoulder and Bethel with a baby under her arm went blithely into the Western Ghats near Bombay. "A ghat isn't only a place where a body is burned; it is also a steep eroded valley, rather like a small Grand Canyon of Arizona, which you go through to get to the mountains," Dr. Bob explains. "The jungle was so thick the trees met in a green canopy over our heads and all paths looked alike. Three people had recently gotten lost in this maze where two of them had died from exposure, but that didn't stop us from exploring when we heard a strange fowl crowing in the depths of the forest. But we did take the precaution of laying a paper trail so we could get back out again. When you're young, living dangerously is meat and drink. Nothing can happen *to you*."

When Sally Beth was born in 1944, they simply packed her up also, took off for the far fields and mountains; now there were four of them to explore the exciting world around them. Imagine being *paid* for having a continuous picnic!

They traveled 5,000 miles in India, exploring their adopted country further even than their own United States, listening for new bird calls, learning the ways in which the small creatures built their nests, how they ate and mated. Young Bobby soon proved himself his father's own son. "He didn't have to decide to be a biologist; he was born one!" Dr. Bob, who signs his letters to his son as "The Original," says proudly. When Bobby was only three, he and his father were standing on the green quadrangle in front of a mission station in Bombay, watching the sparrows hopping about, looking for bugs and worms. Young Bobby asked, "How do you catch a sparrow, Daddy?"

"Oh just creep up on it, grab it, and you have it," Dr. Bob told him, absently.

Half an hour later Bobby came into the living room with a baby sparrow clutched in his small hand. Bethel and Bob were bug-eyed, demanding, "How did you do it?"

"Oh, I just did like you said. I crept up on it, got it in a corner, and grabbed."

Bobby was eleven when he first went on a collecting trip for birds and ferns as his Dad's assistant. At fourteen Bobby went alone up into the hills back of Mussoorie, discovered under some rhododendrons, bent down by the snow, a Gould's short-wing which up to now had been found only in Sikkim. "He extended this bird's range by 1,000 miles! The husky lad could already out-walk me, leave me far behind," Dr. Bob recalls proudly.

Together the two achieved a record for speedy cooperation. Once when Bobby was in his teens, he and his father on an ornithological trip skinned eighty birds in one week, twenty-one in one day. His Excellency the Governor came over to see their collection; impressed, he rewarded the scientists by sending down gourmet meals. "One evening we shared a whole peacock," Bob says, still smacking his lips in remembrance of the feast after weeks of boiled rice and tsampa tea prepared by the native porters in their mountain camps. "Imagine! We had breast of a jungle fowl, shredded venison, and all the good things that went with them. This wasn't the Ritz but fifty miles from a turning wheel or a road!"

Best of all they appreciated Gopal Kali, the elephant His Excellency sent down so that the bird hunters could comb the high grasses and the swamps as well as the forest for new birds, could cover twice as much territory as was possible on foot.

"But it did seem rather ridiculous," Dr. Bob confesses wryly, "charging through the forest on this great beast, looking for something no bigger than a sparrow!"

Young Bobby's heart had been nearly broken because he could not go on his father's first ornithological trip into Nepal where the expedition was first aware of the needs of the sick at Tansen. The Flemings still had no permission to start a medical clinic, when they were allowed to take a second "birding" expedition to Nepal in 1951. This was very much a family affair. Young Bob who was fourteen and Sally Beth who was eight went along with their parents, as did another family of friends. Dr. Carl Friedericks, who had recently arrived from China to work in India, followed two weeks after the Flemings, bringing his wife and three small children, the oldest five and the baby only three months.

They were met with hospitality at Butwal where the governor sent a *dandi*, a small box with four bearers, for Sally Beth to ride in. The *dandi* was obviously too cramped for a large woman to ride in comfortably, so Dr. Bob hired a horse for Dr. Bethel. Never having ridden horseback in her life, she got on dubiously, trying to keep down the skirt of her cotton dress, to stay on the horse as it climbed swaying precariously up the narrow winding path. She didn't dare look down over the stirrup to the frightening valley below. After they had crossed what Dr. Bob called "two little mountains only five or six thousand feet high," the way grew steeper; Bethel, clutching desperately at the reins, could only shut her eyes to the sheer drop only a few feet away. Suddenly the horse gave a desperate lunge to make the top of a ridge, the surcingle broke; to her horror Behtel felt herself sliding backward. She was too frightened to scream.

"Dad! help! Mother's fallen off her horse!" Bobby yelled.

Bob tore up the path fearing to see both horse and rider at the bottom of the precipice, only to find his wife sitting speechless in the middle of the road with her rumpled cotton frock above her knees. She had slid off, saddle and all, over the horse's tail and found herself shaken but intact. They found a new surcingle for the horse but Bethel refused to mount again, insisting, "If I'm going over that precipice, I'll go on my own two legs!"

The guest house the family occupied at Tansen proved to be furnished with only one large table, because, they were told blandly, the rest of the furniture had been removed for a Rana wedding. Fortunately the Flemings had taken along the children's mattresses, heavy blankets, a folding table, and four chairs, so they made out nicely. The two families, the Flemings and the Friederickses, spent a gay Christmas together, exchanging odd Nepalese presents from the Tansen bazaar.

Bob's Christmas present to Bethel was a bag stuffed with straw for a mattress which was much appreciated.

When Tansen people found out that not one but two physicians had arrived, the crowd of expectant, pathetic patients was even larger than in 1949. While the two Bobs were off collecting ornithological specimens, Dr. Bethel and Dr. Carl set up a temporary dispensary where their one table proved invaluable for operating. General Rudra Shumshere had to send down troops to keep the patients in line, make sure the sickest got the first attention and were not shoved aside.

"We did everything from repairing a hideous harelip to removing stones from a gall bladder," Dr. Bethel recalls. "Most patients complained of a pain in the abdomen which could be anything from a tumor already suffered for years to worms which were the result of contaminated food or water. The Methodist and Presbyterian boards had given us antibiotics and we operated on hundreds of patients outdoors where it was more sanitary than inside on mud and dung floors.

"Those Tansen people need us," Dr. Bethel worried to Dr. Bob when the two families, the Flemings and the Friederickses, were safely back in India, complete with birds, children, and straw mattresses. "Let's write again to the government headquarters at Kathmandu to see if they won't please let us open a permanent dispensary in Tansen."

But still no answer came from the Nepalese government. Dr. Bob tried to believe it was a hopeful sign when he was invited to head a third ornithological expedition, this time into far western Nepal during his next Christmas vacation.

The father of one Rana student sent to study at the Woodstock School after Dr. Bob's first visit to Tansen, His Excellency Dairya Shumshere Jung Bahadur Rana, had become governor of Kailali-Kanchanpur, the extreme western region of the *terai*. The governor arranged for Dr. Bob and Bobby to visit him there in order to collect birds up north along the Doti hills. Naturally the two Bobs were aflame with excitement to go, but Dr. Bethel insisted firmly that she would not spend another Christmas alone. She announced that she and Sally Beth would join the party at Dhangarhi, a town just over the Indian border in Nepal, on Christmas Eve for a real American celebration. "Look for a pine tree and we'll bring the Christmas tree decorations!" she ordered.

"No ornithologist had ever visited this far western region before," Dr. Bob explains, "so I was thrilled to go. I took Bobby and a classmate, Richard Parker, and our Indian cook and set out for my third trip to Nepal in November 1953. I think now I had courage to take the boys into the wilderness with no doctor but then it didn't occur to me to worry. You can imagine how excited the boys were when the governor met us at the border town with an elephant for them to ride!"

They made Dhangarhi their headquarters for four weeks. On the trails they met groups of Nepalese country people from the north coming south for the winter, putting up leafy lean-tos where they and their cattle would stay until spring. Walking through the woods they passed a shrine to Lord Siva hung with small bells and tridents where large groups of Hindus, mostly pilgrims going south to India, stopped to pray. Evenings around their campfire forty village children sang them folksongs. The Nepalese adopted these strangers into their family group so cordially that "It was like discovering blood relatives you'd never had the good fortune to meet!" says Dr. Bob.

The boys and Dr. Bob traveled slowly through the countryside with an oxcart carrying their belongings, making side excursions when they found an exciting bird trail. "Once I got separated from the others, lost the oxcart, and landed alone in a perfectly strange village," Dr. Bob recalls nostalgically. "Dusk was falling, and when I asked the villagers for a guide to help me locate the rest of the party, they said, shocked, that no one ventured on that road after dark for fear of the tigers. This seemed a good enough reason for staying the night. I had no food, blankets, nothing, but the villagers eagerly brought me rice and boiling water, vegetables and *chapati*. One householder offered to let me sleep on his stone veranda where he built a fire; he brought me one blanket and, when he saw I was still shivering with the mountain cold, brought me another. I settled down snugly with my boot for a pillow and a large friendly warm black dog for a welcome bedfellow."

At Belauri, the capital of Kanchanpur province, with a population of 1,000, the party were offered one of the well-built brick houses, but preferred to put up their own tents in a mango orchard beyond town. The first night they were kept awake by unearthly cries of something that turned out to be nothing more lethal than a Pallas eagle. "We also found annoying the screams of swamp deer, the grunting of wild pigs, and the roars of tigers in the tall grass beyond our tents, but you soon got used to it," Dr. Bob remembers. "We collected blue-bearded bee-eaters, spur-winged plovers, rose-winged herons, egrets, terns, flycatchers, parakeets, and many other species of birds. The boys thought it as much fun as living in a circus; . . . you got to ride the elephants instead of watering them!"

Dr. Bethel had determined that this Christmas the family would be together if she had to climb Everest to locate "her boys." Dhangarhi was not far over the border into Nepal but getting

there from Mussoorie, India, was complicated; she and Sally Beth
had to change trains several times and the connections had to be
planned carefully to arrive on Christmas Eve. She and Sally Beth
also took along with them—besides the bedding without which
no one travels overnight in India—boiled water, fruit and other
food, and Christmas presents and decorations, for there would be
no rushing out to the Five & Dime for tinsel at the last moment.
Bethel half-baked the huge goose for their Christmas dinner, since
no refrigeration was possible, and made a couple of mince pies.
She packed the food and the candles that make a real Christmas
tree into several tin trunks, along with the presents for which Sally
Beth had shopped in the Landour bazaar. Happy and excited,
the Flemings spent too much time visiting with friends at Bareilly,
so arrived at the station with only ten minutes left before train
time to weigh in all the assorted baggage, to get it and themselves
aboard. The train for Tanakpur, she was told, was waiting on
Track Three. Bethel ordered the coolies ahead to put the luggage
on the train, rushed to find a second-class compartment where she
settled Sally Beth and the hand luggage, then got off to make
doubly sure the heavy luggage was aboard. But she could see no
coolies and no trunks!

"Mother! Mother! The train's going! Get on!" Frantic eight-
year-old Sally Beth was standing screaming in the compartment
doorway. Bethel swung herself aboard the moving train: better
to lose the luggage than Sally Beth.

"Now we won't have any Christmas!" Sally Beth wailed. "All
my nice presents . . ."

Impulsively Bethel reached up, pulled the emergency cord, and
the train stopped with a jerk. There was a fifty-rupee fine for halt-
ing the train unduly but she just couldn't see that goose and those
mince pies going off into heaven knew where.

The conductor came, raging, down the aisle. "Who stopped this
train?"

"I did," Bethel confessed. "Because my luggage is not aboard."
It didn't sound like a very good excuse even to her as she wondered
frantically how she could dig up fifty rupees, which was more than

her slender purse contained. Then she remembered that conductors are people, too. Maybe he even had children of his own. Bethel's smile would charm a tiger out of the jungle to purr at her hand. She explained, one parent to another to the conductor, "My little girl and I are meeting my husband and son to celebrate our very special Christian festival, the Day Our Lord, Jesus Christ, was born. It is our biggest holiday for children. Couldn't we please get off, now?"

The charmed conductor helped them down the steps, even carrying their heavy luggage. Safe but knowing that now they'd never reach Dhangarhi by Christmas Eve, Bethel and Sally Beth stood there disconsolate on the platform. Missing the train meant they might at best make it by noon on Christmas Day, and where, oh where, were the goose and the mince pies?

"Mother, there's our trunks!" Sally Beth cried.

The amazed Bethel stared at the beaming porters arriving for their pay. "That other train was for Allahabad. This train Tanakpur, Memsahib." It had never occurred to Bethel there might be two trains, one behind the other, on Track Three! She and Sally Beth reached the Nepal border complete with all their precious luggage on Christmas Eve as planned. It was fortunate they did; not only Dr. Bob and the boys were waiting on the platform for them but his Excellency the Governor, dressed superbly to receive foreign guests.

"He drove us in great style in his jeep to Dhangarhi," Bethel relates. "It was the first time I'd ever seen anyone driving a jeep in white gloves! The boys, of course, chose to ride back to camp on the elephant."

Dr. Bethel remembers this as "one of those perfect Christmases you look back on in after years" when the children have gone off to college or to build their own lives and parents are left with the ghost of the Christmas past. Yet this memory is theirs forever, to take out, to admire, to relive in every nostalgic detail. "The feast, with all its trimmings, was spiced with love and laughter. The gifts the boys had brought for us were peculiar, to say the least. Sally Beth and I had been able to shop in Landour but all the boys could do was comb the village bazaar. Bobby got me a lovely little tray that cost only five annas—about a nickle in our money—but it was such a pretty shape I later had it silverplated. Bobby's tray was just the right size to hold a sugar and creamer for tea." Dr. Bethel stops to laugh, to confess, "I guess what I really mean is that the gifts which young sons pick out for you, on their own, cannot be measured in annas or dollars! Big Bob couldn't find anything in the bazaar that I could conceivably want so he gave me a big jar of honey from their expedition store. The rodents had almost taken over our tent so Bobby's gift for Sally Beth brought down the house . . . a mouse trap! None of us will ever forget that Christmas together in Nepal."

The Flemings and their children may now be separated by thousands of miles, but they are still very much together in their sensitiveness to world needs. Last June, Dr. Bob Senior, "The Original," sent a letter of congratulations to his son Bobby, "The Duplicate," who had just taken his doctorate in biology at Michigan State. Today he is the second Dr. Robert Fleming to be teaching in Woodstock School, Mussoorie, India, where his father taught science for twenty-five years before he crossed the Nepal border. College freshman, young Sally Beth, plans after graduation to train as a nurse and to go back to Nepal.

Chapter Five

Early Days in Kathmandu

The United Mission to Nepal did not start with a 200-bed Shanta
Bhawan Hospital, however, but with a tiny clinic in a Kathmandu
front parlor.

One morning three months after the Flemings' return from
visiting the Roses at Kathmandu, and with their request to open a
medical mission in Tansen still unanswered, an official letterhead
arrived in Mussoorie. Dr. Bethel couldn't wait till Dr. Bob had
finished his science class to tell him about it. She sent a messenger,
who burst into Dr. Bob's classroom, with a piece of paper upon
which she had scribbled, "The government of Nepal has asked us
to come! Bethel." The damp place on her signature was a tear of
pure joy.

"Class dismissed!" Dr. Bob cried and rushed home to hold in
his own hands the longed-for invitation to start medical work
beyond the Himalayas. But uneasiness tempered the Flemings'
rejoicing as they read more closely the terms on which they were
to be admitted to the mysterious country of their dreams.

We are glad to inform you that His Majesty's Government will be
pleased to have you open medical work in Kathmandu and
Tansen on the following conditions:

1. You will finance the entire project yourselves.
2. You will charge no fees for any of your medicine or your
work.

3. You will train Nepalese in various branches of medical science.
4. You will hand over your work to the government of Nepal at the end of five years. . . .

They were to be allowed to start medical work not only in Tansen as they had asked but also in Kathmandu, the capital city.

"You see, we didn't ask big enough. The Lord's Plan for Nepal was greater than we knew!" Bethel exulted. Then Dr. Bethel and Dr. Bob, coming down to solid earth, stared at each other over the official-looking paper. What would the always needy Mission Board in New York say about going to all the expense of setting up a medical dispensary which would be theirs for only five years? A so-called "charity hospital" in India was expected to give only 5 percent of its services and medicines, free. In Nepal this new clinic would have to be 100 percent free. Even if by some miracle the Mission Board did agree to furnish equipment and cash for medical work, how could Dr. Bethel possibly train an adequate medical staff of Nepalese in so short a time? Yet how could Bob and Bethel refuse so wonderful an opportunity?

Bishop J. W. Pickett, the Flemings' immediate superior in the Methodist Church in India, felt that they should go. He argued, "If Nepal is willing to take a step like this, we should be willing also to take a step by faith." The Paul Roses at USOM also urged the Flemings to accept the somewhat guarded invitation. "Take it and trust to the good sense of the Nepalese government," Paul Rose wrote from Kathmandu. "Do your best for the five years and then see what happens."

Living within sight of the mountains of India as the Flemings had in Mussoorie, something of the majesty and tolerance of that vast landscape had already gotten into the veins of both Bob and Bethel. They felt that to go with healing to Nepal was more important than what particular Christian creed first crossed the border into that mysterious Hindu-Buddhist country. After his first trip to Tansen in 1949, Dr. Bob had written thoughtfully for his students in his sociology classes at Woodstock School:

Protestant Missions tend to follow two patterns. On the one hand, emphasis is upon the evangelical approach. Missionaries are carefully trained in a college or seminary in a thorough knowledge of the Bible. Gospel songs and literature are characterized by an evangelistic fervor. . . . There is a certain note of urgency. . . . All other phases of missionary work are subsidiary. . . . Immediately following the war of 1939–45, two thirds of those coming to India belong to this group.

Missionaries who follow the second pattern usually belong to missions which have been in India a longer time and whose work is more widely spread. They have studied theology along with sociology, psychology, and anthropology . . . education, medicine, agriculture. They look to service for others which would meet the need of the entire individual, his spiritual, also his mental and social life. Planning the mission program is on a long-range basis with less emphasis upon the immediate and more upon the future. Those of the second group often consider themselves as research persons upon which their Indian colleagues may call. They often hold advanced degrees from recognized institutions in America and other countries. . . . [This kind of missions] is a real witness to the fact that Christ is unique and when His principles are adequately practised, the world becomes a better place in which to live.*

Bishop Pickett who was of this latter school of thought insisting that this first mission to Nepal must be like the missionary journeys of the early church, lay men and women dedicated first to Jesus Christ. Doctor, teacher, nurse, agriculturalist, any witness should be allowed to go. "What does it matter by what path he may have climbed to the hilltop of Golgotha? It is the Cross that is important!"

"We must not make the same mistakes we did in India," the bishop insisted earnestly to the church officials and to the Flemings. "You happen to be American Methodists; more impor-

* Robert L. Fleming, *India Past and Present* (Mysore, India: Wesley Press and Publishing House, 1950).

tant, you are Christians. We must aim at intercredal, international cooperation not competition." Perhaps, he mused, it's a good thing that they could not preach, except through the triumphant life of service. They were to remember there is not only the Cross but the crown: a Christian should be happy.

Bethel and Bob Fleming, in their excitement at their opportunity to serve, were already living in an atmosphere as rarefied as that on the peak of Everest. If need be, they would have climbed up to the steep Chandragiri Pass, walked back alone down the precipitous slopes to the lush Kathmandu Valley teaming with sick people who needed them, with nothing but Dr. Bethel's instruments and medical knowledge. They did not even wait for official sanction to send their reply.

"Relying entirely on faith that the Lord had led us this far, we wrote back at once to tell the Nepalese government that we would come," Dr. Bob says.

"Who can limit the Plan?" Dr. Bethel asks simply. Then, as usual, Dr. Bethel's wise brown eyes and Dr. Bob's very blue ones meet; the look that flashes between them is a hand held out to each other. Thus for a quarter of a century they have walked together fearless of anything life can offer. For this is a true marriage of body, mind, and spirit, a creative marriage which daily gives the lie to the pessimism of the angry young men whose language of defeat fills hefty volumes, pathetic pages of frail heroes who blame their failure on inheritance, on environment whether in city streets or desert islands, on anything and anyone but themselves. People like the Flemings make their own environment. They have dug down to the Rock upon which a man may safely build his home. Thus hand in hand they climbed eagerly into unknown Nepal.

On a bright October morning in 1953, Dr. Bethel attended the Delhi Methodist Conference of which she and her husband were both members; she sat alone as Dr. Bob could not leave his Mussoorie high-school classes. She listened, breathless, as a new appointment was read out, to go where no Protestant missionaries had ever been assigned before:

"Dr. and Mrs. Robert Fleming to Kathmandu, Nepal!"

For an instant the great audience sat in startled silence, then the entire assembly rose to their feet in a thunder of applause.

"That November Bethel and I started off with little or no financial backing to start our clinic in Kathmandu," Dr. Bob recalls. "True, the Methodists had advanced us $500, petty cash among nine million people. We had only our salaries, one pocket set of instruments that belonged to Bethel, a few medicines, and the faith that if we were following the Plan, more help would come."

The Flemings have built their many hospitals and clinics in Nepal by faith every day for the past nine years and the Plan has never failed them. Even today the tourists who come to see Shanta Bhawan Hospital are so impressed they tell of it all over the world and voluntarily send back help. As she shows international guests through her wards and laboratories, Dr. Bethel explains casually, "That electrocardiograph machine is Baptist, the new X-ray machine is Methodist, and the Menonite conscientious objectors sent us by the U.S. government built that stairway up to the third floor so we wouldn't have to carry a woman in labor through the operating room to get to the delivery room." The Plan has always been sufficient for the day, whether they needed blood transfusions or a full-time resident surgeon like Dr. Robert Berry, "whom the Lord sent with His love," Dr. Bethel explains. An architect just happened to stop by on his way home to Norway in time to plan the two well-baby clinic buildings she wanted at Sundarijal. A busy dentist gave them three months' help on his vacation. Can you run a 100,000-customer business by prayer? They do it daily in Nepal.

The medical work at their first clinic grew in geometric progression. The Presbyterians and several other groups who had workers already along the Indian-Nepalese border joined the Flemings. Formal arrangements for the United Medical Mission to Nepal were completed in March 1954, at Nagpur, India, where Ernest Oliver was appointed the first executive secretary for the new venture. He was well fitted for the job, for while in the British Army during the war, he had become friendly with those brave little fighting men, the Gurkhas (as a matter of fact they come from many parts of Nepal besides Gorkha), and had learned from them to speak Nepali. His salary was paid by The Regions Beyond Missionary Union. In less than five years, medical work in Nepal was backed by seventeen different churches or Christian lay groups from twelve countries. They had become one of the largest interfaith lay missions in the world!

"Strange how the Lord prepares little people to do His great will," said one visitor to Shanta Bhawan recently as she looked over the 400 patients crowding the Saturday clinic, the waiting line in the hospital lobby for the ward beds. "After thousands of years the sun of opportunity rose behind these great mountains. The promise is eternal, the same yesterday, this moment, and tomorrow—'and the earth shall be filled with the glory of God. . . .'"

The trip from Mussoorie to Nepal was hardest for Dr. Bethel since she was not only mother and housewife but a busy physician. Manlike, the two Bobs thankfully escaped the confusion of moving by taking off for West Nepal to collect more birds, en route to their new home in Kathmandu. Dr. Bethel had to attack the practical problem of packing up their belongings collected over twenty-five years, of moving to a city to which all of their furniture had to be carried by native porters over the Himalayas into the Kathmandu Valley.

"If they can carry in Chevrolets for the Ranas to ride in, I guess they can manage our grand piano," Dr. Bethel said hopefully. Dr. Bob loved to play, to sing in his rich tenor voice, and Sally Beth was learning to accompany her father, so leaving the piano behind would be like deserting a member of the family.

In addition, Dr. Bethel could hardly just walk out of her responsibilities in India. She had to stay in Mussoorie to finish the fall semester, until someone could be found to replace her as physician at Woodstock School and in the Landour Community Hospital.

The four Flemings had agreed to meet at Rabi Bhawan with the Roses for Christmas. Bethel had little time to pack until school closed on December 17th, the day she and Sally Beth would have to leave by train in order to get to Kathmandu for the 25th. To complicate things further, the Maharajah's daughter in Landour had her baby prematurely and nothing would do except for Dr. Bethel to stop packing and take care of her. The delivery was a difficult one, not safely accomplished until December 16th, the day before Bethel and Sally Beth were scheduled to start their trip to Nepal.

As before, they would have to ride on four different railroads, change to a native bus, then climb on foot over the Chandragiri Pass to Thankot where the Kathmandu road began.

"That last day was a madhouse," Bethel recalls. "I packed twenty-seven trunks and big pieces and it was four in the afternoon before I got the coolies off to carry the stuff to the end of the road where the Maharajah, penitent at delaying me, had loaned me a truck." But when Bethel arrived, breathless and exhausted, the driver refused to load so much luggage on his precious truck. What to do? The train they had to catch left Dehra Dun in less than two hours.

Bethel, desperate, told the truck driver, "I'll hire a bus to take what you can't get on." She had to offer the bus driver thirty rupees, which seriously depleted her travel funds, but she had no time to bargain. She warned him anxiously, "Hurry, please. We have all this stuff to weigh in before the train that connects for Raxaul leaves at six-thirty."

She and Sally Beth climbed up on the front seat of the Maharajah's truck, started off at a great pace, only to have the truck stop dead. "We're out of gas," the Maharajah's driver announced gloomily. Bethel waved the bus coming up behind them to a frantic stop, ordered the transfer of all the rest of the luggage, but the driver refused any extra load.

"I cannot do this, Memsahib. This is a chartered bus, direct to the station!"

"But I'm the one who chartered it!"

"That makes no difference," the driver insisted with the stubbornness of an Indian insisting upon his rights. "I did not agree to take on new freight or passengers!"

"Well, can you give the truck a push to the gas station?"

This the bus driver consented to do, then he drove off, having done his duty as he saw it. By the time Bethel and Sally Beth arrived at the station practically hysterical with worry, the train connecting for Raxaul had already left; there was no other until the following day. Bethel was regarding her mountain of luggage despairingly when the stationmaster came up with a new dilemma. "Doctor, you have only one lock on those trunks. Each is required to have a lock on both ends! But I have good news for you. A new carriage is being connected which will be detached at Allahabad where you can make connection with Raxaul; but the train is leaving in only fifteen minutes."

Bethel stared at him. "But what will I do about the locks?" It was impossible to put new locks on twenty-seven trunks, weigh them all, and get them aboard the train in fifteen minutes: she would have to trust the Maharajah's truck driver. Bethel gave him ten rupees to buy the new locks and put them on, made him promise to send on her precious luggage on next day's train. With the conductor screaming at her that he'd already held the train ten minutes—and who did she think she was?—Bethel found a second-class compartment for Sally Beth, the cat, the dog, and the hand luggage of which there was, if not a mountain, at least a small hill, saw that the cook had a seat in the third-class compartment, and sank, exhausted, into her own seat. She certainly hoped that the truck driver would keep his word, for everything the Flemings owned in the world was in those twenty-seven trunks.

The trunks actually arrived the next day at Allahabad but with more problems attached as well as two locks. In her haste, Bethel had neglected to get baggage receipts for them, and on an Indian railroad, no receipt, no luggage. By the time she got that difficulty straightened out, it was noon and the twenty-seven trunks had to be transferred to the other railway leaving for Raxaul in only one hour, during which everything would have to be retagged by the new railroad officials. Was there no end to this comedy of errors?

"I just had that stuff all weighed at the other station. Couldn't you possibly accept it as written? Here is my receipt," Bethel pleaded with the new stationmaster, wishing by now she was an elephant with one trunk instead of having twenty-seven. "Here, look!"

The idea worked. Worn but triumphant, Bethel got on the next train, slid off into the deep sleep of exhaustion. Unfortunately they had to change cars to one with a narrower gauge at four the next morning. Bethel wearily had to wake up Sally Beth, sleep-walk her off the train, together with the cat mewing angrily in her basket, the dog barking on his leash, and the cook no help at all in seeing about the twenty-seven trunks. This time the stationmaster announced there wasn't room for so much luggage in the van. But Bethel, having fought her way this far, was not to be balked. She tipped a crew of porters to make room in the van, and once more she and Sally Beth, the cook, the cat, the dog, and the twenty-seven trunks took off toward Nepal.

Friends met them at Raxaul, the border town where they spent the night, with the cheering news that Bethel and Sally Beth would not have to take the native bus to Bhimpedi because a jeep and trailer were being sent down for them. "Happy day in the morning," murmured Bethel. "It looks as if all of us may get there in one piece, after all." But it turned out that the trailer would hold only half her luggage. She stood on the station platform in a daze of fatigue trying to decide which of the twenty-seven trunks held her and the children's clothes and which the eggbeater and blankets. She didn't have the keys to the new locks of course; all she could do was count, eeny, meany, miny, mo, and hope she was right. Her left-behind trunks were not delivered in Kathmandu until the end of January. Such was moving day in the Himalayas.

It was thick dark when Bethel and Sally Beth got out of the jeep at the end of the road at Bhimpedi which now became a precipitous mountain path. Bethel had already arranged for them to stay in the Guest House on the ridge at Chisapani Garhi, so they started off into the night, a long dim procession of weary Flemings—Bethel, Sally Beth, their cook, cat, and dog—followed by the small army of porters carrying their belongings.

"Sally Beth was worn out . . . she was still a little girl, not quite ten . . . she rode in her *dandi*," Bethel recalls. She herself was over fifty, not exactly young for a woman to be setting out to climb an 8,000-foot pass over the Himalayas after all she had been through the past few days. "I walked beside my *dandi* because I'm too big to fit inside such a little box. I stumbled along in the pitch blackness feeling out one step at a time, thinking I couldn't possibly make the next one. I was exhausted, discouraged, tired to my very bones. Suddenly the darkness blossomed out with a flower of light, then another, and another! The servants had lighted great clumps of what looked like cat o'nine tails, stood bowing and waving the lights along our way. I lifted my head, walking a little straighter. '*Namaste!*' I called back to their smiling greetings. *This was Nepal! I was here!* So we arrived at the Guest House, Sally Beth and I, welcomed like two princesses."

Rabi Bhawan held out even more welcome rest for the weary Flemings after Bethel and Sally Beth had walked across the Chandragiri Pass and down the other side of the mountain to where the jeep again waited to carry them from Thankot to Kathmandu, to American soap and a tub of hot water.

"But I don't think our friends the Roses were expecting our livestock," Bethel recalls ruefully. "We had to keep the cat in our room and keep a close watch on the dog. After the two Bobs walked in from their collecting trip, we all celebrated Christmas together, then we started looking around for a place to begin our medical clinic as soon as possible. I wanted especially to do prenatal work among the women. I had treated so many botched jobs among the Tansen patients, women with clumsy abortions, childless women afraid they'd either lose their husbands by divorce or have to accept a fertile concubine in the home. The children also desperately needed medical attention because of malnutrition in the midst of plenty; in a rich valley overflowing with ample crops, they had to be taught how to use what they had for a balanced diet. This was why I as a woman doctor had come to Kathmandu, and the medical work must not be delayed even to find ourselves a roof of our own."

Dr. Bethel rested only a few days before she and Mrs. Rose climbed into the American jeep, bumped over the road to

Bhatgaon at the edge of Kathmandu where they decided to ask the district magistrate for his help and advice in finding a home for their new clinic. They followed a narrow road of flagstones between the brick city buildings with their glassless windows staring like black hostile eyes, and came out onto a courtyard where ancient stone gods carved thousands of years ago stood silently watching these brash young Westerners. Bethel suggested, "Let's ask that nice-looking man over there if he can tell us where to find the magistrate."

"Yes, I can help you find him," the nice-looking man smiled. "I *am* the magistrate, Badri Prasad Thapalia."

"Mrs. Rose from Rabi Bhawan and I am Dr. Bethel Fleming," Bethel introduced them. "We are looking for a place to open a medical dispensary for women and children. Have you any suggestions?"

"*Namaste!* You are welcome. I have heard you are here." The magistrate offered Dr. Bethel first a room in the temple courtyard in Hanuman Khola. Hanuman is the monkey god, especially sacred in Kathmandu, and the priests wearing their saffron robes in his service were going in and out of the picturesque temple with its gilded pagoda roofs, while pilgrims crowded the rest rooms that lined the square, eating, drinking, spitting, and praying. Bethel tried to picture adding to this confusion a long line of anxious patients such as the police had had to keep in order when word got around Tansen that a doctor was available. . . .

"It's very nice here," Bethel murmured tactfully, "but . . . do you have any other suggestions? Perhaps we should see other places first, a little less crowded perhaps, before deciding?"

"There is that large house, just over that little stream." The huge rambling brick structure was already occupied by a family of 150 members but they obligingly offered to move into the back rooms, to leave the front rooms for the dispensary. Dr. Bethel could move in any time, the magistrate assured her; the quarters would be free of charge, he added proudly. This was just as well, as Bethel had no money to pay for rent. The magistrate, eager to help, offered his own daughter as interpreter between doctor and the patients, who would understand only a little of Bethel's Hindi. Bethel went back to Rabi Bhawan with a warmth about her heart from the friendliness of the Nepalis, so eager to do what they could to help themselves. What more could you do than move out of your own front living room?

Word spread around that the new clinic would open January 7th. The American women from USOM in Kathmandu, startled at the meagerness of Dr. Bethel's medical equipment, gave her a modest sum to buy extra instruments. Warned by the crowds of patients at Tansen, she wired the Community Hospital at Landour, India, for a temporary loan of three nurses. Three missionary nurses, one from South Dakota, a second from Canada, and a third from India, answered the call for help. Dr. Carl Friedericks arrived also to prepare to open medical work in Tansen. "So from its very beginning, the United Mission to Nepal had volunteers from several nations working together," Dr. Bethel points out. "On New Year's Day, Bob and I, Dr. Carl, and the nurses went to Bhatgaon to clean up the place, to put fresh papers on the shelves, and to sterilize our equipment for the expected avalanche of patients. Only twenty women and children, however, arrived on the opening day. Kathmandu was trying us out, waiting to see if our strange new medicine really worked." Dr. Bethel diagnosed and prescribed for the patients while the nurses carried out the treatment.

"An old lady with pus dropping out of both her eyes was our first patient." Dr. Bethel adds with a small shiver. "Imagine my concern when I found out that she was the chief midwife for that section of the city!"

The number of patients increased rapidly as the confidence of the neighborhood grew that these foreign doctors and nurses who cured illness "for free" really were as good or better than the Nepalese "compounders" or native medicine men who had to be paid. Soon the clinic treated fifty patients a day, and after a few weeks 200 were lined up each morning in the narrow street, waiting for treatment. Dr. Bethel had to get some order into that milling mob, so a nurse went down the line, gave the most obviously ill pink cards to insure they would be seen that day; the others were given white numbered slips, so if there was not time to see them before dark (the electric-light bulbs were too dim to allow diagnosis, so night clinics were impossible) they would be attended to first on the following day. Some of the Buddhists thought these slips were Christian prayers like those printed in their own prayer wheels, but the nurses patiently explained those were not magic numbers on the cards.

When Dr. James Mathews (later to be elected Bishop of the Methodist Church) came up from India to see how the new Kathmandu clinic was making out, he was all but elbowed away from the dispensary door by 270 patients, women and children struggling for their pink and white cards. Dr. Bethel said with a chuckle later to Bob, "I think the good man was a little shaken. Anyway, he says he's going to report to the Board that we need more help."

During this avalanche of work, the Flemings and the nurses still had to find a place to live: they couldn't impose on the Roses' hospitality forever. Dr. Bob had been appointed superintendent for the Kathmandu area to attend to all but medical details. While Dr. Bethel was busy in the clinic, he tramped the streets for miles looking for a home. The native brick houses were sturdily built but had dirt and dung floors, no electricity, and, worse, no plumbing at all, not even an outhouse; the neighbors merely used the back lane to relieve themselves. Bob finally discovered a landlord who would put in a bathroom; they put up a sign, "Medical Mission," and the Flemings were at home. The location was inconvenient: to get to the clinic they had to walk through the fields along a narrow pathway of nightsoil and other oddities thrown out from the houses. "Not exactly a sterile approach," Bethel joked wearily when she walked home after attending to 200 clinic patients in one day.

It was becoming more and more evident that they had to have a hospital to which to send patients so desperately ill that they needed in-patient care and nursing. But how could they build and equip a proper hospital with no funds and less than five years to go? As usual the Flemings talked their problems over with the Lord, and as usual the way opened.

"You don't have to know the whole Plan," Bethel explains. "Only the next step."

The government officials who had been watching their efforts with great interest offered the Flemings the use of one wing of the cholera hospital which had recently been emptied of patients.

The previous year's epidemic must have been pretty bad. The soiled leather mattresses were beyond recovery, so the Flemings took them out on the lawn and burned them, while a frantic little policeman hopped up and down in agony because they were "destroying government property." They sterilized the metal beds with a blowtorch borrowed from Rabi Bhawan; also sterilized was a wasp's nest discovered under one bed just in time. Walls and floors were so filthy they had to be scraped clean. Miss Isla Knight, one of the Christian nurses (she is still in charge of the long lines of clinic patients at Shanta Bhawan Hospital), was down on her knees, trying not to vomit as she scrubbed.

"I hope you realize no one could *pay* me to do this!" she snapped to Dr. Bethel. "I'm doing it of my own free will!"

They spent most of their initial $500 for paint for the cholera ward, green for the walls and a cheerful red for the beds, and decided to have "a grand opening" on February 20, 1954, at which they invited the Nepalese public health minister to preside. Unfortunately, just two days before the big event (for the Flemings anyway) the government cabinet was reshuffled; there was no new health minister as yet. Bishop Pickett was coming up from India and could be depended upon to pinch-hit, but Dr. Bob and Dr. Bethel had set their hearts on having a Nepalese play the major role in their opening.

"Why don't you invite the prime minister His Excellency, M. P. Koirala?" another member of the new cabinet suggested.

"But would such an important man accept our invitation at the last minute?" Dr. Bethel worried. "Especially a secondhand one!"

"Mr. Koirala is very understanding, he knows the value of medical work," she was assured. So the belated invitation was sent off posthaste. The Flemings spent their small remaining hoard of coins to buy ten native mattresses at seventy-five cents each in the bazaar, and the very last rupee went for a red ribbon to stretch across the hospital-wing door for the prime minister to cut . . . if he came.

The opening had been set for three in the afternoon. At a quarter of the hour, everything was ready, including dainty sandwiches and tea supplied by the American ladies at USOM. Since the Flemings could not afford to buy sheets for the beds, they had borrowed from the government red blankets which they tucked in carefully to hid the deficiency. But would any of those important Nepalese they had invited come? Bethel and Bob needn't have worried. Cars began to roll up to the cholera hospital door, letting out field marshals, generals in full uniform with medals, high government officials, USOM personnel, and other friends; even the Nepalese foreign minister was kind enough to lend his presence. But no prime minister. The foreign minister urged Dr. Bethel, "Give His Excellency a few more minutes of grace." But how long could one keep all these important people waiting?

The welcome roar of official motorcycles, then a squealing of truck brakes sent the two Doctor Flemings hurrying to the door. A truckload of attendant soldiers had arrived and, yes, Bethel could see the official flags on the fenders—the big black car behind the soldiers was that of the prime minister!

"Thank you, Lord!" Bethel said silently as Dr. Bob rushed outside to greet His Excellency, for M. P. Koirala's backing for their hospital was second only to that of royalty.

Nine years later to the day, a modern Hospital for Contagious Diseases was opened by King Mahendra, before a distinguished international audience from the diplomatic corps and Nepalese government officials. This was actually the old cholera hospital entirely rebuilt on the same site.

Like all recent government buildings, the stucco walls of the new hospital had been painted pink—"shocking pink" the Kathmandu newspaper had grumbled when even the new supreme court building had been painted this gay color. But at least new government buildings could be easily identified, and perhaps warm rosy pink was more welcoming than stark white for the awed patients being ushered into immaculate wards with high hospital beds to save the nurses' backs. Where, nine years before, the Flemings had had no sheets and primitive plumbing, the new modern hospital had bathrooms where water actually flowed from the taps, white-tiled examining rooms for diagnosis by Nepalese doctors and nurses, trained either in Europe, the United States, or India. It was almost impossible to believe that such a short time had passed since the Flemings had scraped and blowtorched ten beds, and waited for the prime minister to cut their one-rupee red ribbon!

"Look! One of these beds is still red like we painted it!" one of the mission nurses remarked excitedly to Dr. Edgar Miller, now chief of staff of Shanta Bhawan Hospital and its official representative at the dedication of the new hospital. "Why isn't Dr. Bethel here to see all this? To help celebrate?"

"She had to go to the Sundarijal clinic," Dr. Miller explained. "Some of the patients walk for a week down from the mountains to consult her. She said she couldn't fail them."

His Majesty, King Mahendra, had reason to be proud as he walked up the red carpet to the dais erected for him, acknowledging the applause of various members of the diplomatic corps including the American Ambassador Henry Stebbins; all knew that Nepal and the United States had worked closely together to make this medical transformation possible. The Contagious Diseases Hospital is only one branch of the 200-bed Bir Government Hospital, well-equipped in both operating rooms, wards, and trained personnel, through the joint efforts of East and West. As the Nepalese national anthem blared from the band, followed by "The Star-Spangled Banner," the King stood erect with both the Nepalese flag and Old Glory waving in the mild breeze.

King Mahendra is tall for a Nepali, and holds himself like the monarch he is. Most Nepalese men wear tight-fitting white trousers (apt to bag in the seat) with their white shirttails hanging out;

over that the average businessman or teacher wears a coat and shoes if he is affluent enough to afford them. The King wears the national costume but with a difference. This particular morning he was well tailored in gray: gray tweed coat over his high-necked snowy cravat, tight gray trousers, and a cotton Nepali cap debonair and gaily flowered. He was accompanied by Queen Ratna in a delicate floating sari, wearing the dark glasses she and the King use as protection against the stark Kathmandu sun. Next to the Queen sat the Princess, wife of Prince Himalaya, lending more grace to the occasion. The women sat quietly, letting the King give the welcome sign, *"Namaste!"* to his guests.

"This is a great occasion, Your Majesty!"

As the superintendent of the Bir Hospital, the young and handsome Dr. Prasad, stepped forward to greet the royal visitor, Dr. Miller noted on his program that the superintendent's first name was also Mahendra. Dr. Miller realized suddenly, "That's the young surgeon to whom Bethel loaned our Shanta Bhawan operating room—with only his own word as to who he was!"

Dr. Bethel is never one to stand on red tape when a patient needs help but the elastic of medical ethics was certainly stretched a bit on the day she and Dr. Prasad first became friends.

"We at Shanta Bhawan had the only well-equipped operating room in Nepal in 1956," she explains. "One day a young Nepali came into my office; I didn't know him but I liked his clean-cut earnest face. He said he was just back from doing pediatric surgery in London and that the young son of one of his friends had an acute appendix.

" 'You don't know me, Dr. Fleming, but could I operate on the boy in your operating room?' he begged.

"I hesitated. I could hardly turn over my hospital to a complete stranger I knew nothing about, but this young doctor was so desperately in earnest. . . .

"I'll scrub up with you," Dr. Bethel told him quietly. "Bring in your patient. Both of us will operate."

She stood by to assist while the brilliant young Nepali doctor operated and the small boy lived. Now as friends as well as heads of two great hospitals, they assist each other in diagnosis, call upon each other whether for X-ray plates, opening a new clinic, or only for a special nursing bottle for a premature baby. Regardless of age or nationality, more than professional red tape binds them together. Dr. Bethel did not need to leave her Sundarijal patients to celebrate the opening of this new Contagious Diseases Hospital; she was there in spirit in her Nepali friend, who said in his dedicatory speech how their constant effective help "has earned our respect for the American people."

Another important person was missing from this ninth anniversary of the opening of the Christian clinic in the old cholera hospital—His Excellency, M. P. Koirala, who had done more than cut the one-rupee red ribbon and declare the mission hospital open for service to his people in 1954. He had taken a look down through the years.

He now acts as ambassador for his country not only in Washington but to the United Nations. On a recent trip home to Nepal, Ambassador Koirala revisited Shanta Bhawan Hospital, now equipped with nearly 200 beds (including the auxiliary hospital, Surendra Bhawan, next door), with a staff drawn from many nations.

"When I, as prime minister, decided to help the United Mission to start work here in Kathmandu, there was much opposition from many sides," admitted the ambassador as he looked out over the doctors, nurses, and technicians assembled on the hospital lawn to do him honor. "The beginning may have been a small one, but just as the seed is tiny, not very impressive, it grows in good soil to bear delicious fruit, so the United Mission has blossomed into service to us all. The cholera hospital was untouchable; Dr. Bethel Fleming made it touchable. Those who opposed you would not say anything against you now. You have established yourselves in your own right in the hearts of the Nepali people whom you serve."

Chapter Six

Nepal Spells Adventure

Travel has greatly changed since the Flemings crossed the Chandragiri Pass on foot, slid down the snowy mountainside to Kathmandu, though it is still possible to walk into Nepal from India and China as many Hindu and Buddhist pilgrims do, as well as refugees escaping from Tibet. However, there are now daily flights to Kathmandu by either the Indian or the Royal Nepalese airlines from Delhi or Calcutta as well as from other cities. But even the official brochures admit that travel in Nepal may still be an adventure. After listing the airplane schedules, the travel leaflet adds blandly, "Other means of transport are porters, bullock carts, buffalo carts, elephants, asses, sheep, goats, and yaks."

In addition to these assorted methods of travel, buses, trucks, and American jeeps run daily over the Rajpath, the King's Highway, built and completed by the Indian government just in time for the coronation of King Mahendra in 1956. This "motorable" road runs from the Indian border to Kathmandu and is only about ninety miles long, but it frequently takes two days to make the trip, depending upon how many washouts or mountain landslides there have been or whether or not a huge trailer carrying freight lies stuck at a sharp turn of the road with a thousand-foot cliff dropping off to one side.

With less than 400 miles of motorable roads in the whole country and with plane and radio connections only between the principal cities, with machines which frequently break down with no spare parts to repair them available for weeks, the problem of communication is overwhelming. In fact, Kathmandu is almost as much a mystery to many of the Nepalese mountain villagers as it is to the rest of the world.

The traveler who goes by jeep over the Rajpath frequently has to be washed off to be identified when he arrives at Kathmandu, with his face, clothes, and body a mummy of dust and sweat hardened into mud. The most comfortable way to get to this capital city is to fly to Goucher Airport, which is today as modern as Logan Airport in Boston if not quite as large. The plane trip from New Delhi to The Valley, as its inhabitants call the rich alluvial plain surrounding Kathmandu, is one of the most beautiful and exciting in the world. The plane is only a small mosquito buzzing busily down the vast aerial runway between the lofty snow-capped mountains on either side, many of whose peaks are over 20,000 feet high. Here the traveler gets his first glimpse of the great "snows." In the monsoon season of heavy rains or in case of deep mist or a dust storm, the plane cannot fly on schedule, since trying to navigate this precarious mountain route without clear vision could end only in kindling upon a desolate mountainside. The planes are mostly ancient DC3's, almost twenty years old dating back to just after the Second World War, but they are trusty, husky, kept in good repair, and flown by expert pilots. Yet some planes lack not only pressurization but heat, so when the plane mounts to 6,000 feet, the passenger's ears begin to pop and he digs shivering into his luggage for extra sweaters to supplement the heavy blankets the stewardess has already thoughtfully distributed.

But the scenery is so breathtakingly magnificent, minor discomforts simply do not matter as the traveler gazes, awed, at the towering "lords of the sky," tall, majestic, and a little frightening, upon whose dazzling snowy peaks the gods make their high homes. Sometimes Everest is visible, sometimes not, but the flight from Calcutta rarely misses seeing the tallest mountain in the world.

To look below is almost as fascinating as at the snows, for the mosaic of the many-colored fields and farms down in the deep valleys, embroidered up the mountainsides till some of the crops seem to stand almost vertically, makes a lovely intricate pattern of squares and rhomboids. There lies a bright green rice field, here a yellow square of flowering mustard, again appears a deeper blue-green, perhaps to prove that, even in Nepal, "cabbages is beautiful." All of these fields have been laboriously terraced and cultivated for thousands of years by the patient hands and primitive hoes of the farmers who make up over 80 percent of the country's populace. Those mud-village dwellers down there, whose homes are hacked from the very ground they cultivate, eke out an existence on a few rupees a week (a Nepalese rupee is about thirteen American cents) but they are as firmly planted in the good earth as their own seeds; they have always the gods of the sky looking down upon their small doings. Who could tell who is happier, the traveler in the noisy plane shattering the ancient silence, or they down below, rich in time and uncluttered peace?

As the plane nears Kathmandu, the pilot seems to be heading directly for a mountain; the traveler thinks of downdrafts that could smash a plane to matchsticks in a matter of seconds, but before he can let out his held breath, the plane has made an abrupt turn and is gliding down into the lush valley of Kathmandu and toward the black tarmac of Goucher Airport.

If the traveler turned right around to return to New Delhi on the same plane in which he arrived, the trip to Kathmandu would have been still worth his while. But this rich valley, which is only about 4,500 feet above sea level and used to be a great lake, has a special magic which draws the imagination as the moon the tides. There is enchantment in a mountain always peering over one's shoulder, a sense of uncluttered leisure. Brooding over this sprawling lovely capital city rise the brown and green Mountains of the Moon and other lower Himalayas, while behind these "hills" on a clear day is visible a breathtaking circle of snowy peaks, everlasting, awesome, some of them too sacred even to be climbed. Is there a more beautiful city in the world, with infinity at the end of every muddy lane if one but lifts up his eyes?

Yet Nepal, with its gentle valleys and violent peaks, is a place of fantastic contrasts. In the fertile *terai* along the Indian border still lurk tigers, rhinoceros, wolves, elephants, and the even more dangerous mosquito whose bite causes a particularly vicious malaria that may drive a man mad before he dies. This danger is, however, disappearing rapidly before the DDT guns of the World Health Organization and the use of modern drugs, though Dr. Bob Fleming himself recently nearly lost his own life from a recurrent attack of this virulent form of malaria. Naturally that did not prevent his going back to the *terai* to hunt for new bird specimens or to pick the site for a needed medical clinic among the scattered villages where he has made many friends on his ornithological trips.

So varied is this beautiful little country that almost anything one may say about it can be true. Nepal is alternately mountain cold and hellishly hot. It is a very old country whose artists have carved buildings seldom equaled for beauty and workmanship; it is also a disease-riddled country, trying to cure and educate its almost entirely illiterate people, to make the jump from the Middle Ages to the present in one great leap.

Nepal is far more than a picturesque small monarchy strategically situated between India and China. It is a confused state of mind which wavers between a sincere desire to become a modern unified nation, and a reluctance to give up a culture thousands of years old which has held people together in the convenient layers of the caste system, obedient to the powerful astrologer-priests. It is desperately trying to work out an educational system that is modern and yet does not disdain the beauty of old legends, to discover that form of government best fitted for its particular needs.

The country has been open to foreigners only about thirteen years. Up to 1951 few Westerners were admitted to this tight little kingdom which was ruled for the last century by the Rana Maharajahs (they kept the King, who appeared in public only at religious festivals, a virtual prisoner in his own palace). Westerners were either restricted to the area of a few miles around the capital city or had their every footstep dogged by government "observers." The British Resident, for example, was allowed to travel only twelve miles from his large white home in Kathmandu where his homesick wife had planted a nostalgically beautiful English garden.

Under the Ranas, Nepal had developed almost none of the national consciousness which King Mahendra is now trying to inspire. Since most of the villages were scattered among rugged mountains or in far-off valleys many days' walk from each other, many villages did not even understand each other's language, and spoke of "going to Nepal" when they meant to Kathmandu. To them this was not their capital, but a foreign market in which to sell their wares. They considered themselves Gurkhas, Sherpas (the famous Tigers of the Snow who guide the mountain-climbing expeditions), Rais, Lepchas, or one of the many other racial groups, rather than Nepalese.

Disunity was caused not only by the lack of roads and communication but by the vast difference between the economic condition of the common man, whose average yearly income is about thirty-five dollars, and the enormous wealth of the ruling Ranas who lived regally in their great sprawling Victorian palaces. While 95 percent of the nine million Nepalese could neither read nor write, the Ranas sent their sons to Eton and then perhaps on to Cambridge, England, or to Harvard, Massachusetts. There is no denying the fact that the "ranarchy," as the government of the prolific Rana family has been called, used the national income for their own ends without trying to improve the lot of their less fortunate compatriots. Instead of setting up primary schools for the children of the Kathmandu Valley, one Maharajah built himself a 1,500-room palace while another collected a personal library of 30,000 books. The contrast between the illiteracy and the grinding poverty of the average Nepali and the education and wealth of the Rana family was as great as the distance from the low-lying *terai* swamps on the border of India to the top of the 29,029-foot peak of Sagarmarth (Everest).

Yet in spite of all this, the Nepalese were a comparatively happy simple people in a beautiful land cut off from the tumult of the

outside world, and the sins of the Ranas, so often castigated, were
not so much theirs personally as a result of the fact that the Middle
Ages simply lasted longer in Nepal, shut off by the high Himalayas
from the rest of the so-called civilization bent on developing atom
bombs.

Although the political power of the Ranas was curbed when
King Tribhuvan came to the throne, threw open his country to
foreign aid, to education, industry, and travel, this entry into the
world of today brought with it other problems. Westerners and
Easterners, Indians, Russians, Chinese, Americans, Europeans,
have come bearing aid and differing ideologies, both social and
political, all foreign to Nepal. The Americans offer a new brew
salted with strange ideas of democracy and the rights of the individual however humble he may be, while the Russians and Chinese
maintain that the state is more important than any individual.
How is Nepal to choose without offending any great nation? Small
wonder that even today the Nepalese are still wary of foreigners.
Tourists are allowed only a seven-day visa, fly in and out like birds
of passage, leaving their dollars and rubles and taking away a sense
of enchantment. The great mountain-climbing expeditions—
European, American, Japanese—have to enter into long, involved
financial and travel arrangements with the Nepalese government.
Even an accepted foreign resident of Kathmandu cannot fly the
ninety miles from Kathmandu to Pokhara, about as far distant as
Boston from Springfield, Massachusetts, without special permission
from Singha Durbar.

Some of this caution may be due to concern for the safety of
the foreign visitors in a still dangerous countryside where it is
routine to read, in the blurred print of the Kathmandu newspaper,
that a farm woman on her way to cultivate her rice field has been
carried off by a man-eating tiger or that a climber has disappeared
under an avalanche of ice, magnificently entombed. But much of
this red tape is the result of the justifiable fear that the twentieth-
century intruder may upset the status quo.

Actually these international intercredal missions, such as the
Flemings' at Shanta Bhawan, and the staff of the mission serving
in hospitals and clinics all over Nepal who have no political ax of

their own to grind, are giving the Nepalese their first conception of what a really Christian democracy may be. Why have these special silent Christians succeeded so signally in a Hindu-Buddhist country like Nepal when in too many "emerging nations" such as in Africa, trying desperately to forge a national consciousness out of the confusion of differing tribes and dialects, Christian missions have been frequently labeled as "colonial," have been spat upon? Why is there this free flowering of mutual understanding between Europeans, Americans, Japanese, and Nepalese in a proud land where the Flemings do not even use the word "Christian" in the title of their hospital? Is it not because the quiet gospel of faith and work speaks in the only universal language? "What you are speaks so loudly I cannot hear what you say. . . ." When billions are being spent on foreign aid not only by governments but by private foundations, does not this experiment in silent Christian missions in Nepal raise vital queries about the psychology of giving and receiving aid, important to be understood by all nations, both giver and recipient, both East and West?

Certainly there is room for all, for medical help is still as desperately important as it was nine years ago. Disease today stalks the now well-paved city streets of Kathmandu so openly as to appall the Westerner suddenly glad he listened to his doctor and had so many "shots" before he started out. Over 90 percent of the population have some form of tuberculosis, pulmonary, bone, or another variety of this now preventable and curable disease; in some villages its incidence is 100 percent due to the damp houses in which the Nepalese live, as well as to their lack of proper hygiene and diet. A balanced diet would be easy to attain in the Kathmandu valley where the topsoil is so rich that a trained farmer can raise from three to four crops a year. But if a pound of buffalo meat costs more than his day's wage, if the tiny eggs his hens lay are so valuable they must be used as cash, how is the average householder to devour his proper protein? Beef from the holy cow is forbidden to the Hindu, and the Mohammedans of course cannot eat the pigs (neither can the Westerners, because of trichinosis).

"Public-health improvement must go hand in hand with im-

proved education and communciation, a slow business," Dr. Bethel
points out, her eyes on the woodcutter staggering along the Kathmandu street under a load of branches so huge they appear to
have skinny legs of their own. This mountain man left home before
daybreak, may not get back there until tomorrow morning with a
few coins or a length of cheap cloth in his hand as payment for
days of toil. "The pitiful thing is that the enormous goiters dragging at the throats of those men and women could be avoided by
adding to their diet six to eight drops of iodine a year!" Dr. Bethel
says. "Maybe half a dozen barrels of iodine for the whole population would eliminate goiter entirely in Nepal as it has done in
Europe! But with no means of explaining the emergency in far-off
mountain villages which it takes weeks of arduous climbing to
reach—where the people cannot read directions—how are you going
to distribute the iodine or be sure it is used properly?"

One health problem is so common it is treated wholesale at the
Shanta Bhawan clinic. Out in the corridor a nurse routinely pours
worm medicine from a great bottle, using the same measure for
each child without even touching his lips, into a long line of child
patients whose mouths are wide open like hungry birds in the nest!

"All the barefoot children here get worms," Dr. Bethel explains.
"Tape, hook, ring, pin, whip; amoeba is the hardest to get rid of.
They get worm medicine as a matter of course before they are
treated for whatever else is wrong with them."

Another reason for bad public-health conditions is that Nepalese
homes, except for those of the Ranas', mostly have no plumbing.
They use the paths through the fields, the open street drains, or
their own backyards to evacuate. It is not unusual to see a whole
family of children lined up by mama along the city curb doing
their daily duty into the gutter.

The situation is not without humor, however; sometimes the
Nepalese smiles slyly at the strange ways of the Westerner, intent
upon improving him. The Hindu is careful to use only his right
hand to eat or to serve a guest, since his left hand is used to pour
out the water he substitutes for toilet paper. The Nepalese neighbors had a good laugh at one of the visiting doctor's wives at

Shanta Bhawan who bought several of "those darling little brass pots they keep by their front doors," to take home as souvenir vases for her friends in the States. The pretty little pots were what the Nepalese take with them when they retire to the fields.

Providing a balanced diet is a constant problem for the mission housekeepers, not only in the hospital kitchen, but in the private quarters of the staff doctors' families. United States government workers (except for the Peace Corps who shop at the native bazaars and live as nearly as possible as the Nepalese do) may buy almost any frozen western delicacy from the PX which is kept well stocked by government jeeps and trucks which shuttle almost continually from the wharfs at Calcutta to Kathmandu. For the average worker at Shanta Bhawan (to whom, of course, the PX is closed) practically the only edible meat he can afford is water buffalo, which costs only about sixty cents for a two-pound hunk hacked off by the local butcher. An occasional chicken is a celebration, for the Nepalese are loath to sell the source of eggs that are as good as cash. Usually Dr. Bethel comes home from her huge Saturday clinic of 400 patients, carrying carefully in her hand a couple of eggs offered in grateful payment.

The staff table as well as the trays of Western patients at Shanta Bhawan Hospital are laden chiefly with curried rice, toast which tastes like mildewed cardboard since the Nepalese often store their grain in bins in their damp houses for indefinite periods, oranges as small as marbles, tiny bananas about as long as a man's finger, and an occasional pullet-sized egg. If the coffee, imported from India, ever saw a coffee bean it must have been merely a passing acquaintance. But there are always tea and biscuits in the afternoon, and for dinner the water buffalo challenges the cook to new ways of disguising its leathery tasteless consistency.

"I've learned fifty-nine different ways of cooking water buffalo: hamburg, stew, soup, run through the pressure cooker and then called steak . . . buffalo meat, hot, cold, lukewarm . . . oh the heck with it!" one distracted young wife of a Shanta Bhawan doctor wrote home to her mother.

The Flemings have a special problem in feeding hospitably the many visitors who come to inspect the hospital and stay to tea or dinner. Doctors, scientists, mountain climbers, bishops, porters, Ranas, curious Americans arriving daily by plane—anyone is apt to appear at their always-open door, from the head of a great Foundation with world-wide interests flying up from India in his private plane to an old Dutch lady who walked miles from the end of the Rajpath before she collapsed at the hospital from sheer exhaustion. She announced she had been warned in a dream to go to see Nepal. The Flemings enjoy their assorted visitors with sincerely wholehearted hospitality, but it must be admitted that to feed them all on a mission salary of only $200 a month, with no special fund set aside for entertainment, taxes even Dr. Bethel's ingenuity. But nobody minds if the soup is watered to feed a few more hungry mouths, or if extra gravy is added to the buffalo stew, for the sauce of friendship spices every bite.

The acute problem the winter of 1962–63 for all except the Embassy and USAID Americans who were supplied by their own government was the shortage of both kerosene and gasoline, due to the cold war still going on between China and India. Both commodities, important in the icy winter of the Himalayas, come up to Nepal from India and were in very short supply since, as India explained, their Army troops, high in the Himalayas, freezing on guard duty at the icy borders of Tibet, had first claim. The shortage at Shanta Bhawan was so acute that though water ran down their walls and stood in pools on their concrete floors, none of the doctors' quarters had kerosene for heating, merely enough for cooking. Not even the hospital wards or private rooms for patients or staff quarters could be warmed.

What kerosene there was at Shanta Bhawan had to be hoarded to run the sterilizer in the operating and delivery rooms, to fill the patients' hot-water bottles, and to cook food. Gasoline, due to the same cold-war scarcity, cost a dollar a gallon, when one could buy it—an enormous price to run a mission-hospital ambulance. Frequently the commercial gasoline pumps in all Kathmandu were entirely dry. If it hadn't been that Dr. Bob had a Nepalese friend who owned a gasoline station and notified the American doctor the moment a new supply arrived from India, the hospital cars would not been able to function.

The most welcome of invitations from an officially employed government housewife to a fellow American mission friend was: "Come up to dinner in time to have a hot bath first."

Cooperation among the 400 Americans now living in Kathmandu was nothing new. It had been traditional since Father Moran, a Roman Catholic scholar priest from Chicago who came to Kathmandu in 1949, the same year that Dr. Bob was allowed into Tansen to collect his birds, welcomed these Methodist missionaries warmly when they opened their first medical clinic in the capital city in 1954. The Flemings were only too glad of further medical aid to Nepal when Dr. Stanley Sturgis, a Seventh-Day Adventist, arrived from the States with $20,000 in his pocket to build a twenty-bed hospital in Banepa. The Flemings had already started a flourishing medical dispensary in that strategic village where the road ends and all the great mountain expeditions have to shift to proceeding on foot over mountain paths. With government approval, the Flemings turned their dispensary over to Dr. Sturgis in great relief that more trained medical leadership had arrived where it was so badly needed.

It is interesting that at Shanta Bhawan Buddhists and Hindus can be as tolerantly friendly to Christians as the other way around. Morning prayers in the Shanta Bhawan Hospital chapel for the Christian members of the staff begin at the shivery early hour of 6:45 A.M. when usually both Dr. Bethel and Dr. Bob may be seen hurrying across the compound to lead the worship or to sit and listen, to pray or sing the hymns in Nepali. The chapel is comfortably full, for besides the Christians of all creeds, although they are not required to attend, the little Hindu and Buddhist nurses love to sing the tuneful Christian hymns in their own language. Wrapped in their heavy blue capes with the gay scarlet lining against the mountain wind, they sit on the hard benches caroling lustily, for all Nepalese seem to sing as naturally as they breathe; the little nurses in their bright uniforms and white caps let their young voices soar to greet the dawn as naturally as the early birds twitter in the jacaranda tree outside in the hospital garden. It is joyous to be young at Shanta Bhawan with enough to eat and a big job to do! Up and up rise their gay sweet voices until it seems as if the Mountains of the Moon beyond the open windows are humming too. Then both the foreign staff and the little Nepalese nurses in their red and white saris made warmer by bright scarlet sweaters clatter and chatter off down the long hospital corridors to start the day with their patients, to follow the Christian doctors on their ward rounds.

In a country where proselytizing spells jail, Catholics and Protestants, however their theologies may differ, cooperate closely. The Western congregations have frequently held Easter sunrise services together before a great flowery Cross high on a Kathmandu hill. The same great room in Rabi Bhawan, the American headquarters, serves as a chapel every Sunday, first for the Roman Catholic Mass for all Westerners, and then for the Protestant services led by a Methodist minister. The intricate carving on the lovely wooden altar used by both congregations was made by a Nepalese, while from the high molding around the walls of this former Hindu palace small ancient sun gods look down, showing no surprise, upon the kneeling Western worshippers.

Father Moran, as a well-known educator in India, was originally invited to Kathmandu by the Nepalese government to conduct the Cambridge examinations for the students of Trichandra College (which is now a university). He stayed on to start St. Xavier's School at Godavari, which has such high scholastic standards that the students include many Ranas, some foreigners, and even a former "Living Goddess," a Hindu girl who is worshipped until puberty when she becomes again merely human. This scholar-priest is the first American to become a Nepalese citizen and has been decorated by King Mahendra. Yet he does not presume upon this friendship. Because of the law against proselytizing, Father Moran will not allow his Nepalese students to attend Mass without special permission from their parents. The good Father is a gay and familiar sight racing about the crowded Kathmandu streets on his motorcycle, his black robes floating out behind him and a beret perched debonairly on the side of his head, with his free hand precariously off the handlebars, as he waves at his many friends on the sidewalks.

Father Moran loves to tell the story of how his Catholic home-made ambulance brought Protestant Dr. Bethel Fleming her first patient when she made up her ten beds with no sheets in the old cholera hospital in 1954.

"I had just got back to Godavari from attending the formal opening of this brave new little hospital in Kathmandu when our village schoolmaster burst into my office at the school quite beside himself," Father Moran related. " 'My wife is dying, Father!' the poor man cried. 'She's been twenty-four hours in labor. Help me!'

" 'I'm no doctor, I'm a priest,' I told the frantic husband. 'But I know where there is a good doctor. Wrap your wife up and I'll take her there.'

"Two of my schoolboys, a Baptist boy from Iowa and a high-caste Brahmin boy from Kathmandu, helped me take out the seats of the school jeep, put in a mattress . . . add a Catholic priest and a Hindu patient and that's some ambulance! I took off fast, then slowed down to a crawl, afraid of each rut lest the baby arrive before we got there. Believe me, I handed that poor woman over to Dr. Bethel, wiping the anxious perspiration from my forehead and heaving a great sigh of relief."

"It was the most difficult delivery I ever had," Dr. Bethel told Father Moran when he went back the next day to see if his ambulance patient was still alive. "I thought several times we'd lose both mother and baby, but now they're just fine." The little Nepali mother was lying there with the baby safe in the crook of her arm, the tiny girl was wrapped in one of Dr. Bethel's tea towels because that was all the linen the doctor had on hand. When Dr. Bethel put down her finger, the baby's little wriggling red fist closed around it: the two mothers, Nepali and American, smiled at each other as if they knew a secret. "The baby's name is *Ishwari*," Dr. Bethel told Father Moran. "*Ishwari* means *God-given* in Nepali, as I guess you know. That's what this special baby is, all right."

"You want to know why the two Doctor Flemings are so much beloved in Kathmandu?" Father Moran asks, then answers his own query heartily: "Because they're the kind of people they are; they take off their shoes when they go into a Nepali's house, they sit down on the floor with him and eat his food. They're gentle, considerate, make no pretenses, and do a good job ... in His name. At that, I guess a tea towel to wrap a baby in is as good as swaddling clothes in a manger."

"Make no pretenses and do a good job." These new pioneer doctors, Dr. Bob and Dr. Bethel, understand that the kingdom of heaven is not situated either in Washington or in Kathmandu, but in the hearts of men.

Chapter Seven

A Dream Comes True

The ten beds in the cholera hospital were in such demand that a newly vacated mattress was hardly cool before another patient moved in. Makeshift cots were set up in the corridor and more wards and medical staff were desperately needed. It was to be two hectic years before the mission moved from this crowded clinic to the sixty-room Rana palace that was to become the spacious Shanta Bhawan Hospital. This metamorphosis was to come about in a strangely roundabout way via the United States where the Flemings' son, young Bobby, was brushed by the pale skirts of death in a Michigan hospital.

The Flemings, due for furlough every five years, had spent seven years in India and Nepal, climbing mountains not only of granite and ice but of prejudice, working at top speed with every nerve stretched taut for months at a time, living on a restricted diet. The Mission Board insisted it was high time they came home to the States for a rest. Young Bob was to enter Albion College in Michigan as a freshman that fall. Sally Beth had been too young on her last visit to remember what her home country looked like; sometimes Dr. Bethel thought that the little girl was more Indian or Nepalese than American, which was fine, yet she must also have some contact with her own roots. A substitute doctor came up from India to run the cholera hospital for Dr. Bethel, and Dr. Bob's job was assumed by the executive secretary. So the Fleming family sailed together for New York from Calcutta.

"Rest!" sputtered Bethel wearily three months later to her husband. "Do you realize, Bob, we've talked about Nepal in forty states since we got back!"

At first it had been wonderful just to watch comfortable well-fed Americans driving along with the healthy children in their motorcars, just to drink real coffee which gave you a morning lift, to sleep in comfortable bedrooms where no dampness dripped from the walls, where you pressed a button and there was warmth and light. But the more they told other people about their home in Kathmandu and their hospital, the more homesick the two Flemings became. Medical groups and churches, Rotarians, colleges, public school assemblies had eagerly invited them to show their pictures of the grandeur and mystery that was Nepal, to tell their vivid stories of the tuberculars, the lepers, the desperately ill where there were so few doctors and nurses for so many millions who needed them. Dr. Bethel, yawning and stretching one morning after a late lecture, remarked ruefully, "At least in the cholera hospital we got to sleep nights. . . . Oh, there's the phone."

Dr. Bob's face grew white as he listened; he hung up the receiver with frozen fingers. He told Bethel slowly, "Bobby's in the hospital at Ann Arbor. He's to be operated upon tomorrow; they want us to come to sign the release."

"Operated upon!" gasped Bethel. "Bobby . . . whatever for?" He'd looked so brown and husky when he strode up the gangplank at New York. On his last holiday he'd easily outdistanced his father, "The Original," on their last treks through the Nepal mountains looking for birds. Yet the infections of the Orient were insidious, creeping up on the unwary; 90 percent of the Nepalese suffered from . . . She gasped, "Not tuberculosis? Not Bobby!"

"Pulmonary," his father agreed heavily. "The routine X-ray they give college freshmen showed it up. It's had too much of a start. They want a resection to remove the upper lobe of his right lung. We'll take the next plane to Michigan."

There are times when being both a doctor and a mother is a mixed blessing; you realize what can happen. But Dr. Bethel was smiling as she walked into her son's hospital room; she observed the surgeon operate and congratulated him upon his skill. If she was white to the lips, the other doctor did not suggest her resting —he knew that she couldn't until she knew her son was safe. All through that long hot summer the anxious mother stood over young Bob's bed, fanning him when he panted for breath. Gradually she watched him grow stronger; then he was sitting up. "This fall he'll be able to go back to college," the surgeon promised.

Dr. Bethel drew a long breath of relief. When desperate illness hits home, it hurts not only the patient but the whole family; yet it also helped a doctor to know how other parents of sick children felt. It must be even harder for the Nepalese mother who couldn't even understand the explanations of what the medical treatment was trying to accomplish. No wonder the Nepalese mothers curled protectively around their babies in their cribs! It was full time that she and Bob got back to Kathmandu, to their job. Already Sally Beth had missed the fall opening of the Woodstock School in India where she was to study when her parents returned to Kathmandu.

The first ship on which the Flemings could get passage back to India was to sail in January, a month away. Not all their time here had been lost for they had collected much-needed equipment. They would take back with them a new X-ray machine and an improved electrocardiograph, even if there wouldn't actually be room for them at the cholera hospital. If young Bobby hadn't been sick perhaps by now they could have raised the cash to rent the bigger hospital they needed so badly, Dr. Bethel thought ruefully.

One morning she found in her mail a welcome letter from an old classmate of hers at the Women's Medical College, Dr. Elizabeth Miller, inviting the Flemings to visit her in her home in Wilmington, Delaware.

"Let's go, Bob," begged Dr. Bethel. "I suppose we ought to make some more speaking engagements before we sail but . . . well, it's been a long hard summer. I'm tired."

Dr. Bob put his arm around her. "Bobby's all right now. You can relax."

"I know." She laid her cheek against his. "Elizabeth Miller is such an old friend of mine. . . . Goodness, Medical School seems worlds away where we were such close friends! I understand both she and Dr. Edgar Miller whom she married have been unusually successful. I don't mean just money; they've done a lot of original research work." She sighed. "Not that money isn't kind of nice to have." She glanced down at her dark blue serviceable dress she'd worn almost all the time they'd been in the States; it'd be a wonderful lift to afford a new dress to go to see Elizabeth, but the sleeves of Bob's jacket were threadbare. He needed a coat more than she did a dress. Oh well . . . It was she herself that Elizabeth wanted to see, not her clothes. She'd have the blue dress cleaned and pressed—even missionaries had a little pride.

Dr. Bethel had no inkling that by going to see the Millers she would do more for Nepal than a hundred lectures. She and Dr. Bob relaxed gratefully in the Millers' lovely fifteen-room home, rode gratefully to see the sights in their comfortable cars (both Elizabeth and Edgar had their own Cadillacs to visit patients), enjoyed the Millers' lovely children and grandchildren in their comfortable homes. It was pleasant to be just guests, not medical pioneers for a few days. Dr. Elizabeth and Dr. Edgar had become an amazingly successful team in Wilmington, each with an enormous practice, she as a gynecologist and he as a heart specialist. And now their son was taking up medicine too. Truly the most satisfying kind of an American family, they loved their jobs and each other. Yet they made time to get reacquainted with their old friends, Dr. Bob and Dr. Bethel Fleming, to listen, fascinated, to their problems of trying to diagnose strange oriental diseases in Nepal with inadequate equipment, too pitifully few doctors and nurses.

One of the Flemings' greatest assets is their ability to share their dream of their medical work in Nepal with other people through their own radiant happiness in their tremendous job. Dr. Bethel and Dr. Bob draw people of great ability to volunteer to help simply by being themselves. For their good doctor friends, the Millers, the Flemings drew fabulous pictures of how exciting it was to pioneer in medicine in almost untouched fields; over the

Miller dinner table they explained how they could hardly wait, after this lovely rest, to get back to their enchanted home in Kathmandu, the land of the mighty snows, on whose peaks the Lords of the Sky lived in ice and glory, and where each sunset was a foretaste of what heaven must look like.

"Kathmandu used to be called Kantipur, the City of Glory. Guna Kana Deva gave the city its ancient name in 723 and it fits the place. When you watch the sun set behind two tiers of mountains, the lower ones fading into mysterious violet, while the snows are still swimming in a golden-rosy haze, you can hardly believe in such beauty." Dr. Bob stopped; there were simply no words big enough to paint a sunset in the Himalayas for the Millers.

"That's the bright side of the picture; there's a darker one, unfortunately." Dr. Bethel sighed. "Almost every known disease is rampant in Kathmandu, typhoid, goiter, elephantiasis; just to walk down the street gives a physician a course in oriental medicine! Curing the sick in the City of Glory is almost too big a job for anyone to tackle! You can just take one short step at a time."

As Dr. Bethel looked down the table at her old friend, Dr. Elizabeth, small, gay, and wise, and then at the big calm-faced Dr. Edgar in whom so many sick people trusted, her heart gave a sudden lurch as a wild crazy idea came into her mind. They needed a bigger hospital in Kathmandu than the ten-bed cholera wing; but, more important, they needed a grade-A staff of doctors to make the new hospital one of the most outstanding places of healing in the East. If Dr. Elizabeth and Dr. Edgar could only go back to Nepal with them . . . Oh no; it was too fantastic even to put into words. . . . The Millers really had nothing left to wish for: a big practice; their children nearby, with a houseful of happy, healthy small people whom they loved; a luxurious home far different from the Flemings' own primitive mud-brick house with its temperamental plumbing, its icy rooms in winter. . . .

"Bethel, what are you daydreaming about?" Dr. Elizabeth asked her guest suddenly. "I know that look in your eyes of old. What are you after?"

"You!" Dr. Bethel wanted to shout but she didn't quite dare;

she asked, trying to keep her excitement out of her voice, "You two once planned to go to the mission field when you were students, didn't you, Elizabeth? When you and Edgar were first married?"

"Why—yes. But I had a $5,000 college debt to work off first," Dr. Edgar interrupted. He is a large dark-haired man with keen brown eyes that automatically diagnose a patient even before he speaks, but his doctor's voice is gentle. "Elizabeth and I both had volunteered for foreign mission service. But by the time our college obligations were paid off, the children had come, then our parents grew old, needed help. Oh, I don't know. . . . We were tied here—I guess."

Dr. Bethel hardly dared breathe. She blurted, "How about you two coming back with Bob and me to Nepal? To practice?"

Shocked and startled, the two successful American doctors stared at each other down the length of their candlelit table bright with crystal and silver. Even Dr. Bob looked startled. Well, of course . . . it had been only a wild dream. . . .

"Well, Edgar, what about it?" Elizabeth asked suddenly in her gay voice. Dr. Bethel drew in her breath sharply, unbelieving. Dr. Elizabeth is a tiny woman, as small as her husband is big, but her brown eyes light up when she smiles and she moves quickly, lightly, with a vitality that burns like a flame. She reminded her husband, "Mother is gone and the children have grown up, have their own homes; *nobody really needs us here any more!* I wanted to go to China when I was a medical student and you wanted India. *Why not compromise on Nepal?*"

"We're only fifty," Dr. Edgar agreed. The dream was lighting his face too. "Lots of good years left. We might as well invest them where they really count." He grinned at the two excited Flemings who could hardly credit their own ears. "When do we leave?"

It was not quite as simple as that. The Methodist Mission Board to whom the Millers applied for foreign service in Nepal were stunned by the request. Who ever heard of sending out missionaries already past the fifty-year mark, *a grandmother and a grandfather?* Especially to an untamed country where even hardy mountain climbers frequently collected strange fevers? Three experienced doctors with an impressive list of medical degrees after their names to take care of a cholera mission hospital with only ten beds. . . . According to their agreement with the Nepalese government, even this small beginning might have to close up shop in a few years! It was impossible. It was out of this world. . . .

"When do we leave?" the Millers inquired patiently. "It isn't as if this was the first time we'd applied to the Board. Our application blank is twenty-five years old! We know much more about medicine and what makes people tick than we did then. We're far more valuable."

The Mission Board finally threw up its hands, agreed to sponsor them. After all, nothing in this fantastic silent mission to Nepal seemed to go according to the rules. But the experiment worked. How it worked!

The Millers put their lovely home on the market, sold their Cadillacs, turned their practices over to competent hands, kissed the children and grandchildren good-by, and set off to meet the Flemings at the wharf in New York where the ship should take them and their household goods to Calcutta on the first step to far-off Kathmandu. Dr. Elizabeth Miller chuckled, "You know, Edgar, I feel like a bride again! This is another honeymoon!"

"A busman's holiday, dear," he told her. If he had known how true this prediction was to be, that they'd be almost too busy in Kathmandu to talk to each other, if they had known the terrible homesickness for children and grandchildren who were growing up strangers, would they have had the courage to pull up stakes? Fortunately a wise man faces the future a moment, an hour at a time. And of course they were part of the Lord's Plan they prayed only to understand.

Meanwhile Dr. Bob and Dr. Bethel Fleming had gone back to Michigan to pack their own luggage for Nepal, to collect Sally Beth from a friend's where she was visiting. Suddenly a cable came from the executive secretary in Kathmandu that threw all their plans into confusion.

"Sixty-room Rana palace Shanta Bhawan available for new hospital. Have option till December 31. Yearly rent $2,500. Can you raise necessary cash in States?"

A new hospital with sixty rooms! That would mean they could accommodate 120 in-patients at least! And they already had the experienced, wonderful Dr. Millers to help organize the new staff. . . .

"But today's December 15th!" Bethel figured, frantically. Where could they get $2,500 in two weeks? They scrabbled about in their purses; they owned about twenty-five dollars between them. "Yet $200 a month is a very reasonable rent for such a big palace. We've got to do something!" Bethel and Bob consulted with their eyes in the way they had of talking without words.

"We'll need a big church that can afford to sponsor us," Dr. Bob decided briskly. "That Methodist church where we spoke in Barrington, Illinois, perhaps?" He reached for the phone. "I'll call the minister."

Over the long-distance telephone Dr. Bob explained feverishly about the marvelous offer from the Nepalese, how they needed $2,500 immediately to rent the new hospital. To Bob's great relief the minister didn't say, "Have you lost your mind?" He merely protested mildly, "Our missionary budget for the year is already set up. And it's hard to get hold of people in the holiday season, but I'll call a special meeting of our official board. I tell you, why don't you and your wife come back down here, show us your pictures again, and talk to the board yourselves?"

Dr. Bethel had been anxiously watching her husband's face while he phoned. When he told her the minister hadn't actually promised anything, just invited them to come, Bethel reminded him how many good things had happened to them at Christmas time—a visit to Kathmandu, the celebration at Dhangarhi. "Well, we never got a Christmas present of $2,500!" Dr. Bob reminded her. "That's a year's salary! The Barrington church has already subscribed its foreign budget." He sighed. "Shut the suitcases, will you? I want to check over our slides."

They showed their slides and talked fast about Nepal which

seemed mighty far away on the map but which belonged to the Lord's big family. Did these people want a part in the new kind of mission that preached in deeds of healing rather than words? They already were taking back with them two doctors, specialists, to start a modern staff; now all they needed were walls and a roof to shelter the extra patients, doctors, and nurses. The new hospital would be called Shanta Bhawan, the Palace of Peace.

When the Flemings finished speaking, they walked out of the room so the official board could deliberate in private. They went back to the parsonage, but they couldn't sit still; they walked the floor till the minister came home with the great news: The board had voted not only to pay the yearly rent for the new hospital but to add the two Doctor Flemings to their own official church workers! Next Sunday the church calendar would be printed to read: "*Dr. Robert and Dr. Bethel Fleming, our staff members in Nepal.*"

"It was the grandest Christmas present we ever had, a church home in the States, a big new hospital in Nepal, and Dr. Elizabeth and Dr. Edgar Miller on the new staff," Dr. Bethel smiles quietly: the calmer she seems, the more deeply she feels. "If Bob and I had been shouting Methodists you could have heard us back home in Kathmandu! The best of it is, those wonderful people in Illinois still pay our rent, every year for nine years! Every single member of that congregation is on the staff of Shanta Bhawan as much as Bob and I."

"I noticed that the girls lost no time moving us from the cholera hospital into the new palace." Dr. Bob's eyes twinkle as he teases the two doctors, Bethel Fleming and Elizabeth Miller, classmates still in this new experiment in the Orient. "Shanta Bhawan was ours from February 1, and Bethel and Elizabeth hustled us in by the 6th, bag and baggage. Or perhaps I should say, stethoscope and prescription pad."

"It wasn't that easy," protests Dr. Bethel. "This big place had no heat and not enough water for the operating room which had to double also as a delivery room. We didn't have enough nurses for the patients who began to flood into our ward beds and no way

of communicating with the nurses if we had them except by sending chits by messenger running down those long cold corridors,
up and down the winding stairs. Imagine sixty sickrooms with no
bells and no heat!"

But the necessary staff soon began to gather, literally from the
far corners of the earth: doctors, trained nurses, dietitians, workers
from Japan, Sweden, Norway, Germany, Canada, Great Britain,
and Scotland, from India and the Middle East as well as from
north, east, south, and west of the United States. Their many
creeds became merged at Shanta Bhawan into the single litany of
Christian service. Their cash salaries might vary with their home
boards, but their real pay was in seeing a child breathe easily again
after pneumonia; in watching an old-time Nepalese gentleman
bow six times regally before he left the hospital recovered from a
heart ailment; in seeing a leper with his disease arrested walk home
again to his welcoming family. The workers' periods of service
varied also: a dentist who volunteered his services for two months;
a trained nurse from India for six months; graduate fellows sent
from England and the United States to study oriental medicine;
as well as trained machinists and carpenters who stopped by to
have a look, stayed to help.

"It's like the New England weather," Bob Fleming says jokingly.
"If you don't have what you want at Shanta Bhawan just wait a
minute!"

Red tape is to Dr. Bethel something to be rolled up into a ball
and tossed away when a patient's welfare or peace of mind is concerned. She is apt to come into a ward with a Tibetan baby, rosy-
cheeked and smelling to high heaven of mustard oil, on her arm,
taking the patients' minds off their own troubles by asking, "Isn't
she a doll?" The baby is from the hospital's Saturday clinic which
goes on all day and sometimes after dinner with five staff doctors
working at to speed. Or possibly she has firmly tucked under her
elbow a squirming Tibetian puppy, tiny as a toy, which she has
collected on her rounds as payment from a grateful patient. Or
maybe the gift in her hand is a couple of eggs still warm from the
hen. She makes medicine not a fearful import from the West, but

a natural part of everyday living, and each patient, be he lama sitting up in bed reading his sacred books and humming to himself Buddhist prayers or an orthodox Hindu lady with her scarf drawn tightly up over her head, holding herself apart lest she be defiled by these strange Christians, is a member of her big family.

So many visitors come to the hospital that an official hostess had to be appointed (she lives in the former concubine quarters of this Rana palace) to take newcomers through. Dr. Bob often guides special guests, and of course when visiting physicians arrive from Japan, Russia, England, the United States, or Ethiopia, medical etiquette demands that Dr. Bethel leave her patients long enough to make them professionally welcome. As she goes the rounds, she manages to make even inanimate objects personal.

"That kerosene sterilizer in the operating room was given by a church in Philadelphia, U.S.A.," she will remark casually. "The laboratory microscope came from Tokyo . . . the Japanese do such a wonderful job with instruments these days. Most of the anti-biotics over there on the pharmacy shelves are given to us by drug companies; they are perfectly good for months yet, but cannot by law be used in the States. Some mixtures have to be shaken for an hour to bring them back to use, but then they work beautifully. Shanta Bhawan Hospital itself stays open only because a Methodist church in Illinois pays the $2,500 rent every year, on the dot. A Presbyterian church in New Jersey pays the rent for Surendra Bhawan, our new hospital for women and children we have just opened next door. The training school for nurses has its dormitory and classes there, too."

Awed by the long line of patients who have stood patiently in the clinic corridor since early morning, by the great wards where bed after bed is filled by Nepalese patients whose faces turn to the Dr. Bethel's as naturally as a morning glory opens to the sun, the visitor's reaction is frequently, "What can I do to help?" Two American tourists, an artist and a schoolteacher who dropped by on their way around the world, came back to offer to run the hospital kitchen, free of pay, for a year. "And that," comments Dr. Bethel, "is a hard, unspectacular, vital job." A German mechanic who came to Shanta Bhawan out of curiosity, listened with shocked ears to the sound of the ambulance's engine, decided to stay long enough to get it running smoothly; after six months he is still there, doctoring carburetors and weak tires, keeping the vitally necessary jeeps and hospital vehicles running as smoothly as their age will allow. A retired doctor came to visit and stayed for a year, paying his own expenses and those of his wife. More used to society teas than the spartan hospital fare, the wife ended up by starting occupational therapy and English lessons for the long-term patients.

"We can use anyone who can help," Dr. Bethel says placidly, fitting the newcomer into her program. Even Sally Dyhrenfurth, wife of the famous mountain climber who was later to lead the first American expedition to conquer Mt. Everest, once spent a tense three months working in the Shanta Bhawan laboratory while her husband was cutting his way up perilous mountains of ice.

Most heads of hospitals treating nearly a thousand patients a week would throw up their hands in horror at such a shifting personnel; Dr. Bethel merely wonders where she can dig up another bed for the new worker to sleep. The staff, paid and volunteer, sleep on the roof of Salisbury Bungalow, the interior of which has been divided into quarters for the five resident doctors and their families; others climb up narrow winding stairs to screened verandas in Shanta Bhawan; hostess and technicians use the former concubine quarters, while the graduate nurses hang up curtains in the former stable which they call "Bethlehem."

Dr. Bethel has kept her promise to train the Nepalese in medical techniques. A training school for nurses was started at Shanta Bhawan with a highly experienced Menonite nurse, Miss Lena Graber, as its head; the Indian and English technicians took on apprentice workers in the laboratory; arrangements were made for young American medical-school graduates to spend part of their internship at Shanta Bhawan. "The best is none too good for Nepal," Dr. Bethel argued. "We must keep up with the latest in medicine. Thank heaven, we have Dr. Edgar Miller here as chief of staff;

all our doctors can teach with experience. Now that we also have a resident surgeon, Dr. Robert Berry, we are covered for major emergencies, day and night."

Dr. Bethel insists upon standards of medical care so meticulous that one of the Fellows sent by a great medical firm for four months' training in Nepal remarked rather dazedly that he had not seen better nursing techniques in the famous Philadelphia hospital where he had interned. He had expected to help educate backward Kathmandu but instead Shanta Bhawan was teaching him!

When the Flemings and Millers first moved into Shanta Bhawan, a joint apartment was furnished for them up on the top floor of the hospital where the two families could escape from the hurry and bustle of the downstairs wards; wide windows and a veranda boasted a view of the mountains to rest their eyes . . . after they had climbed the three steep flights of stairs at the end of a long day. They had separate living rooms and bedrooms but a joint kitchen which sometimes presented problems when their Nepali cooks failed to agree. Often Bethel and Elizabeth gave the cooks a holiday and did their own cooking to get peace. They took turns entertaining the guests from all over the world who flew in unexpectedly almost every day to see what Nepal and Shanta Bhawan Hospital were like.

"I'll never forget the time I was stirring porridge in my kitchen when I looked up to see John D. Rockefeller peering over my shoulder," Dr. Bethel says with a chuckle.

"John D., Junior?" she was asked by an awed listener.

"No, Third. I invited them to stay in our apartment, I was so sorry for them."

It took Bethel to be sorry for the John D. Rockefellers!

"Their hotel room was so frigid that winter morning when they flew into Kathmandu," Dr. Bethel explained. "Bob and I had been invited to go to the airport to welcome them. We knew they'd reserved a room at the hotel weeks ago and as we drove by, Bob suggested we stop a moment to be sure everything was ready for them. It's a good thing we did. We found that a big tourist party

had arrived the night before, had browbeaten the management
into giving them the warmest room available so the Rockefellers
had been shifted to the big ark of a palace room where the American ambassador had stayed before he had an Embassy to live in.
He'd been so congealed with cold he'd had to beg a friend to let
him sleep on their living-room couch!"

"This will never do; the poor Rockefellers will get pneumonia,"
Dr. Bethel said worriedly to Dr. Bob. "We'd better ask them to
stay with us at Shanta Bhawan. The Millers are away so they can
have their suite and I'll feed them."

Dr. Bethel smiled. "The Rockefellers were glad to come once
they'd inspected that icebox of a hotel room. Only one thing
worried them: they were afraid that having engaged the room so
far ahead, they might not be able to cancel it."

"Why didn't they just buy the hotel?" the listener suggested.
"At least, they could have paid for the room even if they didn't
use it."

"Oh no, they're very thrifty people. They're dears, really," Dr.
Bethel protested warmly. "His wife called him 'Johnny.'"

A year later a check had arrived for $10,000 for Shanta Bhawan,
a generous sort of hostess gift, you might call it. The Flemings
used the money to build the long low white clinic where now
hundreds of patients flock every week. Wealthy Ranas and lepers
without a rupee, Peace Corps and Embassy, international mountain climbers and Sherpa porters, and the John D. Rockefellers,
III . . . it took Doctor Bethel Fleming to mother them all!

The Flemings make use literally of the promise "And I, if I be
lifted up, shall draw all men unto me." Silently, luminously what
they are speaks compassionately, much as the lighted Cross shines
all night in the hospital quadrangle, sending pale fingers of light
into the hospital rooms, reassuring the patients who cannot sleep:
"Someone cares that you are here. You are not alone."

"Everyone gets perplexed and overwhelmed at times. Especially
in a hospital like this. He asks himself, 'How can a loving God
allow such poverty, such agony and death?' Perhaps he even goes
a step further and decides, bitter and angry, that there is no loving

Heavenly Father," Dr. Bethel says with understanding. She agrees realistically, "Pain and death are facts a man must face; but so is God. If a man accepts life whole, with faith, a merciful God can turn even pain and death into victorious living. Muscles of the spirit can atrophy if they are not used. A man must reach for something bigger than himself if he is to stretch to his full stature."

Chapter Eight

Getting Acquainted in Tansen and Gorkha

Few dreams take on such lovely substance as when Dr. Bob
Fleming was invited back to Tansen by his friend, Dr. Carl
Friedericks, to lay the cornerstone in 1959 for the mission's new
fifty-bed hospital to be built there. It was only eight years before
that Dr. Bethel and Dr. Carl had operated here on a dining table
under the blue sky in the village square while Dr. Bob hunted
bird specimens in the surrounding mountain slopes; now Dr.
Friedericks' plans called for a large modern hospital any city in
the world would be glad to have. But there was still no road to
Tansen, this city of about 8,000 people 100 miles west of Kathmandu. The building materials that could not be made locally
and all the medical equipment would have to come in slowly
upon the backs of porters. The hospital staff would have to have
steady heads to walk in also over the precipitous mountain paths,
in places so steep that steps had been carved in the cliff for the
traveler to climb. The easiest way to Tansen from Kathmandu is
still to take a plane back to the Indian border, then to ride a rickety
bus for fifty miles, finally to walk two days. When Dr. Friedericks'
seventy-year-old mother-in-law came to the cornerstone-laying, she
had to be carried in on the back of a porter in a large basket.

Dr. Carl, a big hearty man with so much energy he seems to
give off sparks, takes mountains in his stride. He and Dr. Bob had
walked all over this up-and-down country, had picked out the
spot where their dream hospital could best rise, and now their

plans were taking shape in this great brick building. "A little bigger than the cholera hospital, eh, Bob?" Dr. Carl slapped his friend affectionately on the back, remembering the time he had helped to blowtorch the ten beds, to paint them red. "But, you know, I kind of miss those days when the kids were young, crawling around the mud floor of our first house here. Three of them are off to school in India now. A house with only three kids isn't really a home."

"I know," Dr. Bob agreed. "Sally Beth's leaving soon for the States to start college. I can't believe how the last few years have flown by in Nepal. We won't have the cash for her to come home for four years. Bethel's already begun to worry for fear Sally won't have the right clothes, won't fit in with American freshmen. The last time we went home, when she saw TV she asked, round-eyed, 'Who's Bob Hope?' "

"She'll make it O.K.," Dr. Friedericks insisted. "One thing our kids do have is the international know-how; they can hold their own anywhere in the world, given a little time to adjust. Look at mine! Carl Jr. was born in Germany, Betty in Korea, Dick in the United States, Chuck in India, Anne in China, and young Jimmy right here in Nepal!"

Mrs. Friedericks had been the real pioneer in the early days in Tansen, taking care of five children in a native house with a mud floor, with no electricity, running water, or plumbing! And then there were six, with a baby to watch every instant to be sure he didn't put anything in his mouth or walk barefoot to get worms or worse. Every mouthful of water had to be boiled, greens had to be washed in disinfectant, skinned knees had to be treated at once for fear of infection with strange fevers to which Western children had not yet developed an immunity. A missionary mother in Tansen needed forty-eight hours a day to look after things properly; yet now the family had shrunk so, she almost wished those early days back. At least they had all been together so she knew what to worry about instead of just wondering what was happening to her little flock.

"We had such good neighbors from the very beginning," Dr.

Carl told Dr. Bob. "When our stuff was late arriving, the chief Hindu priest loaned us some of his furniture so we would have a place to sleep; he came every day to visit us. Without his help and advice we'd have done a lot of things wrong, but from the start, this Hindu was the chairman of the neighborhood hospital-aid committee."

Their furniture had finally arrived, piecemeal and piggy-back, but Dr. Carl had little time to help his wife settle in; he had barely plucked the children out of their carrying baskets when the first patient arrived. The doctor set up a clinic in a native house with, of course, a mud floor and no glass in the windows to keep out the flies or the curious neighbors.

The news that medical help was now available flamed like wild-fire up and down the mountains. One man with a compound fracture of the leg was carried twenty-eight days by his friends to reach Dr. Carl. Tubercular babies were rushed to the hastily set-up medical dispensary; patients began to flood in, day and night—heart cases, patients with goiter, many lepers both young and old, hesitant, afraid to hope, whose frightened families had turned them out. The procession was endless, demanding, and wonderful. It soon became evident that Dr. Carl had to have help. Several Nepalese young men volunteered to train as medical assistants and the busy doctor started classes in biology, hygiene, public health, parasitology, medical ethics, and laboratory procedure. But his friendly visits to the Nepali homes helped the doctor as much as his lab did the patients.

"It does little good to try to do public-health work until you know the customs of the people, the way they can best be approached to guide them into better ways," Dr. Carl explained to his wife. Actually, he was talking to himself but that is what a good wife is, a mirror to reflect back a man's ideas and ideals. The mirror worked also in reverse, for Dr. Carl helped her with the children; the only American family within a hundred miles had to stay together. After his strenuous hours of professional work, Dr. Carl played and romped with his boys until sometimes it was hard to tell which one was father and which son. By osmosis the children learned tolerance of customs different from their own, made friends with the small Nepalese. Dr. Carl explained, "Don't make fun of the other kids because they don't play baseball! Play their games too. We must *offer* them only what is good in our modern medicine and ideas, not try to force our ways on a country where we are guests."

"Aw, Pop!" the oldest boy protested. "You told us that in China and in India. You think we're dumb?"

Dr. Friedericks' first hospital at Tansen had twenty-two patients crowded into the eleven beds, one head at each end. The government suggested, "Why don't you build a bigger hospital?" The villagers, called in for consultation by Dr. Carl, all agreed that the best building site was on a ridge near the city's water pipe. Although it can still be reached only over mountain paths, the present hospital, completed in 1963, has not only all the modern X-ray, and up-to-date laboratory equipment but the same kind of international staff as Shanta Bhawan. A doctor from Japan, sent and financed by a lay association of Christian doctors in Tokyo, has made history by his discovery of crab flukes, formerly unsuspected, in the lungs of afflicted Nepalese. The X-ray machine, which had to be lugged in on the backs of porters and took forty days to put together for use, is the first of its kind for diagnosis and treatment of the constant stream of patients in this vast area where the new hospital serves not only the city of Tansen but the 8,000 inhabitants of the neighboring city of Pokhara and the surrounding mountain villages.

Dr. Friedericks, who is as modern as an atomic reactor, keeps up with medical research and new drugs, but he is still careful to consult with the Nepalese community, to take its advice, based upon years of experience, on everything from how to increase the water supply to how to prevent juvenile delinquency by keeping the local youth as busy on village improvements as is his own staff at the hospital. He points out how well this system works from a long-range point of view.

"The public-health survey our Japanese doctor is making from village to village, to teach the Nepalese officials to analyze the water supply, to understand why certain health customs, such as living in damp houses, defecating near public wells, a merchant coughing blood over his wares in the market place, even the children's going barefoot, cause worms, dysentery, tuberculosis, would be impossible unless we had already learned to talk to these people in terms of their own experience. Now they have come to trust us in Tansen; but advance takes patience and mutual confidence in each other's integrity.

"Our leprosy work is under a British doctor who takes the eight-hour trip by horseback every two weeks to the government leprosy colony at Malung; he and the horse sort of skid down the hair-raising mountain path from 4,000 to 2,000 feet. The average distance each man patient walks to get to our hospital is twenty-five miles, the average woman patient walks twenty miles, and each child patient averages a forty-one-mile walk. The worst of the lepers the doctor frequently brings back on his horse to our hospital; some are sent back home cured but their families refuse to take them in. But the whole world helps us here in the Nepal mountains! The Bread for the World movement which started in Germany has sent us a clinic worker, and our business manager is a Dane. The wife of our Japanese doctor doesn't understand English but she can speak Nepali! This has become the lingua franca for all of us, as it should be in Nepal."

Keeping so many nationalities working together smoothly calls for all Dr. Carl's tact as it does Dr. Bethel's at Shanta Bhawan. "Sometimes we do collide and the sparks fly," Dr. Friedericks admits. When he grins his face lights up like a movie marquee, flashing excitement. "But you know why there's so little real friction? *Because we are all laymen!* Theological questions or creeds are never discussed; we are not concerned with talking about the things that separate us, but with what we all have in common. This means tolerance not only among ourselves but for other religions and customs."

Because Tansen is not yet in as close touch with Western ways as Kathmandu, these problems of adjustment between East and West are accentuated. It was a Tansen judge who sent to jail the

Christian Indian minister and the eight Nepalese whom he had baptized but only after the high court had considered their case for three months. Under the ancient Nepalese laws designed to protect the Hindu way of life, the judges had no choice except to jail them all, Dr. Carl explains.

"These people were not concerned in any way with our United Mission Hospital; it is interesting to note that they actually were not baptized into any Western creed at all, but into an Eastern one. The preacher Prem Prdhan is a Nepali who served in the Indian Army, got interested there in a Christian group who are anti-Western, who want to do things in their own way. After being a pastor in India, he came back to Nepal under the National Missionary Society of North India. He and the people he baptized were not too badly off in jail for they lived under about the same conditions they would at home, with a place to sleep and food brought in by friends. They could walk in the jail quadrangle daytimes but at night were locked in. The lay Christians were pardoned by the King before their year was up, but only one of them was fined—because, as a Christian, he had served rice and water to his small Hindu son, thus defiling him. After three years in custody the preacher is now being brought down to Kathmandu, walking down with his guard. What will happen I do not know, but only the King can pardon him."

It is impossible for Dr. Carl to be pessimistic for long. "Religious freedom under the constitution is sure to come eventually: it is part of the slowly evolving democratic process," he insists. "The Christian Church, if and when it comes, will grow up indigenously, in a way especially suited for Nepal, perhaps with a sort of panchayat system such as the King is inaugurating politically. We at Tansen obey the law of the land; we mind our own business which is preventive and curative medicine. We find our hands plenty full trying to live what we believe."

When the projected new road is built which will link Pokhara and Tansen, the big new hospital will be even more useful than it now is. Dr. Carl Friedericks is not at all sure he wants to live in such a crowded area where it is only a fifty-mile drive between cities; he has begun to cast longing eyes toward starting new pioneer work in more remote mountain villages where people can't drop by in a jeep. The government has recently authorized the building, beside the new government road, of a new Technical Institute where the United Mission will train young Nepalese engineers, businessmen, and technical specialists.

"The Nepalese have decided to keep church and state separate in the future, to permit no more mission schools to be built, rather like our own Supreme Court ruling against reading the Bible in public schools," explains Dr. Friedericks. "So the Institute will not be under the Board of Education, but under the department of Industry and Commerce. But when the government needs engineers to build a bridge, we'll have 'em. Or road supervisors. The Institute will be a pilot project to encourage small businesses." He grins ruefully. "Progress, thy name is Babel! I'm an anomaly, an office-shy 'loner' who just happens to run a big hospital. Too many highways are being built around here. Pretty soon a man can't stretch without bumping into a city slicker!"

It is not given to many pioneers to see the forest that has grown tall from the seedling trees they planted, but Dr. Bob, Dr. Bethel, and Dr. Carl have watched their work grow not only by years but by months, weeks, even every day. Where the need is great and the goodwill is clear, friendly cooperation burgeons. That the Nepalese government respects what Christian laymen are trying to do for their people was plainly shown when in 1958 they agreed to give the United Mission a new ten-year contract to stay on in Nepal. The terms were somewhat more liberal than the first ones. They included:

1) The mission workers are subject to the laws of the land.
2) They must also obey the rule of their own directors who are responsible for their conduct.
3) The mission must pay its own way without government help.
4) Government permission is necessary for new projects.
5) Staff must not engage in extracurricular activities.
6) Government must give permission for sale of any property.

7) The government may nationalize all institutions at any time, paying compensation.

8) This agreement may be reviewed and revised.

9) Preference must be given in employment to Nepalese citizens.

Agricultural, medical, and educational cooperation has also flourished in the Gorkha District, seventy miles northwest of Kathmandu. When Jonathan Lindell, now executive secretary for the United Mission, began pioneering there shortly after Dr. Carl went to start work in Tansen, there was still no road. Lindell had to go seventy-one times to the authorities at Singha Durbar to get permission to climb the mountain paths to advise the Gurkha farmers how to grow better crops, to teach the village children to read and write, to start a medical clinic. He and Dr. Bob had earlier wandered about here, collecting birds and making friends in this romantic country, where even today the Gurkha farmer still wears his great curved warlike kukri attached to his belt, though he uses it now more often to cut down a tree, to harvest his grain, or to delicately pare his toenails than to knife an enemy in battle. This does not mean he has gone soft; merely that he is a practical man. If attacked he would still spring to arms fiercely to protect his home, in spite of the fact that a Nepalese kukri would be about as much use as a rusty cannon in the Ticonderoga Museum fort in Vermont against an atomic missile.

Adapting to this new precarious world in which we must either get along together or all perish together, Lindell came to live in a Gurkha village to learn as well as to teach. On his first trip in from Kathmandu, he had to ford six rivers, climb cliffs so steep he did not dare look down, but was obliged to keep his eyes on the top rim lest he get dizzy and fall. Once arrived, Jonathan knew that these independent Gurkhas could be reached only if they wanted to be. He and the village authorities inspected every possible site for the new mission medical and agricultural clinic which would, Jonathan insisted, belong to them; together they decided upon Ampipal-bhanjyang, "The pass of the mango and peepal tree," as the place to build. At first Lindell had to live in a tent, for he could not buy bamboo to build a proper village house. According to time-honored custom, the bamboo had to be cut by an old man in the dark of the moon on a certain month, and then must be given, not sold, to the new villager from America.

When Mrs. Lindell trekked in with her two small daughters ten months later to join her husband, the bamboo hut was up but had no glass in the windows nor any door, and its one room was lighted only by native yak-butter lamps. The mud floor made a shambles of the little girls' clean clothes five minutes after they were dressed in the morning. The village people were so curious about their outlandish Western neighbors that Jonathan Lindell tacked paper over the windows so the family could get some sleep at night. The villagers promptly poked holes in the paper to go on with their fascinating peep show, then would double up with laughter. One morning the Lindells missed one of the little girls. They found her outside with the villagers peering through the poked holes in the window covering. She explained, "I wanted to see what everyone was *looking* at that was so much fun!"

Knoll House, the Lindell's permanent home of stone and native dried bricks, was built after the boys' school had been started; first Jonathan taught his classes out under a tree, then in a two-room hut which was expanded as materials were obtained locally, bricks of mud, wood from the jungle. Only the tin roof of Knoll House, the Lindell's permanent dwelling, had to be carried in from Kathmandu in great shining wings sprouting from the backs of the porters. Runners also arrived with building tools, schoolbooks, fruit-tree seedlings, and seeds to start off the agricultural advisory service for the farmers. The villagers themselves formed a local school committee and worked together to build shelter not only for the primary and middle schools but for a school designed to give advanced training to student-teachers who were, in turn, to start schools in other nearby villages.

So many enterprising businessmen started shops to serve the increasing numbers of workers and students that the government opened a post office. By the third year of hard work, fifteen Christian workers had arrived at the Gurkha headquarters—agricultural experts, nurses for the dispensary, teachers, and social workers. At the medical dispensary, in the schoolrooms, in the village committee meetings, in the homes, Jonathan Lindell calculated that these Christian workers were in touch with nearly 500 Nepalese a week. Yet these specialists were still too few to answer all the eager questions of the villagers:

"Will you really be childless if you plant bamboos on any but the south side of your house?"

"Scabies, bedbugs, worms, rats . . . how do you get rid of them? Will the gods mind if we spray with DDT?"

"Is there any other fertilizer than dung?"

"How can we spare our children from the fields and chores to go to school?"

"Is manual labor any less honorable than a white-collar job?"

"Why am I my neighbor's keeper? What do you mean by 'conscience'?" . . .

"This awakening is the raw material out of which new Nepal must be made," Jonathan Lindell insists. "Development depends not only upon material things but upon the men who make use of them. The springs of better things, when they come, flow from the hearts of men. You can't change people by arguing; they change themselves when, from being self-centered, they become God-centered. In the last analysis, the better life is not only an economic but a moral problem, a question of *man's inability to handle what he already has . . . to control himself!*

"Building character is as much the job of Christian workers as medicine, education, or planting better fields, his *raison d'être*. All the material aid one generous nation may offer another does not change the root nature of either the giver or the recipient," Jonathan Lindell points out.

"Man's inability to control himself leads to graft, intolerance, even to using food for political ends, frequently to resentment instead of gratitude by the receiving nation. This is not to say that all government aid is selfish . . . far from it . . . or that Christian laymen are any less human than government workers; they may be identical. But the *emphasis* is different, on character rather than markets."

At one of the village discussion groups, a pensioned Gurkha

soldier who had been several times around the world, who knew Hong Kong, Singapore, Southampton, who had fought beside the white man in Italy but who had preferred to come home to his native Nepalese mountain to end his days, asked Jonathan Lindell curiously, "What are these 'space laws of the spirit' you talk about, Friend?"

Jonathan Lindell hesitated. By law, he could not speak to these people of his own religion; he could only hope his sincerity as a good neighbor in this village would shine through.

"The first law is, I think, a man has to accept his responsibility for those worse off than he is," Jonathan Lindell told his Gurkha fellow villagers, carefully.

"Second, every man must learn that liberty demands law, a law that applies to himself as well as to his neighbors whether they live next door or over The Black Water [the sea].

"Third, a man must believe that before God all men are equal. That goes not only here in Gorkha but back in my home in the United States. Is not the myth of the white man's superiority over the black man as much a superstition as thinking a witch doctor can cure worms?"

"You and your family live here like one of us," the old Gurkha soldier said gravely. "These are good laws." He looked up as a loud halloo! came from a runner racing down the nearby hill. "Someone approaches, in trouble, I think," he added as four men appeared in the distance, carrying a litter carefully down the rough path.

The runner, breathless, flung himself down beside the committee meeting under the mango tree, gasping, "It is my son whose hand was pawed by a bear! A week ago. By now it stinketh. Is the doctor here?"

"No. There are only nurses." Jonathan Lindell got to his feet to go to meet the litter on which lay a moaning boy whom they had been carrying for a seven days' climb—one does not measure distances by miles in Nepal but by the up and down, and by days. . . . Lindell stared down, appalled, at the boy's mangled black and swollen hand. Even a layman could see the telltale angry red streaks running up the boy's arm. Unless the gangrenous hand was taken off the boy would die. But would the nurse have the knowledge and the courage to do this major operation? "Take the boy to the clinic," Jonathan Lindell ordered the faithful bearers. "The nurse will put him to bed." He laid a hand on the distracted father's shoulder. "Don't worry, we'll do the best we—"

"Another runner approaches!" interrupted the Gurkha elder under the mango tree. "It is a day for foreigners."

This foreigner was a man from the next village, bearing news. Four people were climbing over the mountain, two doctors from Shanta Bhawan accompanied by two of their former patients. One patient had been cured of a pain like a rat gnawing in his chest and the other was the small girl who had run to show the ancient doctors—they must have at least fifty years—her greatest treasure which had been given her in the Shanta Bhawan children's ward at some strange *puja* or other. It was a picture of a Lady in Blue holding a very fat Baby with a circle of light around his head. The Memsahib called her husband, "Ed-gar dar-ling," though which was his first name and which his last who could tell? He had sent a message to Jonathan Lindell. . . . Edgar! Jonathan Lindell grabbed for the note scribbled on a torn sheet of paper:

Dear Jonathan:
Elizabeth and I hope to make it by dusk. Please have beds ready, no dinner, only sleep. We are exhausted.
Edgar Miller

"Before ye ask, I will answer. . . ."

"What are you muttering?" the Gurkha elder demanded of Jonathan. "It is a prayer?"

"A quotation from our sacred book," Jonathan told him. "It means that help is coming."

It was after dark when Dr. Edgar and Dr. Elizabeth arrived, barely able to drag one foot in front of the other; they were taken at once to the clinic. Neither of the Millers were surgeons but they found the boy's condition critical. They must operate at once; tomorrow would be too late. The nurse rushed about sterilizing one of Mrs. Lindell's butcher knives, Dr. Elizabeth held the boy's arm steady, Jonathan Lindell focused the flashlight by which the doctors worked, while Dr. Edgar knelt on the mud floor of the little clinic, amputated the boy's hand with the butcher knife, and saved his life.

Today the clinic includes not only a resident doctor and several nurses, but trained agricultural and social workers. One of the latter, Mary Candy, has recently completed the first social survey of a Gurkha village ever to be attempted. Social customs never before put on paper are not only fascinating but significant, proving that ancient ways are not all unsuited to today, but may be modified and built upon to meet modern conditions rather than summarily discarded, leaving no law at all. She writes:

"The people of Pyersingh are not poor in a country where thirty-five dollars is the usual yearly wage for a farmer; they are just about average. The land is mostly flat about the village; some of it is thickly wooded, and terraces have been built up to 7,000 feet on the mountainside which rises abruptly from the plain. Houses are of mud and stone, or of mud and bamboo with thatched roofs. The chief drawback is that since the roads are mere tracks, there is no way to barter or sell much of the grain or produce which they raise.

"Most villagers own some land. A man is wealthy if he has fields that produce more than his family can eat of dal, rice, potatoes, buckwheat, and vegetables of various kinds which are unsalable because of no nearby market and have to be given away. There are plenty of citrus fruits in season, lemons, oranges, pomelos, guavas, bananas, and pears, so the family need not lack for vitamin C.

"With the practical good sense of the Nepalese, the measurement of the land does not depend upon size alone but upon its fertility. When a man wants to buy a new field, he considers both before he agrees to the price asked. Measurements are indigenous to Nepal. One *hal* is the land which it takes one day to plow; one *doko* is land which produces one *doko* or basketful; one *kodali* is the amount of land a man can hoe in one day with the heavy awkward native hoe or *kodali*. If the land is good, two *hals* should support a family of three. Two *hals* of terraced land cost from 400 to 500 rupees (about seventy-one dollars, two years' average income) as compared with the rich valley of Kathmandu where land may go for as much as 2,000 to 3,000 rupees, for the ground is more fertile and near the market. Also in Pyersingh the farmer not only has to cultivate his crops but also to fight off the hungry monkeys and porcupines, which means he often has to sit up all night after a hard day's hoeing.

"Buffaloes are kept for manure, milk, and *wray* (a sort of whey). Chickens are kept both for eggs and for eating, goats and cows for milk, manure, and eating. Only the out-castes, however, eat pigs. Most farmers keep their own seed from year to year and either barter or sell their crops privately. Brahmins do not plow their own land but pay the low-caste farmers one fifth of the crop to work the land.

"Gurkha pensions are the chief source of cash for the village, amounts varying from 15 to 300 rupees a month, depending upon the old soldier's length of service and rank in the British or Indian Army. Fathers are anxious for their sons to enlist, for this means a regular income for the rest of their lives; Gurkha soldiers also learn to read and write Nepali and often English which is a great help in their careers. Government village schools are increasing, with each pensioner asked to subscribe out of public spirit, according to the size of his monthly income. Parents pay from one to three rupees a month for each schoolchild and each family contributes one rupee a year whether it has any schoolchildren or not.

"Village customs concerning marriage and inheritance have come down from ancient times. A man may have as many wives of his own caste or concubines as he can support, but a woman is somewhat more limited. If a wife has a baby by another man, she may go to live with the father, but her own husband must be paid compensation. If in turn the father of the child does not want to keep the mother, he may persuade another man to take her, who in his turn pays the father for the privilege. Thus a woman may live with as many as three men, one after the other, each paying for the privilege of her company, before being considered a harlot. But if, by any chance, she has a child by a man other than in her own caste, the police or village panchayat interfere with appropriate punishment. Such are the social laws at Pyersingh.

"Political power is held by the panchayat which consists of from eight to ten men representing the nearly eight villages; the members of this local panchayat serve without charge and have the power to try ordinary cases of misdemeanors against the law. More puzzling or more important cases may be sent to the district panchayat or even to the governor of the area. Out-castes have a headman known as *Kotwol* who acts as intermediary between the out-castes and the other villagers.

"Each village has a headman, or *Mukia*, who has as much or more power than the panchayat. His office is hereditary but must be confirmed by the local panchayat. The *Mukia* rules on routine cases of inheritance which often can become very tangled in this land where polygamy is common. He decides which land shall be held in trust and by whom it can be inherited. No widow can sell her land until she is fifty, unable to have another child. If a childless widow remarries, she forfeits her inheritance from her first husband; if she has a son, the inheritance goes to him, a boy being considered of age when he is fifteen.

"In times of emergency, the *Mukia* can exert great influence. When a case of smallpox was discovered in Pyersingh, the villagers were isolated in caves, given a special place to draw their water. The Christian dispensary at Gorkha sent word that smallpox vaccine was available but no one took advantage of the offer for six weeks. There were ten more cases and two deaths before the *Mukia* led the frightened procession of all his people to the dispensary for vaccination, stood by sternly until each villager had his shot, keeping records to be sure all had been immunized. On another occasion, when a mad dog threatened the neighborhood, the *Mukia* even ordered all dogs in the area killed, an unheard-of act among people who cherish dogs as sacred.

"Medical inquiry disclosed that 80 percent of the people had been formerly treated only by wandering mendicants with local herbal medicines. Lamas were paid to perform *tantra mantras* (prayers) which drive off the bad magic, a sensible course by people who believe that sickness is caused by evil spirits. Yet once they discovered that smallpox vaccination really worked, the villagers flocked to the Christian dispensary to cure bad eyes, ears, or aches in stomach, or elephantiasis. Infant mortality is still very high at Pyersingh since sterilization of milk and food is unknown."

Mary Candy ends her report on this typical village in Gorkha District with several conclusions:

"Inbred superstition cannot be broken down in a moment. To secure the confidence of the villagers is more important than haste. We may assist them by 1) Education. 2) Agricultural specialists. 3) Doctors and medicine, especially those concerned with child health and public-health clinics. 4) More cooperative efforts introduced into the village so that the villagers may help themselves. The Nepalis are a gay, gallant, resourceful, ingenious, and spiritual people who can grasp the meaning of spiritual truth."

As Dr. Bob Fleming points out: "If Christianity is any good, it will speak for itself to such people."

Medical help is hard to bring to isolated mountain villages like Pyersingh. When Dr. Bob Fleming set out to investigate conditions in Okhaldunga in the far western part of Nepal, he had first to fly back to India, then trek eight days on foot into the mountains, incidentally gathering more birds by the wayside for his collection which now includes 627 species, stuffed, labeled, and cherished by the Chicago Natural History Museum of which he is now Field Associate in Zoology. He hopes to raise this number to a round 800. He is saving duplicates of each species to start a Nepalese Museum of Natural History in Kathmandu to display their native flora and fauna. Already he has taught students how to mount and prepare over 1,000 ferns for this permanent exhibition.

After Dr. Bob's survey, with government permission, a new dispensary was opened up in Okhaldunga in May 1961 by Dr. James Dick and his wife and a nurse who took the long walk into the mountains to live in the village. The need proved so great that now six buildings are going up to shelter more patients, nurses, and a staff of twenty agricultural workers. An English farmer and his wife have started another modest agricultural center in remote Dandeldura. An anxious call for help came from Bejang State, 250 miles northwest of Kathmandu. Dr. Bob, trekking in as usual to investigate conditions, had to cross "a fearfully narrow bridge, high above a swirling current, with nothing to hold onto! All but two of our porters refused to attempt it alone and had to be led across by hand." When a native refuses a bridge, it's really dangerous; so how were nurses, doctors, and medicines to be safely transported to such remote villages? Dr. Bob cherishes the hope that to serve these districts a "flying doctor service" may be set up which can airlift the worst cases into Shanta Bhawan just as the mountain expeditions fly in their injured by helicopter.

"It's easier to cut down trees to make a small airport than to build 250 miles of road," Dr. Bob argues. "The people themselves could make the landing place. Look at what they have done to help themselves in the past nine years! Take Gorkha, for example. There were 196,000 villagers living in that area much as people did in the Middle Ages. Three men walked in at first to consult with the villagers, an American [Jonathan Lindell], a Britisher, and a Nepali who asked the villagers flatly if they would welcome the Westerners coming to their section. After two days, fifty-three villagers from these mountains signed a petition of invitation three feet long; this amounted to a covenant that these native people would work with the new team from the start. The villagers not only helped select the site for the mission work but set the price they paid the headman of the village for his land.

"The three men and a cook accordingly settled into a tent on the new land, hired a runner, gathered a dozen boys under a tree to start a school. That night people gathered around the tent to listen to hymn-singing and Bible-reading. The next morning a distracted mother brought her badly burned baby for help . . . and the medical dispensary had begun."

Truly, "If Christianity is any good, it speaks for itself."

Chapter Nine

Poets, Queens, Ambassadors Get Sick, Too

The three-year-old baby with dark congested face and terrible breathing lay upon the hospital bed, fighting for his life. As the doctor hurried down the long ward with its twenty beds and patients, overhead glittered the gay incongruous crystal chandelier of the former palace and upon the walls silent hunters rode painted elephants, hunting painted tigers. The doctor could hear the baby's harsh strangled breaths. Diphtheria—probably brought here too late. He was a beautiful child, well-rounded limbs, dark curling lashes and hair which his mother squatting by the bedside put out a hand to brush anxiously from her small son's damp forehead. Her eyes lifted to the doctor's were black pools of terror demanding, "My son is dying! Do I dare trust him to you?"

The doctor studied the baby's congested face. "I'll have to do a tracheotomy here," the doctor decided. "There's not even time to take him to the operating room." He called, "Nurse! Instruments, please. At once."

The moment the cut was made in the baby's tender throat, the tube inserted, he drew a deep gasping breath; in no time at all he was breathing evenly, deeply, and the soft natural rose began to come back to his rounded baby cheeks. "It's almost worth coming 9,000 miles to see his mother's face," the doctor thought. She laid a hand on the doctor's arm and her eyes shone with gratitude, almost worship, as she saw her child snatched back from the evil spirits who had been carrying him away from her. They did not speak each other's language but between the mother who loved the child and the doctor who had saved him there was no need of words.

But the little boy still was seriously ill; at all costs, the tube must be kept open or his breathing would stop. The doctor stood by the bedside tending him as if the small boy were his own; he *was* in a way, since through his skill the child had been born again. The doctor left the baby only briefly to go to the aid of a patient three beds away who was hemorrhaging; but he was back in a matter of minutes to inspect the tube, to be sure all was well. If only they had more nurses! Only three Nepali nurses, two girls and a man, had been graduated, so far, from this new hospital training course and they were all too busy with twenty patients in each ward to give anyone their entire attention. For twenty-two hours the doctor stood by the small boy, emptying the tube, watching the baby's every breath as did the mother who was still squatting beside the bed on the floor. The child was sleeping sweetly now, the doctor saw; if only his mother watching him so fiercely and tenderly could be told what to do, had the skill to do it! But this was impossible; he didn't dare risk it. The small patient was doing fine. It was the doctor who was swaying with fatigue, and he had other very sick patients he could not neglect; he'd better get some sleep while he could.

"Don't leave this boy any more than you have to," he warned the nurse. "Keep that tube open."

"Yes, Doctor." He was a good nurse who knew his business. If there were only ten of him, twenty. . . . Yawning, the doctor patted the small boy's shoulder, smiled at the mother, and stumbled sleepily away. Too weary to undress, he threw himself down upon his bed. It seemed only moments, but it was actually two hours later when someone shook the doctor awake.

"Doctor, come quick. Baby is worse!"

The doctor began to run. When he reached the bedside he grabbed the child's wrist, listened for a pulse. The child was dead. Red rage swept over the doctor so that his hand shook as he pulled out the tube; it was full of phlegm: this baby had choked to death.

But he need not have died! It was murder, black murder that's what it was. . . .

"I am so sorry, Doctor." The nurse's face was horrified. "I had to leave him. The patient down there had another hemorrhage. Could I let him bleed?"

With great effort the doctor thrust down his anger. What could a good nurse do, save the one and let the nineteen die? "It was not your fault," he told the nurse heavily. This was one of the bitterest disappointments of the doctor's career. Back at his old hospital in the States, this baby would have had a special nurse watching every moment to see that the tube was kept cleared; here that was impossible. Whose fault was it that this beautiful baby had died? It cost $200 a year to train a Nepalese nurse; the hospital simply did not have enough money. Whose fault was that? Many of his wealthy patients back home paid that much for a winter coat, more if it was fur. If only he had stayed longer with the child himself! But he was not as young as he used to be; he couldn't take twenty-four-hour duty any more. The boy's mother had drawn her scarf over her head, was rocking back and forth in silent terrible grief; the doctor leaned to put a compassionate hand upon her shoulder. What did it matter whose fault this was? The child was dead.

The doctor was Dr. Edgar Miller and the hospital was Shanta Bhawan, and the time was three years after he and his doctor-wife Elizabeth had arrived from Wilmington accompanying his friends, Dr. Bob and Dr. Bethel Fleming, to Nepal.

"We were right to come, Elizabeth. Only we didn't come soon enough!" Dr. Edgar's face was haggard as he told her what had happened.

"We came as soon as the call was clear, Edgar," Elizabeth Miller comforted him. "We'll train more nurses. The Nepalese are clever, quick to learn." Incredibly she smiled; she had to lead his thoughts back to normal. A doctor could not identify himself with every patient and go on living. "But I must admit that the Nepalese have such *different* ideas. . . . I have one little lady in my ward who won't eat a bite of food unless I sample it first. We eat bite for bite. She has to eat or she'll die, so I won't be home to meals this week."

"Elizabeth! You mean you're eating Hindu food, prepared by a *sati*? Over the cow-dung fire? You'll pick up amoebic dysentery! I won't permit—"

"Oh hush, Edgar. I take a pill when I get back home. She's a nice clean little lady."

They gave so much more than pills and hypodermics, these Christian doctors; they gave companionship, tolerance, understanding, even their blood if needed. And they gave laughter. Why not? A merry heart doeth good like a medicine. . . . They gave parties in their big apartment on top of Salisbury Bungalow where Elizabeth had scattered about as many of their own things from the States as possible, to make it home.

She was the one responsible for taking over Salisbury Bungalow, the other big house in the Shanta Bhawan compound, so that it could be divided into apartments for the rapidly expanding staff of doctors and their families. Dr. Elizabeth had written to friends in Salisbury, Connecticut, about the vacant Rana dwelling house, and the church had written back by return mail to say they'd take over the yearly rent of $1,800. "If you folks can give your whole lives to Nepal, surely we can manage the dollars," her friends wrote back. There were now five full-time doctors on the hospital staff living there, and still they hurried from ward to clinic and back again, all day from early morning till late at night, trying to keep up with the flood of patients.

For Shanta Bhawan served not only the Nepalese. So many Europeans and Americans from the Embassy, USAID, and the Peace Corps came to this hospital, where competent doctors were available, that a special room, the Memorial Room—furnished by the American Women's Club of Kathmandu—had been set aside for such patients. At first Dr. Bethel took care of all the Westerners but, after all, the Nepalese sick came first and there were so many of them. The Embassy staff finally got their own doctor who also used the Shanta Bhawan laboratories and beds and was available for consultation. Then came the mountain expeditions from England, United States, Japan; whenever one of these climbers froze his feet or fell off a cliff, he was evacuated by helicopter to Shanta Bhawan. There simply was no end to patients who needed them.

"It's like Alice in Wonderland. We have to run to stay where we are," Dr. Bethel says. "But I wouldn't want it any different."

The number of Nepalese nurses in the training school grew to twenty, then to thirty; the resident surgeon Dr. Bethel had prayed for became a reality when Dr. Bob Berry and his gay young wife, Margery, arrived with their three children. Rooms had been built on for them at Salisbury Bungalow, but the walls were still so damp they wept moisture for weeks even in fair weather and the Berrys had to step over puddles on the floor when it rained. The children all got sick; Dr. Bob and his wife had the flu, with high fevers.

"The family haven't all had a well day really since they arrived in Kathmandu," Dr. Bethel said worriedly to her husband. "Maybe they'll have to go home. But not only is he a good surgeon; they're just the kind of people we need. He's brought new techniques to the operating room and Margy's so pretty and so gay. She makes friends without trying."

Margy Berry did the hospital proud when, slender and svelte in her raw-silk suit and white gloves, she went to the Embassy for tea or represented Shanta Bhawan at a reception for the Royal Family. White gloves were protocol at Nepali formals and Margy tucked a yellow flower in her dark hair, as the Kathmandu girls did. "You don't have to wear Queen Mary hats to be a missionary!" Margy said. Although sometimes the mission was criticized for being "too social," how could you treat patients competently until you got to know, firsthand, how the Nepalese thought? Friends trusted each other and a patient's mental attitude was important for getting well. Yet socially in demand as they were, the Berrys rarely missed a Tuesday-night Bible-study class at Shanta Bhawan and Dr. Bob Berry had prayer in the operating room daily, a custom Dr. Bethel had begun at her first small clinic.

The Memorial Room at Shanta Bhawan was my home for my

first five weeks in Nepal. Dr. Bethel's casual remark that the Lord's Plan for me to learn the truth about the hospital, its patients, and its problems might be better than my own turned out to be true for, thanks to the Flemings, Kathmandu in all its color and variety came to my bedside. The three of them, Dr. Bob, Dr. Bethel, and Sally Beth, made a gay parade to my room every day, either to tell me new tales about their early days in Nepal, or perhaps Dr. Bob wanted to show me a tailor bird he'd just stuffed. He'd point out, "See how he sews his nest together? Leaves sewed over and over by one species, under and under by the other. Pretty neat, isn't he?" Usually Sally Beth would be singing some gay doggerel as she pushed behind my head the specially soft pillow I'd been wanting. The Flemings brought their friends: generals with decorations on their broad uniformed chests; lovely Ranees in saris so delicate they floated like pink clouds around their wearers, who had real diamonds in their aristocratic noses. Maia, the barefoot maid who raised the dust daily around my bed with her broom of twigs and then washed floor and furniture with a particularly evil-smelling disinfectant, taught me the Nepali words for "hot water" and "I sleep now, please." Jungjean, the daughter of Chumbi, the Sherpa friend of Sir Edmund Hillary, who had flown with him around the world to see if the "yeti" skin was really that of the Abominable Snowman, came to give me a Tibetan coin as her "get-well" gift. Embassy staff members, Peace Corps boys and girls, of whom there were usually several in the hospital suffering from some kind of digestive upset, Nepalese doctors and police-men came to cheer up the poor lonely sick American. I learned more about the real Kathmandu in these informal chats that I did later at a formal appointment in some office at two P.M. where the official had to be so careful about what he said the words might as well be a tape recording. Casually I collected strange stories about queens, ambassadors, famous mountain climbers, and village farm women brought down from fantastic mountain heights by helicopter to be healed at Shanta Bhawan.

Most illuminating and relaxed were the evening talks with Dr. Edgar Miller, to whom Dr. Bethel had assigned me as a patient, who would knock on the Memorial Room door after he had completed his night ward rounds, when the hospital lights were low and only the luminous Cross was still bright in the quadrangle. For these were tales of his everyday job, vivid, unrehearsed.

"The Russian Embassy rang me up one morning to ask for an appointment for the ambassador to see me," Dr. Miller related. "It seemed strange to me that the Russian Ambassador should choose a Western Christian hospital, but, of course, at Shanta Bhawan we are not concerned with a man's politics. But the appointed hour came and His Excellency didn't show up. I was annoyed, because my time is valuable, so when I met him later that week at a reception, I asked why he had stood me up. He explained that he'd had to go out to the airport to see the King off on a trip out east. It's true that the entire diplomatic corps goes to Goucher Airport whenever the King comes in or leaves town. 'Besides,' the Russian ambassador told me, smiling, 'I hate doctors!'

" 'Indeed?' I answered. I had the un-Christian hope that he wouldn't waste any more of my time. It wasn't long, however, before I had a hurry-up call to go to the Russian Embassy. I found the ambassador very ill with a high fever, vomiting, and stomach tenderness. I held my breath after I said he'd be better off in Shanta Bhawan, but this time he came without argument here to this very room. At first we suspected a coronary thrombosis, but when a cardiogram ruled that out, I decided it was a peptic ulcer. However, I didn't want to precipitate an international incident by making a mistake so I persuaded the Russians to fly His Excellency back to Moscow for further diagnosis by his own doctors. Diplomatic me, I put at the end of his medical chart that went back with him: FUO—'fever of unknown origin.' "

Dr. Miller began to chuckle, then his laughter shook his big body. "I was uneasy until I heard what the Moscow doctors had to say about the ambassador, if they agreed with my diagnosis. When I asked the acting ambassador what they had discovered about his boss in Moscow, he seized my hand, pumped it cordially up and down. 'You were exactly right in your diagnosis, Doctor!'

he beamed. 'It was "fever of unknown origin"!' Heaven help us, doctors can't beat diplomats for double-talk!"

"One of the Queen Mothers was here in the Memorial Room for a while. Usually we give her a whole suite of rooms but this time the hospital was jammed to the doors," Dr. Edgar said one evening as he bustled into my room followed by Samson, a slender young boy who accompanied Dr. Miller on his rounds, writing down his orders, seeing later that they were carried out. "Samson's my ears, my secretarial hands, my legs, aren't you, Boy?" They grinned at each other affectionately, Dr. Edgar and his Nepali shadow whose eyes worshipped the big American doctor who was everything that Samson wanted to be. "Run along, Samson, you've had a long day. Beat it to bed."

"The men in the ward, Doctor Sahib. They want I should sing them a good-night song. You like?"

Dr. Edgar looked at his watch. "I *don't* like. It's nearly ten o'clock. Now skip!" The door closed behind the smiling boy. "Handsome, isn't he? And smart as they make 'em. He's half Nepali and his mother is Sikkimese. I don't know what I'd do without him. And he knows it, the young rascal. He plays the harmonium so your feet can't keep still. Even the Queen Mother was amused when she was my patient here. There are two Queen Mothers, you know. King Tribhuvan had two wives; but King Mahendra is so good to both the older Queens I haven't an idea which one is his real blood mother. The King has a big heart, you know. It was he who sent us Bishnu, the little girl with the club feet.

"Bishnu was only three when the King first saw her in a mountain village where he was visiting to listen to the needs and complaints of his people. He gave Bishnu's mother forty rupees to bring the child here to us at Shanta Bhawan, to see if we could do anything for her. Dr. Bethel put the child's feet in casts, then she operated, time after time. Bishnu was here over a year, so long the hospital came to seem to her like home; everyone made a pet of her, and for the first time in her life she had enough to eat;

supper divided by six brothers and sisters doesn't leave very much for the youngest. At last Bishnu could walk straight and even run like other children, but when her mother came from her village to get her, Bishnu cried and cried. She didn't want to leave. She got so hysterical I suggested to her mother, 'You have many children. How would you like to leave us this one? Dr. Elizabeth and I would like a little girl, our own grandchildren are so far away.'

" 'One less mouth to feed! And such a cry-baby! You're welcome to her,' her mother said, much relieved.

"The next time I went to the palace to check up on the Queen Mother, the King asked me how Bishnu was getting along. It's quite a ceremony, going to see the royal family, what with guards snapping to salute, flags flying, servants bowing and scraping, and you naturally having to wait till it's convenient for His Majesty to see you. Once I wandered around in the dog's graveyard. Funny thing, the Hindus burn the bodies of their dead, but they bury their dogs in the palace garden, even give them headstones. The Nepalese have a puja, a 'worship-the-dog' day—I suppose because two dogs guard the door to the Hindu paradise. The Nepalese certainly look after their own. Every time I visited the palace, King Mahendra would ask how Bishnu was. Finally one day I said, 'Your Majesty, would it be all right if Elizabeth and I adopted Bishnu? Our own children have grown up. We could educate her, send her to school. It's good to have someone gay and young around a house. We love that child.'

"His Majesty hesitated a long time, staring at me. Then he said, 'You are a good man. Educate her, call her Bishnu Miller, if you will. It is a good name. But always remember, *she is Nepalese.*'

"So we sent Bishnu as our little girl to a good school in India. But she is a strange child with strong likes and dislikes; one school could do nothing with her; she acted naughty all the time; the next school she loved. I worried about it but Elizabeth said, 'It's the same with any highly strung child; she doesn't feel secure yet, rooted. But I do wish she'd come to feel a real member of our family. Do you think she'll ever adopt *us*, really?'

"Not long after that she came home to us at Kathmandu from

her school in India for the Christmas holidays. We had a Christmas party as usual for the staff at Salisbury Bungalow and Bishnu
came dancing into the room before dinner. Elizabeth had bought
her a new white dress and she looked like a snow sprite in it, flitting
around the room. She never walks, she dances on her new feet she
found at Shanta Bhawan. She settled down finally on the davenport beside one of the guests, beamed up hospitably. We heard
the child ask, 'Does your mother love you? Mine does. Dr. Elizabeth comes to say good night to me every single night. And then
she kisses me!'

"We'd taken Bishnu into our hearts a long time ago, but this
was the first time we knew for sure that she had adopted us."

Another night Dr. Miller told about Peter Mulgrew, a New
Zealander who froze his feet while a member of Sir Edmund
Hillary's expedition to climb Makalu; his feet became so gangrenous that later both had to be amputated by his surgeon at
home. But first he spent long weeks in the Shanta Bhawan
Memorial Room, learning a bitter lesson, slugging his way back
like the fighter that he was.

"Shanta Bhawan is sort of a base hospital for the mountain-
climbing expeditions, British, American, Japanese, whatever," Dr.
Miller explained. "The doctors who climb with the expeditions use
our labs, our X-ray to get pictures of the men before the climb,
afterward to find out how the 'high thin air' affects men's bodies.
Many injured climbers who have challenged the great mountains
and lost are brought back here to Shanta Bhawan by helicopter
where we do what we can for them. They pay plenty for matching
their strength against the mighty Himalayas, not only in their
bodies but in their minds. One American climber who'd gotten
lost in the mountains was so shattered mentally by his experience
that he had to be rushed back by Navy jet to a sanitarium in the
States. Others found here in Shanta Bhawan not only healing for
body and mind but for the spirit. Peter Mulgrew was one of these.

"When Mulgrew arrived here in this room there were ugly
purple frostbites all over his hands and feet and he was still cough-

ing up quantities of blood. He was recovering from pneumonia."

Mulgrew, a member of the Himalayan Scientific and Mountaineering Expedition of 1960–61 led by Sir Edmund Hillary, had developed a pulmonary embolism while he was high up on Makalu. The climbers were within 400 feet of conquering the 27,000-foot peak when they had to make the fateful decision whether to reach the summit or to save the life of Mulgrew. They chose Peter. When they got him down to the lower camp, his fellow mountaineers were horrified. "His eyes were sunken and lifeless; his breath came in uneven shudders and his color was dreadful. Nevertheless, there was still life in him. They pumped him full of hot drinks and oxygen and his improvement was immediate. . . ."*

Peter was rushed with his sick companion, Michael Ward, a Britisher who had also contracted pneumonia, by helicopter (the first to land at a height of 15,000 feet to pick up passengers), directly down to the rice field across from Shanta Bhawan where the doctors and nurses were waiting with their ambulance. After he lay safely between the clean white hospital sheets, Mulgrew was asked what he would most like to have. "Orange juice!" None was available at the hospital but the dietitian rushed to the market, brought back a great armload for juice.

"The poor lad simply lunged for the glass," Dr. Miller remembered. "He was in bad shape. Not only were his feet gangrenous but his frostbitten fingertips dropped off. I don't think he especially enjoyed at first being in a mission hospital. He complained that the Nepali nurses' singing at the early hymn service annoyed him, for (as you know) the chapel is directly under this Memorial Room, and the nurses start off their long day by singing happily in Nepali. Mulgrew grumbled that they woke him up too early. But breakfast was served directly afterward and hospital routine can hardly be upset for one patient who dislikes hymns.

"Peter Mulgrew is that rarity, a completely honest man, a strong brave man," Dr. Miller went on slowly. "I certainly didn't blame him for being discouraged, moody after the tragic accident

---

* Douglas Doig and Sir Edmund Hillary, *High in the Thin Cold Air* (Garden City, N.Y.: Doubleday and Co., 1962), p. 223.

that had happened to him. Nor for being resentful of being thrust into an environment strange to him."

Several other members of this same expedition were patients at Shanta Bhawan at the same time. When he was carried in, Dr. Mike Ward, a surgeon from the London Hospital, took one look at his grimy self and then at the immaculate hospital bed and announced, "I simply can't get in there, I'm too dirty!" He soaked for an hour in a big tin tub they filled with lovely hot water before sighing happily, he consented to climb into bed. The other expedition patients needed mostly rest, nourishing food, and treatment for minor ailments. When Sir Edmund himself got back to Kathmandu, he didn't wait to change his travel-stained shorts or to shave his mountaineering beard before he and the two Sherpas who had carried Mulgrew down the mountain to safety came to see Peter.

"He's a great man, Sir Edmund," Dr. Miller said with admiration. "He doesn't need a knighthood to prove it." Nor did Mulgrew's other comrades desert him. Somehow Peter found out that, along with the whole staff of Shanta Bhawan, who talked about him to the Lord every night and morning, both the Milledges were praying for him to get well. Betty Milledge, the wife of Dr. James Milledge, the physiologist of the expedition, had spent the three months her husband was away on the perilous heights of Makalu working at Shanta Bhawan as an anesthetist. She had recorded some of the nurses' singing on the platters which she had sent out to her husband at the base camps; Peter must have heard them played. "Peter didn't mention his mental struggle to me," Dr. Miller said, "until one day when I came into his room to find a peaceful look on his face, as if he'd climbed his mountain of despair and come down on the other side into a deep and quiet valley.

"'Doctor,' he asked, 'do you think your nurses would sing my favorite hymn tomorrow morning?'

"'If they know it,' I promised. 'What is it?'

"'Eternal Father, strong to save . . .' Next morning they sang this Christian Navy hymn together, the Hindu nurses' young voices soaring from the chapel and Peter Mulgrew, the challenger of mountains, silently in his bed upstairs. It is a song for all brave men who adventure on land or sea:

> From rock and tempest, fire and foe,
> Protect them wheresoe'er they go. . . ."

Dr. Edgar took a long breath, ended his story, "The Milledges are missionaries now, working in Vellore, India. But Peter Mulgrew is back in New Zealand, practicing with his new feet so he can come back to climb again in the Himalayas."

One evening Dr. Miller was very late making his nightly rounds. When it came to be ten-thirty I put out my bed light, sure he'd been too busy with a sick patient to spare time for one who was convalescent. But directly there came the familiar tapping on my door, I put on the light hastily: Dr. Miller came inside, slumped wearily down on the chair beside my bed. His face was gaunt, white with fatigue.

"I had to fly to Pokhara this afternoon to see General Rudra Shumshere, an old friend of mine and the Flemings' who is dying," he explained. "He's over eighty. His sons came to tell me he'd been asking for me; I told them I was almost buried in work but if they'd get the permission from Singha Durbar I'd go. So they did. I knew he already had several more than competent Nepali doctors; there wasn't a thing I could do to help him, really. Sure enough, he was in a coma when I arrived. So I prayed silently that the good Lord who loves us all would give him a quiet passing. And I flew back home."

Dr. Miller ran his hand wearily up over his forehead, rubbed his red-rimmed eyes, but when I said indignantly that it seemed a long way to go for nothing, his eyes flew open, indignantly. "Nothing? His sons knew I was there even if the old general didn't."

He smiled. "The strands of friendship can reach even into eternity. Did I ever tell you about the poet laurate I took care of? How Dr. Elizabeth and I and Mildred Drescher were invited inside the rooms for the dying inside the Hindu temple at Pashupati on the banks of the holy Bagmati River?"

But Christians weren't allowed there! If they even looked

through the open temple door it was slammed shut quickly, it was so holy. Only the family and Hindu priests went with the dying man to lave his feet at the last moment with the holy water of the Bagmati, to wash him clean of his sins. How could these Christians have been allowed in such a sacred Hindu place?

"We'd had the poet laureate at Shanta Bhawan for a long time. He was a wise and good man, a poet who was revered not only in Nepal but in all India," Dr. Miller went on calmly. "He had ulcer of the stomach. I sent him down to India for further diagnosis, but it proved to be cancer, so they sent him home here to Shanta Bhawan to die. When he asked for the truth, I told him; he was a wonderful man you could talk to frankly. I kept him alive for weeks with transfusions till he begged, 'Don't waste any more blood on me, Doctor; save it for those it can really help.'

"As he faced death calmly, he, the Hindu patient, and I, his Christian doctor, got to talking about what it would be like after he went to the River. Did I believe, as the Hindus did, that there were many lives to come in which a man could perfect himself? Christians believed indeed in a life after death, I told him, in a Christ who had died on a Cross and risen from the dead, so that all men who followed his ways might live forever, also. Then would the body be the same as on earth? he demanded. It would be changed, but in what way I didn't understand, I told him. But this I did know: it would be heaven for me to spend eternity with Jesus Christ. It was for His sake I was here at Shanta Bhawan."

" 'Caring for me, a dying Hindu,' " the poet marveled.

" 'He that loveth not his brother abideth in death,' " quoted Dr. Miller. "Finally I had to tell his family waiting here at the hospital, 'It is time to take him to the River.' I could hardly hold back the tears, for I thought this was the last I would see of this brave man. But next morning the family were back at Shanta Bhawan. 'He's still alive; he wants to see you,' they insisted.

" 'But Christians are not allowed to go into the temple of the dying!' I reminded them.

" 'We've already gotten special permission from the temple authorities and from Singha Durbar. Please come quickly.'

"The Hindu poet's last home on earth was a lovely room." The tiredness had all gone from his face now as Dr. Miller remembered his friend. "The room was beautifully furnished; one side was entirely open to the river so you could hear the birds singing and the water lapping against the temple steps. I wouldn't mind dying there myself! With his family clustered around him, we three Christians talked with this good Hindu about the life to come.

" 'I'm almost home,' the poet murmured. 'Tomorrow I'll know all the answers! Don't you wish you were me?'

"We stayed until he dropped off into a coma, and soon afterward a brave and good man went to meet his God." Dr. Miller sighed, thinking of those two gently bred men who had been to him more than patients, the Nepali poet and the general. "Even if I could no longer help as a physician I was glad to go to pay them honor. When the candle burns low, there's so little a man can do for his friend."

Chapter Ten

I Lose a Leper

To make leprosy as respectable and no more frightening a disease than any other to the patient, his family, and friends has been one of Dr. Bethel's major ambitions in Nepal—an ambition she has done much to implement at Shanta Bhawan. Since 2 percent of the population of this little country—approximately 180,000—suffer from Hansen's disease, as this disfiguring sickness which has spelled terror and tragedy for centuries is now known, it is not easy to convince even literate people of the efficacy of modern curative measures. Dr. Bethel's big problem has been to try to get across to a still suspicious public the knowledge that leprosy can now be diagnosed in its early stages, arrested by modern drugs, and that most patients can be rendered non-contagious.

Shanta Bhawan, at Dr. Bethel's insistence, is one of the few general hospitals in the world where lepers with complicating conditions are admitted to the hospital wards; where the outpatients suffering from Hansen's disease use the same clinic—but on a different day—as those with other afflictions.

"Lepers get appendicitis, pneumonia, broken legs just like any other patients," Dr. Bethel explains briskly. "There is today no danger of contagion from patients under proper treatment. In fact, with a few precautions, you can even stay married to a leper and not contract the disease! But I must admit I almost had a rebellion on my hands the first time I sent a leper patient who needed an appendectomy over to Shanta Bhawan. My nurses refused to go near the leper's room so I went to care for him myself. It didn't take long to educate the hospital staff but the patients' families were harder to convince. They get so terrified of the dread disease whose symptoms they have come to recognize that sometimes even a mother will turn her frightened small leprous child out into the street!"

Every Friday the entire Shanta Bhawan clinic is turned over to diagnosing and to treating the lepers. Dr. P. J. Chandy, an Indian specialist on leprosy who heads the Leper Hospital at Anandaban, north of Kathmandu, which was started as a small dispensary the year before Dr. Bob and Dr. Bethel arrived in Nepal, comes down each week to help the Shanta Bhawan doctors with the leper clinic. While Anandaban is supported separately by groups in England and Canada chiefly, the two hospitals have become so closely affiliated in their desperately needed work that their staffs are almost interchangeable. When Dr. Chandy is forced to take a much-needed vacation from his almost twenty-four-hour-a-day job at Anandaban, one of the Shanta Bhawan staff takes over temporarily at his hospital.

Visiting the Friday clinic at Shanta Bhawan with Dr. Bethel is, for the uninitiated Western visitor who has never even seen a leper, an unforgettable experience. The clinic is a long, low, one-storied white building whose apparently endless concrete corridor has wooden benches along the walls to accommodate over a hundred waiting patients. The rest must cue up outside. As the clinic door swings open, the noise, smell, and sight of so many mustard-oiled, ravaged bodies of men, women, and child lepers is like a blow in the face. Some of them are badly disfigured; one has no nose, another no mouth, but many are apparently so normal-looking the average onlooker wonders uneasily how many lepers he may have brushed against unknowingly on the Kathmandu streets. Their hundred faces turn toward Dr. Bethel with a hope so strong it is almost frightening.

"These poor dear people: I wish they didn't have to wait so long," Dr. Bethel says unhappily. "But there are so many of them and only five doctors."

But are these dear people really not contagious? The Western visitor cannot help wondering in spite of the doctor's assurance that the few patients still in the communicable stage are kept separate from the rest. The sight of so many eager lepers crowding into Dr. Bethel's small consulting office makes the nervous on-looker instinctively move back as far as he can get toward the wall. He stares, mesmerized, at the apparently normal Nepali man who has taken off his shoe to show Dr. Bethel how half of his foot has been gnawed away. "Hungry rats," Dr. Bethel explains. "The leper has no feeling in his foot so the rats probably chewed it off while the patient was asleep at night on the floor."

The next patient, a small Nepalese boy, unwraps a filthy rag from a bad burn received when he fell against a hot stove but did not feel the pain. After Dr. Bethel bandages the burn cleanly, with her bare hand she turns the cheek of a worried young girl toward the light for inspection, and the Western watcher feels his own skin crawl in spite of all he can do. Centuries of inherited fear fight unsuccessfully against reason. But Dr. Bethel has no fear.

"You see that dark thickening of her skin upon her cheek?" she says, pointing at the patient's face. "This may or may not mean leprosy. We will send her over to the hospital lab for a test to find out."

Not long ago these leper patients would have been wandering half-starved along the mountain paths, ringing a warning bell and crying, "Unclean, unclean!" Today they are offered a scientific laboratory, an immaculate hospital bed, and a compassionate hand that touches theirs, unafraid. The matter-of-fact approach of the doctor is worth much more psychologically than any medicine.

Dr. Bob Fleming helped Dr. Chandy pick out the site for the new and enlarged hospital now being built at Anandaban to meet the ever-increasing number of leper patients, many of whom have walked for many miles on the stumps of legs or have been carried on litters to get to the hospital for surgery and treatment.

"Dr. Chandy and I tramped all over this valley, looking for a place of beauty which would help the patients to regain their self-respect as valuable members of society," Dr. Bob Fleming recalls.

"To offset the ugly aspects of this disease, we selected one of the most beautiful mountain views in Nepal. We put up tents and stayed awhile to make sure that, besides being enchantingly lovely, this site had plenty of water available for a hospital. But when the villagers in the valley heard we were starting a leper hospital up on the mountainside they were terrified. They sent a petition with 500 names begging the government not to let us build there; they said we'd contaminate the water supply. Contaminate, my eye! When I went down to investigate, two water buffaloes were wallowing in the village water pool, a woman was there washing out a bloody shirt, another was bathing a child who was being violently sick into the muddy drinking water!"

Today the new brick modern buildings are going up rapidly at Anandaban without protest from the villagers who have found that the hospital has improved their water supply instead of contaminating it, and that business in their small shops has increased satisfyingly because of their leprous neighbors. When Dr. Chandy made a brief return to India, Dr. Elizabeth Miller moved out to Anandaban to run the hospital as well as the weekly mission village clinic at nearby Chapagaon.

I was anxious to see both places, but an unfortunate broken ankle, added to my early troubles when I had first arrived in Nepal, had kept me immobile. Eventually, however, my walking cast was taken off and I was able to hobble about the Memorial Room; but I was increasingly anxious to see the rest of the Mission's medical work outside Kathmandu.

Dr. Bethel, Betty, the wife of a volunteer doctor here at Shanta Bhawan, and I were standing by my window one afternoon in February, watching spring come over the Mountains of the Moon. At least the astrologers had announced this was the first day of spring, but the mountains didn't seem to know it yet; they were deep purple against a cold gray sky. Thunder drummed and the clouds were black at each end of the jagged horizon as was most of the range, all except the peak in the center which was strangely outlined in pale muted gray. Suddenly, delicate as a flute piping magic music, a bright ray of sunlight shot down through the clouds, straight into the garden under my window so that the pear tree there in full flower became a white singing glory. The astrologers were right! The golden flute laughing in the sky, the delicate blossoms in the garden, and the great purple mountains merged into one triumphant symphony, shouting, "Wake up, open your eyes! It's spring, *spring*, SPRING!"

I yearned for a new start, too, exploring burgeoning Nepal. I had spent most of a sleepless night plotting. "Bethel," I crept cautiously toward my objective, "since you took off my walking cast I can get about just fine. I hear the ambulance is going to Chapagaon and Anandaban tomorrow. I want to go! If I don't get out of this place pretty soon I'll explode! I haven't had any fever for three days!"

Bethel smiled down at me and then back at the Mountains of the Moon. She murmured evasively, "Sibelius knew nature's dark beauty, too. Look at that gray and silver cloud! He could play it with violins and trumpets. You're Dr. Edgar's patient, not mine."

"Dr. Bethel, you know perfectly well that those two doctors from Denver are riding tomorrow in the ambulance," Betty said, coming to my rescue. "Dr. Elizabeth Miller will be holding the clinic and Dr. Edgar is resting at Anandaban. Even if he isn't on duty, he'd be able to look after one of his own patients." When Dr. Bethel still did not give the required permission for me to go, Betty said, petulantly, staring out the window, "Trumpets indeed! If you ask me, those clouds just look dingy!"

Unexpectedly Dr. Bethel laughed. She told me, "I don't blame you for being restless. You'll probably come back riding flat on the stretcher," she warned. "The road is terribly bumpy and both the clinic and the hospital make a pretty long day . . . but you can try it if you must. Only promise to check back here in Shanta Bhawan and hop straight into bed the minute you get here. Unless I miss my guess, you'll be glad to." Before I could offer my stunned thanks, she picked up her stethoscope, started for the door. "By the way, you may meet that leper lady with the walking cast using that bit of hard rubber that came from yours when we cut it off. Elizabeth put it on after she operated on the patient's foot.

Usually we have to use a piece of rubber out of an old tire, but that's far too soft to walk on comfortably. This leper is getting around fine." Dr. Bethel paused at the door to warn Betty about me. "Keep an eye on her, will you?"

"Sure thing," Betty agreed. She added under her breath, "Never say I'm not a pal!"

Betty had been an enigma to me on the hospital staff. She didn't act or talk like any missionary I'd ever seen. True, she wasn't actually on the staff; her doctor-husband was giving a year of his medical skill to Shanta Bhawan, but as far as I could see Betty was just sticking around as a good wife should. She wore much more expensive clothes than any mission salary could pay for: today she had on a beautifully tailored shocking-pink linen suit, about her slender throat was a gleaming necklace of cut crystal beads, and she kept sliding up and down her smooth arm four beautifully chased silver bracelets. She was always "getting all gussied up" to go to the gay Embassy dinner parties where she was extremely popular, but Betty never got up in time to go to morning chapel or to eat breakfast with the rest of the hospital workers—she brewed late coffee in her own bedroom. She was the only woman at Shanta Bhawan who got her hair washed and set every week.

"Well, I'm off for Tika's," she told me now. Tika was Chinese, the only hairdresser in Nepal who catered to all the Embassy and USAID women and to the wealthy Ranas who were the only ones who could afford her prices. Betty asked, "Did you hear what happened to Tika's two little boys who were in school in India? They got shanghaied at Christmas time."

The war between China and India had gotten pretty hot the previous December, but Tika was not Red Chinese. Her father, a former general in Chang Kai-shek's army, had been executed by the Communists, leaving his family to escape as best they could. Tika had done all right: she'd married in Hong Kong, had had three children, then had drifted finally to Kathmandu where she owned the hotel which housed her beauty parlor as well as an excellent restaurant.

Betty went on, "Her boys were still in class when the Chinese lightning struck India. Tika worried about them naturally; after all, they *were* Chinese and in this war-hate atmosphere you never knew what would happen. It was almost Christmas anyway, time for the boys' vacation, so she sent a man down to bring them home to Nepal, but when he got there, the children were missing. The school didn't know where they were, nobody knew; they'd just vanished. Tika was frantic. She bombarded the Indian Embassy here, pulled strings with all the important husbands of the ladies she takes care of, but no soap. The boys had just disappeared into thin air. Some Christmas present! Finally Tika got a post card written by the oldest boy, complaining, 'The food's terrible here, Mother, come get us.' The postmark was 1,000 miles away in South India! The children had been sent to a prison camp there, but the Indian ambassador here got the boys brought back to Nepal. You bet Tika'll never let them out of her sight again. Well, so long. See you tomorrow at Chapagaon. I'm taking the early jeep that leaves before the ambulance."

Betty left behind her a lingering fragrance of perfume. At crack of dawn the next day, she stuck her beautifully coiffeured head inside my door to warn, "Be sure to go to the john before you leave. There isn't any way to go at Chapagaon, not even a bush to hide behind."

"Heavens! Then what do you do? . . ."

But Betty was gone. In her gay pink suit, with a huge bunch of freshly picked sweet peas stuck into the front of her jacket, with her upswept hair and bright-colored sandals, she looked more as if she were off for an Embassy brunch than going to a village clinic, infected with heaven only knew what kind of strange Eastern germs.

Dr. Bethel was waiting at the Shanta Bhawan door beside the ambulance, a huge Land Rover, to introduce me to Dr. and Mrs. Frank Campbell, both physicians from Denver, he an internist and she a pediatrician, who were to be my companions of the day. They were friends of Lila Bishop, the wife of Barry Bishop, the intrepid mountaineer who was so soon to achieve fame by reaching

the top of Mt. Everest, and then was to be flown back by helicopter to Shanta Bhawan to have his frozen toes and fingers
treated. Lila, not allowed as a woman to be a member of the
American Expedition, was planning a mountain trek of her own.
With six friends including these doctors, she was making arrangements to walk the 400 miles from Kathmandu to Darjeeling, India,
stopping by on her way to call at the 18,000-foot-high base camp
where her husband, Barry, was already waiting for the big climb.

As I clambered painfully up the high steps of the Land Rover
to take a seat beside the two Dr. Campbells, I said admiringly
that they must be experienced mountaineers to be keeping up with
Lila.

"Oh, we've climbed in Colorado, but actually you'd have to call
us amateurs," Mrs. Campbell answered. "We're just going along
for the walk, so to speak. But we want to be sure to take the right
medicines with us in case some of us get ill or perhaps we can
help the villagers as we pass through. We're not very familiar
with oriental diseases, so Dr. Miller is going to fill us in at the
Chapagaon clinic. We'll take a look at the Anandaban lepers, too."

As the Land Rover driver shifted gears to take off, Dr. Bethel
came to my side of the car to explain, "I'm sending a leper patient
along with you for the Anandaban hospital." She smiled at the
back of the ambulance where sat an extremely pretty girl in a red
and white sari, with a red scarf tied over her hair. How on earth
could you tell she was a leper? Dr. Bethel warned me, "I'm leaving
her in your charge. Be sure she gets to Anandaban safely, won't
you? Don't lose her."

How on earth could you lose a leper out of an ambulance?
I wondered as we moved off down the hospital drive. But I didn't
have much time to meditate because the road to Chapagaon was
worse than Bethel had warned. The two doctors turned out to be
the nicest kind of un-ugly Americans, friendly, tolerant, loving
beautiful Nepal, but conversation is difficult while being thrown
from side to side of a high seat of a Land Rover. Finally we
merely held on and gasped. Not more than ten feet wide and raised
high above the surrounding fields, the mud road had once been

paved but now the great stones stood every which way, some even on end. Irrigation ditches had been cut right across the alleged road to bring water for irrigation from one field to the farm on the opposite side, but none of the ditches had been bridged. As we dropped with a thud into another excavation, our ambulance driver explained that wood was so scarce, even if a farmer had the cash to buy boards to smooth out the road for cars, by morning the boards would have disappeared to prop up someone else's house. So the farmer did not bother to bridge the ditches.

"No wonder it takes an hour to go eight miles!" gulped Mrs. Campbell clutching her side of the car. "Do you mean to say that the Shanta Bhawan staff comes out here every week? They're certainly dedicated people. I should think they'd all end up in X-ray with dislocated vertebrate, at the very least."

I grabbed for the doctor's arm, for this time we bounced so hard I even left the seat, but when I turned to be sure my leper lady in the red sari was all right, she beamed. Perhaps her rear end was numb; I wished mine were. As the Land Rover went down this time, apparently into the Grand Canyon, we slammed to a stop.

"Chapagaon," the driver announced.

We crawled down shakily from the high seat, watching the village of Chapagaon drowsily coming to life. The houses of bright orange bricks, two stories high, had elaborately carved window blinds and doorways, decorated by long-ago Newari artists. Only 2,000 years of dirt appeared to be holding some of these ancient houses together. Through the open archways we could glimpse courtyards filled with broken bottles, manure piles, discarded junk, but the glassless windows revealed bright brass cooking and water pots hanging on the walls and polished to a high sheen by sand— soap was too expensive for any villager. The cold of the mountain night still lingered in the dark houses, so the villagers had sensibly moved out onto the sun-flooded sidewalk. Here two women were lifting together a heavy weight, pounding grain in a great metal pot; another girl was carding black and red yarn to weave the typical sari of the country woman—black for practical use but edged gaily with red, a costume which could not be bought in the

Kathmandu bazaar but had to be woven to order. The skirt was slit in the back to show the much-admired tatooing on the wearer's leg. A young mother, stripped to the waist, her brown breasts smooth and gleaming, was sitting there rubbing mustard oil into the naked baby in her lap who waved his legs and laughed: a sidewalk Madonna. A small boy attending to nature beside the road put up his hands to cry, *"Namaste!"* amiably to us strangers. Water buffaloes ambled across the street at will, while men, lazy as limpets, lay dozing beside the orange walls.

The water hole, the center of community life, was more animated. Two thirsty water buffaloes, wading and drinking, had roiled the water to a dirty brown; a woman was washing her long black hair; a housewife was pounding her sari against a stone, using it as a laundromat; while a third housewife was filling her bright brass water pot for tea.

"I hope they boil that water twenty minutes before they make the tea!" The doctor's wife shuddered. At the sound of her foreign voice, an old man scowled up at her and spat deliberately into the water hole. Was he perhaps a retired soldier who understood English, resented her comment?

"Clang, cling, clang!"

A small boy had leaped up to strike at the great bronze bell hanging in the little temple beside the water hole. The shrine was surrounded by an iron fence upon which hung white trousers, saris, all sorts of clothes drying in the hot sun; the Nepalese revere their many temples but are not above putting them to practical use.

There was a long line of waiting Nepalese, standing around all four sides of the village square, men, women, and children, patient in the hot sun.

"Patients for clinic," our driver explained, setting the brakes of the Land Rover and yawning. "The rest are already inside. The clinic is upstairs on that veranda. That man over there with the orange cap loans it to the doctors without charge."

As we looked at the generous Nepali gentleman bustling about, the temple bell rang again. This time the worshipper was a little old lady riding on the back of a stalwart young girl so that the tiny grandmother could reach up to give the bell a good whang. She was evidently well known by the rest of the patients or else it was her great age that gave her precedence, for the rest of the waiting patients did not protest when she rode on her granddaughter's back to the head of the line, with us Westerners meekly following her to discover the way upstairs to the clinic. Inside the front door of the house, already crowded with patients, the room was so dark we had to feel with our feet for the rounds of the ladder that led up to the veranda. When we emerged into dazzling sunshine, the first thing we saw was Betty, standing there in her pink suit wearing her great fragrant bunch of sweet peas as she poured worm medicine out of a large bottle into the open mouths of a long line of children.

"Isn't this smell awful? But I came prepared," Betty said, burying her nose in her sweet peas, but not stopping an instant from deworming the young of Chapagaon. "Hey, boy, what's all that black dirt on the back of your neck?" She brushed with her hand and the dirt took wings; they were flies feeding on an open ulcer on the back of the boy's neck! Betty reached calmly for a bottle of iodine, soothing when the boy howled, "It's good for you. Big medicine!" Then she poured more de-wormer down his open mouth to shut him up. This was the fastidious fashion plate I'd wondered about at Shanta Bhawan!

"She comes every week. The children adore her," a woman's soft cultured voice said admiringly behind me. "They call her 'The Lady Who Laughs.' She dresses so pretty and she smells so sweet."

"Meet Mrs. Ananda," Betty introduced us. "She's the midwife who brings most of the village babies since she and her husband moved here to live. Mr. Ananda is a trained nurse, too. They're Indian but the village has adopted them, so now they're practically Nepalese."

"Last week I delivered the loveliest pair of twin boys," Mrs. Ananda said, then she sighed. "But they both died. It's the custom here not to feed newborn babies for four days, so only the hardiest survive."

"There'll be a couple more in nine months," Betty assured her. "For the love of sweet Peter, is that for me?"

A Nepali girl in a gorgeous lavender sari was holding out to Betty a delicate plate of green leaves held together with colored grasses; also from around her own neck she took a strange necklace strung with alternate popped corn and pear blossoms, and slid it around Betty's neck. The shy Nepali explained, "The plate is from me to you but the necklace is from my god. It will ward off bad luck."

"Well, thanks, Pal," Betty said, overcome with such a wealth of assorted gifts.

"Dr. Elizabeth says, why don't you all come down to the other end of the veranda where she is working?" Janeki came up to us visitors to urge; she is the girl with the efficient hands and the long shining hair braid that is always interwoven with flowers, who helps out in the various clinics as interpreter. "Dr. Miller wants to show the Denver doctors some cases."

Dr. Elizabeth had worked out a technique of examining patients which allowed her to diagnose as many as possible with the least effort. The doctor herself was sitting on a chair while each patient perched on a lower stool so that Dr. Elizabeth could use her stethoscope without bending over. Janeki handed over the proper record cards, meanwhile speeding up the unwrapping of the women patients' patukas (waistbands) which were sometimes thirteen feet long, used to carry everything from groceries and purses to the family treasures.

"Did you ever see an initial case of leprosy?" Dr. Elizabeth asked the two Denver doctors. "Then look at the thickening of this man's skin, the darkening area on his face."

The two Denver doctors hastily took out their notebooks, began to jot down symptoms of half a dozen oriental diseases they had never encountered in the States, asked to know what were the proper medicines they would need on their trip to Darjeeling. So I was left free to study the faces of the long line of passing patients. It was a fascinating picture. There were classic brown profiles of the Newari which might have been Greek; Mongolian faces with broad flat noses decorated with nose rings; women whose ears had been pierced all around the lobe by perhaps twenty tiny holes, each with its jewel of bright glass; some even had an ornament stuck into the ear cavity. How could they hear anything? Some of the babies hanging on their mothers' backs waved lethal-looking little scythe-like knives. "To ward off the evil spirits," Dr. Elizabeth explained. Most of the patients still had red powder in their hair and bright stains on their clothes from the festival of *holi* that had been celebrated last week. Even the King had taken part in the fun; and woe betide any brash foreigner who lost his temper! One Englishman riding through town with his fiancée on the back of his motorcycle had been so enraged at her being doused with red powder that he had sprung off his bike to chase the boys who threw it. Later he had been found unconscious beside his overturned bike and had been brought with a concussion to Dr. Bethel at Shanta Bhawan. It was dangerous to bait the Nepali tiger underneath these calm faces.

Dr. Elizabeth was chuckling as she began unwinding yards of soiled bandages from one beaming old man. "He's almost well again but he does so love a clean bandage! I think we'll give him one more as psychological therapy. One of my friends in Wisconsin knits these bandages for me." She wound the clean yardage deftly around the old man's body, and he trotted off proudly, relieved in mind as well as body. "Now, Poodlie! You back again?"

It was our little old lady who'd been riding on the younger woman's back; she was about half as big as a minute. With her pointed wise face, her gray hair, and the impish twinkle in her black eyes she looked like a leprechaun. Dr. Elizabeth chided gently, "You know perfectly well your rheumatism is better since you used the ointment. It is no longer necessary for you to ride to the clinic on your granddaughter's back. You can walk."

"*Namaste*, Doctor!" Poodlie grinned back at the doctor, showing her toothless gums as she folded her hands in gay greeting. "It is true. But do not grudge me the medicine." Clutching her ointment, Poodlie went to bow "*Namaste*" to each worker before she would leave. The clinic to her was a pleasant social occasion, too much fun to miss, sick or well. The next patient was a frightened girl three months pregnant, but not by a man of her own caste. Janeki translated that she wanted an abortion. "She's got a right to be scared," Dr. Elizabeth said worriedly. "She may be up against prison or some worse punishment, such as cutting off her nose. But what can I do? Nothing of course. They know the risks and the law." I shivered, for this seemed such a savage punishment.

"Where do you come from in the States?" The male nurse, Mr. Ananda, had appeared at my elbow, a tall dark gentleman in a white coat being polite to a guest. I told him absently, "From Sudbury, Massachusetts, a town next to Concord."

"The home of Thoreau!" he cried, his dark face lighting up. "Gandhi admired that man. Tell me, did Thoreau's philosophy influence America as much as Gandhi's did my native India?"

I gulped, stared at him. To sit on a mountain veranda surrounded by leprosy, flies, and adultresses about to have their noses cut off and to discuss the philosophy of a New England sage with an Indian nurse . . . this was fantastic Nepal, all right.

"He made more of an intellectual impact that a political one; yet passive resistance as a non-violent weapon is certainly getting a good tryout in our segregation sit-ins today," I told him. "Maybe Thoreau made more of an impact than we realized. But nowadays we Sudburyites swim in Walden Pond instead of philosophizing about it."

We both looked up at a commotion at the other end of the corridor where the patients got their medicines and paid what they could afford. A fat lady who had sworn up and down she could pay nothing at all for her streptomycin pills, that she was in debt, sick, with no single coin in the world, was just unwinding her patuka from around her stout stomach for the doctor's inspection when handfuls of rupees fell out, paper and coins galore. Janeki didn't even glance at the culprit; she merely stooped, counted out the proper coins for the medicine, and handed the rest back to their red-faced owner.

"Be sure your sins will find you out." A dimple of laughter had come into Dr. Elizabeth's cheek. "Janeki doesn't lose a trick."

She raised her voice. "Stop the line, will you, dear? It's time for lunch."

From her kitchen at Anandaban hospital Dr. Elizabeth had brought a lavish lunch for all the workers, curried rice, tea, and fruit. As she piled up the plates I suddenly felt a great distaste for food and became so dizzy I had to take hold of the window shutter. Five weeks in bed had left me weaker than I'd realized. I knew I had to get out into the fresher air; I'd go down to see how my leper was making out, if she needed lunch. But when I got back to the Land Rover, the driver was asleep on the front seat and the back of the ambulance was empty. My leper lady wasn't there!

I nudged the driver awake, demanding, "Where's your patient gone?"

"She was here a minute ago. I don't know."

"We've got to find her!"

We looked all around the village square, investigated the line of patients still waiting, even asked at the open doors of the villagers, with the driver interpreting my concern into rapid Nepali. Nobody had seen my leper, nobody knew anything; or if they did they were certainly not telling strangers. Alarm prickled along my spine as I rushed back up the stairs to tell Dr. Elizabeth, "I've lost my leper! Dr. Bethel told me to be sure she was safe but she's disappeared into thin air!"

"She'll turn up," Dr. Elizabeth soothed. "They love the hospital at Anandaban."

But I was responsible, I worried. Bethel had warned me. What would I tell her when I got home? "Sorry, but I've misplaced your leper"?

"It's time you folks left for Anandaban if you're going to make it back to Kathmandu before dark," Dr. Elizabeth urged. "You go along. If we find the disappearing patient, I'll send her along in the jeep."

There seemed little else to do. I kept an anxious lookout all along the road but there was no leper lady and actually no bush for her to hide behind. The road from Chapagaon to Anandaban was, if possible, worse than that from Kathmandu, for the way had

Sally Beth, Dr. Bob, and Dr. Bethel Fleming, standing in front of Shanta Bhawan Hospital, Kathmandu, Nepal. (*Toge Fujihira*)

The Kathmandu Valley.

Kathmandu street scene.
(*Toge Fujihira*)

Dr. Robert Fleming examining one of the pheasants he has collected for the Chicago Museum of Natural History. He is also
starting a collection of native birds and ferns for a projected
museum in Nepal. (*Toge Fujihira*)

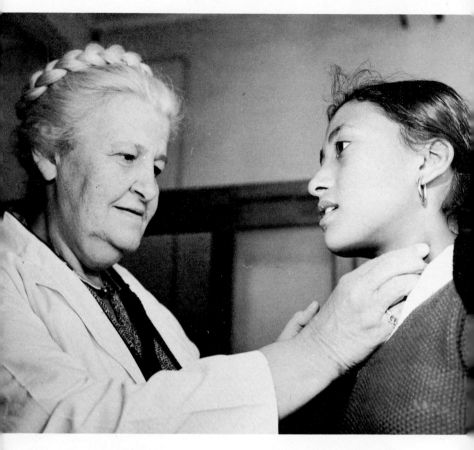

Dr. Bethel Fleming examining one of the 400 patients who attend the Shanta Bhawan Hospital clinic each Saturday. (*Toge Fujihira*)

Nurse feeding baby at Shanta Bhawan Hospital. (*Toge Fujihira*)

Patients waiting in the village street for Dr. Bethel's clinic to open
at Sundarijal.

Mountain scene near Gorkha clinic run by the United Mission
to Nepal. Patients walk an average of twenty-five miles to get
medical attention.

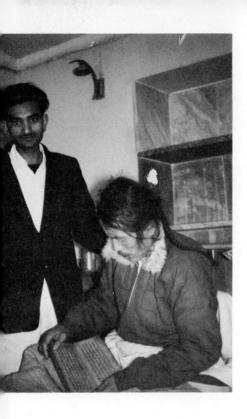

Buddhist lama patient reading his holy book at Shanta Bhawan Hospital while male nurse looks on.

Dr. Bob (right) at the language school he superintends. "Nepal" is word on blackboard.

The Living Goddess of Kathmandu. She is allowed out of her special dwelling only twice a year for the procession shown.

Namaste — Nepalese greeting which means literally, "I bow to you," but also "good morning" and "goodby." (*Toge Fujihira*)

become so narrow that as it mounted up and up the side of the mountain, two cars could not possibly pass. On one side was a sheer rock wall and on the other a frightening drop of 500 feet down into the valley below. When the Denver doctor asked the driver what he'd do if he met another car, he stopped blowing the car horn long enough to answer succinctly, "Back down the mountain." With all those curves and that cliff? Fortunately the traffic was mostly on foot, peasants carrying enormous baskets of vegetables for the Kathmandu market; others had such loads of firewood they appeared to be a woodpile walking; they had tucked ferns under the wood to protect their bent backs, and one man had even decorated the top of his terrible load with bright red rhododendron blossoms. You can't lick people who can carry an incredible burden with a smile and a flower! But where, oh where, was my lost leper?

Up and up and up. Anandaban must be the top of the world. It was. The view was so tremendous that when the Land Rover finally stopped no one got down for a moment; we just sat and stared, drinking in vast unbelievable beauty. The hospital stood on the prow of a great rocky promontory thrusting out into the valley; below lay the village with its terraced gardens making an intricate pattern of dark green, light green, and brown, while all around towered the mighty circle of mountains. Truly this was a spot where the rejected of the world could lift up their eyes unto the hills.

"Welcome to Anandaban!"

Nurse Deirdre Banks was scrambling down over the steep path to the Land Rover to greet us, a slender, dark-haired girl whose eyes had a lonely look as if she'd stared too long at faraway mountain peaks. But she was a wonderfully efficient nurse, courageous enough to live alone in her own lovely little house with the vast valley for her front yard. She ran the hospital with a firm hand, even took over when the doctors had to be away at the clinic. As we climbed up with her to her hospitable front door, she pointed out the long two-story brick building which was the men's ward high above on a ridge, while further down the hill was the

women's ward. The new larger hospital and the houses being built
were not only for patients but for additional staff, a clinical laboratory, and a rest home for the families who often had to walk for
fifty miles to bring a patient to Anandaban Hospital.

"Have you checked in a new patient today?" I demanded
anxiously. "I lost a leper at Chapagaon. I mean, she disappeared
from the ambulance."

No, she was sorry but she hadn't admitted anyone this morning.
Deirdre Banks offered, delicately hospitable, "I expect you'd all
like to wash up. The bathroom's upstairs at the right."

What luxury! It even had a john that flushed. The running
water was not raised by electricity, Deirdre explained, but by some
mechanical legerdemain whereby the water running downhill
generated the power to run the pump which in turn lifted the
water back up the hill. None of us could understand how this
happened; it was enough miracle that the cold-water tap worked.
The big white icebox down in the kitchen was full of ice and
food in spite of the war shortages, for Dr. Elizabeth had discovered
a forgotten cache of kerosene down in the village to run the
machine. Dr. Elizabeth would. We sat upon Deirdre's terrace with
the gorgeous view, thirstily sipping lemonade with real ice in it.

"Well, look who's here!" Dr. Edgar Miller beamed. He had
climbed, unnoticed, up the path carpeted with pine needles from
the doctor's house to join us. He demanded of me, "How did you
get away from Dr. Bethel?" He looked ten years younger than
when he'd left Shanta Bhawan a week ago, so exhausted that he
confessed he'd slept anywhere from fourteen to eighteen hours
a day ever since he'd been here at Anandaban. He complained that
he barely saw Elizabeth; but she was on duty, of course, till Dr.
Chandy got back. She even had to go back to Kathmandu in the
jeep this afternoon, after she finished at Chapagaon, to take over
tomorrow's leper clinic there, then ride back here to Anandaban.
He didn't see how she did it; Elizabeth was wonderful. He still
thought so after thirty years.

Deirdre chimed in fervently, "She not only makes the routine
rounds of seventy patients here every morning but she's mapped
out a stiff program of going over seven patients thoroughly every

day till she has examined them all. A man came in yesterday with a dreadful ulcer I could hardly bear to look at—and I've seen plenty—and a woman with her nose hanging on with a piece of skin which Dr. Elizabeth stitched back on." The nurse's brown eyes slid out to the mountains as she said slowly, "I don't mind the loneliness . . . much; it's being afraid I can't meet emergencies when the doctor is away. Wouldn't you like to see the wards?" she invited the doctors from Denver.

As I trailed after the medical group, I was ashamed to have ever complained of anything as minor as a broken ankle or a pain in the belly. Many of the leper patients, sitting around the low wall of the veranda or on the grass, had lost toes or had no feet or hands at all; some had great holes where their mouths ought to be. Others were blind. A small boy of ten was weeding around a young peach tree bright with lovely pink and white blossoms, with small hands that lacked several fingers.

"That is a very special tree," the nurse explained. "One of the patients planted a peach stone three years ago and now, look! If I didn't stop them they'd cultivate it right out of the ground. This is the first time it's bloomed. Not that we keep many patients long, only those whose families have turned them out or who come from too far away to come back for further treatments."

"How far is too far?" Dr. Campbell demanded.

"Oh, anything more than twenty-five miles."

Lepers, thrown out of their homes, can yet find healing, hope, and a peach tree blossoming against the bright blue sky. . . .

The women's ward was down a steep path along which we slipped and slid to find most of the patients sunning out on the wide veranda. Dressed in bright saris, they looked happy and unconcerned. Three women were sitting on a spread-out blanket knitting bright green and red wool into sweaters with intricate patterns. The wool was the gift of a friend of Dr. Elizabeth, who had written please to send gay colors, not utilitarian gray, black, or white. One smiling round little woman, her right foot in a walking cast thrust out in front of her as she knitted, looked up to nod and smile.

"She's the one who has the piece of hard rubber from your old walking cast!" Nurse Deirdre told me. "She walks and walks, just to show she can. . . ." She stopped because I wasn't listening; I was staring at a girl in a red and white sari, with a red scarf around her head, walking nonchalantly out into the sunny veranda.

"It's my leper!" I rushed over to her. "How on earth did you get here?"

"She walked," the nurse said after consultation in Nepali with the beaming patient. "She got tired of waiting. She says the road was so bumpy it was easier to walk, so she did."

That certainly made sense, but she might have mentioned it to the driver. I'd been so upset. "Don't you feel well?" Nurse Deirdre demanded. Suddenly the world had begun to whirl around my head, and my body felt on fire. "I'm fine," I lied. And there were still two horrible hours to ride back in the Land Rover over that dreadful road. Well, I'd asked for it.

When the nightmare of the return trip finally ended, nothing had ever seemed so gratefully cool as those Shanta Bhawan Hospital sheets which Maia, my little Nepalese nurse, was pulling over my hot body. Was that whirring noise in my dizzy head or outside the window?

"It's the rescue helicopter from the American Expedition," Maia reported running to the window. "It's landing in the rice field across the road! The ambulance is rushing over there!"

"Everything all right in here?" Dr. Bethel came in the screen door, picked up my chart, frowned at the ascending fever curve. I asked hastily, "Is one of the Americans hurt?"

"No, its a badly burned Sherpa woman," Dr. Bethel said. The expedition had been passing through the village when they heard a woman screaming from the horrible burns she'd received when she'd tried to rescue the only wealth she owned, a water buffalo, from her house that was afire. Norman Dyhrenfurth, the expedition leader, had tried to ask by radio for Kathmandu to send the helicopter to airlift the sick woman down to Shanta Bhawan, but static and a storm had prevented his getting through to the valley. Strangely, a ham radio fan in New Zealand had picked up the message for help, had passed it on to Calcutta, which had relayed the call to Kathmandu. As the rescue helicopter whirred off again, Dr. Bethel hurried away to meet the ambulance that was bringing the badly burned woman from the top of the world.

"The Lord's Plan for Nepal is woven of many strands," I thought as I lay there, listening to the helicopter roar away down the valley. "A strand from Asia, from Europe, from New Zealand, from the United States, but altogether the rope of faith is strong enough to reach up to a Himalayan mountain to rescue a village woman and to comfort lepers in a hospital where a peach tree is in bloom." I lay there for a long time, being glad that, however much it cost, I had gone to Anandaban.

"Are you asleep?"

Dr. Bethel was back again. "I thought you'd like to know; it's going to take time of course, for the burns are deep, but the Sherpa villager is going to live." She added, "Doctor Elizabeth says to tell you that your leper lady at Anandaban sent you a message . . . not the one you . . . er . . . misplaced; the one who has the walking cast with your rubber on it. She's sorry she forgot to say, 'Thank you.'"

A leper thanking *me* for a piece of rubber! I couldn't answer: there weren't any words big enough. I could barely see Dr. Bethel through my tears.

Chapter Eleven

Long Live the King

Dr. Bethel and Dr. Bob Fleming were going to a party at the American Embassy to celebrate the "Two Hundred Thirty-first Anniversary of the Birth of George Washington, [to be held] in the garden of Kamal Kunj, Kamaladi" as the melodic invitation from Ambassador and Mrs. Henry Stebbins read to every American in Kathmandu as well as to all official Nepalese. Strangely enough the 22nd of February was a double holiday in Kathmandu, honoring the birth of the first American President and the yearly Festival of the Night of Lord Shiva who has been worshipped by Hindus for over 2,000 years. King Mahendra, as the reincarnation of the god Vishnu, was to preside first at the Shiva celebration on the Tundikal, the great parade grounds in the center of the city, and afterward proceed to the birthday party at the American Embassy.

As the Flemings drove along in their little Volkswagen, they saw that the city's sidewalks were crowded with hundreds of pilgrims wearing the three white lines on their foreheads which stood for Shiva's trident. Many pilgrims had walked for days down from Nepalese mountain villages to worship today at the temple at Pashupatinath; others had traveled for weary weeks up from India. Amid the boom of cannons, the trumpeting of bands, and the flapping of flags, a parade of soldiers, schoolchildren, village headmen and city officials, gay dancers, were taking enthusiastic part in the festival on the common. All castes were mingled, girls in bright silver-tissue saris with real diamonds in their nostrils and humble villagers with equally shining glass earrings; many teenagers wore Punjabi costume, which had become as popular with Nepali youngsters as dungarees among the American adolescents, displaying full trousers, an over-blouse, and a debonair scarf tossed jauntily over the shoulders. Entire families had come, carrying small babies in bright-colored dresses with their eyes outlined with kohl to ward off evil spirits. There were monks wearing red or yellow gowns and natty officers in their well-pressed uniforms with decorations as big as soup plates, dispensing order to the enormous smiling crowd.

His Majesty King Mahendra was the central figure, standing there reviewing the marchers, surrounded by his own Lancers in their bright red and white uniforms, their shiny black boots, helmets with feathers floating behind them as they rode their magnificent horses.

"This is no ordinary parade," Dr. Bethel commented, looking at the happy throng smiling at the small excited boys perched precariously on the top of the wire fence around the Tundikal. "The King standing there symbolizes the new united Nepal. Both for the men from the mountains and for the people of Kathmandu he stands for the national unity in which there is strength. He's rather like a modern George Washington reviewing the Continental Army, with the Minute Men of Concord and Lexington thrown in for good measure. This could be a Fourth of July parade back in my home town! Look, Bob, at those native dancers, with their masks and whirling skirts! Aren't they *fun*? The only things missing are the fire engines howling happily down Main Street!

"Our two countries have a great deal more in common than a love of parades," Dr. Bethel went on as the Shanta Bhawan party stood later on the lawn of the Embassy waiting for the King to arrive from reviewing the parade, for his second great festival of the day. A red carpet ran from the driveway to the royal pavilion that had been set up on the Embassy lawn, on either side of which, drooping in the afternoon heat, stood the two proud flags, the

Nepalese and the American. The flag of Nepal had double red pennants, one showing the white emblem of the sun god, the other the moon god, while the edging of both pennants was deep blue.

"Both flags have the same colors, red, white, and blue, and speak of the celestial! Instead of the sun and moon we have fifty stars," Bethel pointed out dreamily. "Lord Shiva and George Washington, sharing a festival day, although centuries and civilizations apart. What an exciting time we live in when East and West meet as friends!"

The sound of trumpets, the clatter of horses' hoofs brought everyone to his feet. The King was coming! Whenever you heard his Lancers, you knew His Majesty was near.

This is the way a king should arrive, with silver trumpets, proud horses prancing, and banners. Ambassador and Mrs. Stebbins led their royal guests to the pavilion on the lawn, while the band played loudly the national anthem, "Hail most noble and gracious King. . . ." He was both as he stood there at attention, erect and proud in his uniform, surrounded by his generals. "O say can you see . . ." a lump of homesickness rose in Dr. Bethel's throat when the band shifted to the familiar strains. She murmured, "You never know what it means to be American until you see the Stars and Stripes in a strange land!"

Yet she loved Nepal, too, the country of her adoption. It was thrilling to see how *alike* we were, Americans and Nepalese, as well as how different. This was American aid and Nepalese courage in person, not statistics. This was the real thing, flesh-and-blood cooperation between two proud nations which trusted each other. Here we were equal brothers under the Sun, Moon, and the fifty Stars, and under God by whatever name we called Him.

Dr. Bethel's brown eyes slid up to the magnificent panorama of the snows on the horizon. How tiny we must look from those tall peaks up there, the giants with one foot in Nepal and the other in Tibet, like mere ants on the Embassy lawn! Yet intrepid American and Nepalese mountain climbers were at this very moment challenging those proud peaks, together.

> Blessed with victory and peace
> May the heav'n rescued land
> Praise the Power that has made
> And preserved us a nation!
> Then conquer we must
> When our cause it is just
> And this be our motto
> *In God is our trust.*

How many Americans knew these words of the last verse of "The Star-Spangled Banner" and still believed in them? Perhaps the Supreme Court would no longer allow this to be sung in our schools, now they had ruled out the Bible and prayer! Yet underneath all law stood the deep trust of a nation in Almighty God who had forged so many refugees from so many different kinds of countries into a strong nation. Perhaps it was because King Mahendra was actually doing the same thing today, trying to weld so many sects, with differing racial backgrounds, into one strong united Nepal, that he had understood their problems at Shanta Bhawan when they lost their first patient tragically on the operating table, Dr. Bethel remembered. It was important to understand what kind of a man King Mahendra was, and what his plans were, not only for the political future of his country but for religious freedom.

"With King Mahendra rides the future of Nepal." This remark was made by an awed spectator of the colorful coronation procession in May 1956 when the King and his lovely Queen Ratna were riding on the gorgeously caparisoned elephant of state to receive the crown which confirmed that Mahendra Bir Bikran Shah Dev was now monarch of Nepal. Equally important, he was also head of the Hindu religion in his country: Vishnu, the Preserver. It is in this double capacity that King Mahendra is at once the symbol and hope of Nepal's unity in these troubled times. Reverence for his person by both the army and the man in the street is the one fact which even dissident elements in that turbulent lovely kingdom are forced to respect.

If politics is the ship of state, religion is the turbine engine which pushes it ahead. Not only is the King the reincarnation of the Hindu god but he also presides at many of the Buddhist festivals; the two religions have so intertwined during the centuries that there is a Hindu shrine to the goddess of smallpox in the 2,000-year-old Buddhist temple at Swayanbunath. The Nepalese King thus holds in his hands not only the conduct of affairs in this world but the reins of the next. If anyone can make of Nepal a unified modern country, the intelligent, sensitive King Mahendra is that man.

His Majesty rides the ceremonial elephant, but he also rides the airplane, significant of the leap that his country has made from isolation to twentieth-century membership in the United Nations. Yet only thirteen years have elapsed since his father, King Tribhuvan, opened up to foreigners the borders of this lovely mysterious country with its mighty mountains and deep valleys. His hair-breadth escape from his Rana jailer, the Maharajah who held Nepal in his political grip, reads like an adventure story. The royal family, on pretext of going on a picnic, filled their lunch baskets with money and jewelry instead of sandwiches, drove their car for refuge to the protection of the Indian Embassy in Kathmandu. Prime Minister Nehru later sent a plane by which they escaped to India, whence King Tribhuvan returned in triumph in 1951 to claim his throne and to inaugurate a constitutional monarchy. But King Tribhuvan was a sick man. When he died of tuberculosis in Switzerland in 1955 his newly crowned son, Mahendra, was bitterly assailed by his enemies as the King who scuttled democracy, because he dissolved the Congress and suspended the constitution which his father, King Tribhuvan, had sponsored. Mahendra insists that he is merely trying to work out that form of representative government best suited to his country. His big job is to develop a national consciousness, to get his people to think of themselves as *citizens of Nepal*. He argues that the state like every other big business must have an executive head competent to make decisions until such time as he deems his people in condition to take over.

It is no easy task which King Mahendra has set for himself. Consider the physical obstacles alone with which he is faced: lack of motorable roads; villages so isolated the only access to them is by paths or bridges so hair-raising that even experienced porters hesitate to cross the dilapidated contraptions; uncertain radio communications; and the illiteracy of over 90 percent of the population. Airplanes now link the larger cities, but to get to some of the distant parts of Nepal it is actually easier to fly outside to India and then walk back in over the border! For centuries each racial group (Newars, Sherpas, Rais, etc.), even each village, has considered itself a unit with no thought of being a responsible part of the rest of the country. Only a century ago there were separate kings ruling the cities of Patan, Kathmandu, and Bhatgaon.

In his attempt to convert his people to the idea that in national unity there is strength and that only thus can this small country make itself heard in the cacophony of nations, King Mahendra has traveled indefatigibly during the past few years on visits of state around the world. As no other Nepalese ruler has dared he has also traversed his own rugged country-side, north and south, east and west, riding by elephant, airplane, or walking when neither is available, showing himself to the common people to whom the King was formerly only a far-off dream, assuring them, "I am your Father. What do you need?" King Mahendra is preaching a courageous proud gospel to his people: "We must work together, build together, roads, schools, factories, dams, colleges. . . . we must not depend only upon the help of outside nations, as grateful for their aid as we are. What we become as a nation depends upon ourselves."

His Majesty's royal trips around the countryside have not been without danger. Several attempts were made upon his life by malcontents, one of which nearly succeeded. A bomb thrown at the King was instantly intercepted by one of his alert generals who tossed it so far away the explosion did no damage except to shock the horrified bystanders. In Kathmandu as in Washington, tragedy haunts the steps of the head of a great nation.

Once a new Japanese ambassador complained to Dr. Bob Fleming that the dependence of the King upon his soothsayers in conducting foreign affairs was unbelievable. Why, he, the representative of a great nation, dressed in his formal regimentals and glittering decorations, had actually been on his way to present his credentials as arranged at the Royal Palace, when his car had been stopped by one of the King's Lancers! The emissary politely but firmly suggested that since today had turned out to be inauspicious for conducting international business, would His Excellency be kind enough to return to the Palace next Tuesday? There was nothing the Japanese ambassador could do but return to his hotel room to wait two more days for a royal audience, he told Dr. Bob indignantly.

"Did it ever occur to you that the sudden change of plan might have reasons other than the inauspiciousness of the day?" Dr. Bob suggested, with his usual mild way of looking at both sides of a question. "It is quite possible, since there have been several attempts on His Majesty's life, this change might have something to do with security precautions."

While the priests may and do advise, King Mahendra himself, as the reincarnation of Vishnu, is the final authority. Even if he wished to do so, he could not change overnight the culture of centuries. The history books still teach Kathmandu schoolchildren that their lovely valley was made by a god cutting with his sword a cleft in the mountains so that the lake could run out, leaving the holy Bagmati and Vishnumati rivers to run into the Ganges, the holiest of Hindu rivers.

Yet it is the King who is quietly backing the policy of having educational advisers and teachers from the United States and Europe update these schoolbooks to scientific explanations; it is His Majesty who has consistently encouraged the advance of modern medicine for his people, looking forward to the day when this help will no longer be needed, when Nepal can stand alone.

Over and over King Mahendra has insisted that only by adding their own efforts can the Nepalese become economically sound, internationally respected. The three-year plan inaugurated by his government is not content to let outside aid pour into the left hand of his people; it insists that the right hand shall also grasp its own shovel, hoe, or modern schoolbook. King Mahendra announced:

Important targets of the three-year plan are a total of 925 miles of new roads, 23 new air strips, generator of 22,000 kilowatts of power, irrigation facilities for additional 161,000 acres of land, opening of 1200 new primary schools, 3 hospitals, and 10 health centres, additional supply of 9 million gallons of drinking water, self-sufficiency in sugar, cigarettes and footwear. About 16 percent of the plan outlay is to be borne out of internal resources. To meet the remaining financial needs involved we have to rely on foreign aid.

Through these foreign-aid programs King Mahendra's government is unavoidably involved in the East-West struggle between Russia and the United States. As one American official pointed out, "The Nepalese find themselves pressured by different groups, United States and Russia, China and India, each offering a carrot to lead the country in a different direction. Small wonder if the Nepalese are confused." Nepal formerly guarded its independence by turning its back upon the rest of the world; today it plays host to Swiss and American Foundations, International Red Cross, and to many embassies and aid programs, both Eastern and Western.

The United States is developing schools, hospitals, roads; it has installed a 1,500-line telephone system and a "ropeway" made of steel cables, by which 25 tons of freight an hour, three times the capacity of the original system, can be airlifted from high in the mountains to Kathmandu, a tremendous help to the economy. Russia is building a hydroelectric plant and has a fifty-bed modern hospital in Kathmandu, a student-assistance program by which many Nepalese are educated in Moscow colleges, and other major aid projects. India as the nearest neighbor, in spite of the poverty of her own teaming millions, has helped generously: in addition to building the Rajpath, the most traveled road in the country, India recently completed the Phewatal Dam at Pokhara and the Tika Bhairab irrigation project, which is bringing many hundred acres of land under cultivation. China's chief contribution has been in road-building. Having completed a road from Lhasa to the Nepalese border, the Chinese are currently building a seventy-mile road inside Nepal from Kodari to Kathmandu which connects with the Rajpath running to the Indian border. The Chinese say that this new road will make possible the resumption of trade between Tibet and Nepal—which stopped almost entirely after China absorbed Tibet. Many Indians feel however that the road may be another silent gun pointed at their throats. With China on the north and with India bordering on the south, Nepalese foreign policy must of necessity be neutral.

Nepal's historical connection with China, it must be remembered, in the interest of clarity, goes away back to A.D. 646 when the first Chinese emissaries were housed in Kathmandu. The people in the north of Nepal share the Mongolian ethnic roots. The architecture and cultures of the two countries have had much in common. The Nepalese claim they invented the pagoda-style roof which the Chinese later copied from the work of a Nepalese architect imported by the Emperor to Peking. Although the Chinese vigorously deny this, their many temples with curved golden roofs, their high entrance steps guarded by ferocious stone animals or demons, their delicate and intricate carvings argue a common origin. The town square at Patan, just beyond Shanta Bhawan Hospital, is one of the most fantastic in the world, for it boasts almost as many temples and gods as people: here indeed one could shut one's eyes and imagine himself among the golden roofs of forbidden Peking.

But Nepal and China have not always agreed politically: they have frequently invaded each other's territories and demanded tribute. This ancient acquaintance, as well as the size of China, help to explain why Nepal has officially recognized China's taking over Tibet. Yet Nepal had the courage to sign the anti-bomb test treaty even before it was ratified by the United States Senate.

Nepal's ethnic roots go even deeper into the soil of India on her southern border, and the economy of the smaller country is geared to the larger, especially since trade with Tibet has ceased, and the long salt caravans no longer wind down into Nepal.

Many Nepalese resent their country's dependence upon India; as the United States has learned, the giver is not automatically endeared to the recipient. If freight coming over the Rajpath or by air from Calcutta stops, the economy of Nepal rapidly grinds to a halt. The *terai* which borders upon India has almost as many Indian settlers as Nepalese. There, as the dreaded malaria is brought under control, the fertile land is rapidly becoming the bread basket of Nepal, and as such assumes great economic importance. The fact that India has greatly helped their agricultural future and has furthered communication by vital road-building in Nepal has been offset in the opinion of many Nepalese by New Delhi's sheltering of rebels against King Mahendra's government. The ousted Congressional leaders from Nepal under General Subarna Shumshere have set up "a government in exile" in Calcutta and rebel border raids are frequent. India, on the other hand, insists that these are in retaliation for attacks by the Nepalese upon Indian border towns.

King Mahendra has, then, not only to unify his own people but to protect his frontiers, to keep the fine balance between the divergent ideologies of the countries offering aid. Small wonder that he keeps working against time to build among his people a national feeling of responsibility for their united future and the political machinery to implement independence, based upon the panchayat system. Before 70,000 of his subjects at Pokhara His Majesty recently warned:

. . . the general mass of our countrymen must realize the significance of national solidarity and discipline. We have to understand that discipline is not slavery or thraldom, but is the gateway of real freedom. Similarly, freedom does not mean licentiousness or acting arbitrarily. If we correctly imbibe these points, we can easily achieve our targets of implementing development schemes such as the East-West Highway, other roads, industry, the spread of education, hospitals, etc. Only then can we flourish in the independent climate of our own, stand upon our own legs, reducing our dependence upon others.

By April of this year [1963] the National Panchayat, composed of representatives chosen by the people themselves on their own discretion, will start functioning."

The panchayat system which His Majesty is setting up is modeled upon the Indian system with variations to fit the special needs of Nepal. The panchayat starts with the local village where each citizen is eligible to vote for the man he selects, goes on up through special panchayats for the fourteen regions and seventy-five development districts, to the National Panchayat of which the King is the head. In addition, King Mahendra has sponsored new class organizations of laborers, farmers, professional men and women, students, which cut across the lines of caste that have so hindered development of a national consciousness. Admittedly this is at best a limited democracy, but the King is a practical man who knows that democracy must be earned to be valued, that any government must not be improved from outside but must be indigenous. He explains:

I have set it as the main objective of my life to undergo any sort of suffering and to make any sacrifice for the establishment of such a democracy. . . . Let us all put in hard labor and make sacrifices according to our capacity for the completion of the construction of roads, bridges, canals, schools, industries and hospitals, as formulated in the Plan, because on these achievements depend the equal welfare of our future descendants.

If "a man is a patchwork of his ancestors," some historical background is pertinent.

His Majesty, Mahendra Bir Bikran Shah Dev is the thirteenth in line of succession from the great King of the Gurkhas, Prithwi Narain Shah, who conquered the three city kingdoms of Kathmandu, Patan, and Bhatgaon and other small principalities, thus first uniting Nepal under his rule about the time of the American Revolution. The description of Prithwi Narain could almost be that of his descendant, Mahendra: "As Gorkha hill men go he was an inch or so above the usual height, slight of body but lithe and strong, sharp featured, brown eyed, with rather a semitic nose."* The Gurkhas have become world famous not only as magnificent fighting men but, perhaps more significant, as loyal and full of initiative; their word, once given, is sacrosanct. Prithwi Narain proved not only by his success in battle but by his firm administration of his newly united kingdom that he was a true Gurkha.

It is further significant that among Prithwi Narain's most trusted officials was an assistant with the name of Rana, the first of a family which was, as noted earlier, to have a growing ascendency in the future Nepal, and, in fact, to rise to power even above that of the King. Jung Bahadur Rana was proclaimed Prime Minister and Commander-in-Chief of Nepal in 1846; ten years later he had become the hereditary Maharajah of Nepal with such power "that he could appoint and dismiss all public servants, he could declare peace and war, he could himself make new laws and repeal old ones, he was given power of life and death and of all punishments."** Gradually the power of the King declined, so that he became a cipher as far as the government went, and the Ranas took over. The King was retained as titular monarch, however, because as head of the Hindu religion, he held the unswerving loyalty of both the army and the ranks of the common people. On the ostensible grounds that he was too holy to have his life endangered, the King of Nepal was not allowed to go more than twelve miles from his own palace where he was in fact "a prisoner in luxury" of the Maharajah.

The Ranas were effective rulers in many ways: they gradually built up a government sufficiently respected throughout the world to guarantee the integrity of their little kingdom; their police force kept order, and their caravans of laden yaks or donkeys traded

* Sir Francis Tuker, *Gorkha* (London: Constable & Co., Ltd., 1957).
** *Ibid.*

briskly with China and India alike. One of the Nepalese Maharajahs was entertained by Queen Victoria. In the feudal tradition each Rana took care of the health and welfare of all within his compound, slaves as well as his own family. Though the slaves have been freed, the Rana family is today equally a self-sufficient unit.

(Dr. Edgar Miller, who has treated many wealthy friends, as well as needy Nepalese, tells an amusing story on himself: "The Ranas often have more and better medicines in their private medicine cabinets than the little drugstore in the Delaware town where I grew up! Recently I was called upon to treat a patient with high blood pressure but left the hospital in such a hurry I forgot to take my sphygmomanometer. 'Don't bother to send back for yours. We have one,' the head of the Rana household assured me. When it arrived," the doctor admitted ruefully, "the instrument was more modern than my own!")

The political collapse in 1950 of the Ranas as a dynasty was caused not only by the uneasy ideas of personal freedom which had filtered into the country through students who had studied in foreign universities and through returning Gurkha soldiers who had been exposed to democracy, but to quarrels between the Ranas themselves. The office of Maharajah was hereditary; when he died or resigned the title went to his oldest male relative, whether brother or son. Not all the Ranas were of equal rank. A-Class Ranas were the children of wives of equal rank with their husbands; B-Class Ranas had wives whose caste did not allow them to eat rice with their husbands; C-Class were the children of Rana concubines. A-Class Ranas automatically become major generals in the army on their twenty-first birthday, by right of birth rather than training; B-Class became lieutenant colonels, while C-Class Ranas were only second lieutenants. It was natural then for the C-Class to be jealous of the prerogatives of those more fortunately born and to wish to share more equally in their power, wealth, and social standing. They reasoned that if the King was brought back to power on his rightful throne, the strict Rana order would be upset and they would have a better chance of getting ahead.

Accordingly they joined with other dissident groups, including students, have-nots in both India and Nepal to upset the status quo. They got more of an upset than they reckoned on.

Nevertheless, the Ranas are still a power to be reckoned with in Nepal, both economically and politically, because they control much of the wealth and because all of them are highly educated in a country that desperately needs trained leadership. They send their children to the best schools in Europe, and live in their white Victorian palaces behind high compound walls much as they have always done. Many of them are developing a sense of responsibility toward their less fortunate compatriots, are backing the efforts of the King in education and technical training for children regardless of rank or social status.

King Mahendra's first and second wives were Rana sisters. When his first wife, her Royal Highness, Indra Lakshmi Devi Shah, who bore him three sons and three daughters, died in childbirth, the King established in her memory a modern maternity hospital in Kathmandu. This excellent hospital was at first run most efficiently by an Irishwoman but has now been turned over to the management of an equally competent Nepalese woman. In 1940 the King, a monogamist although polygamy flourishes in Nepal, married the lovely Queen Ratna. She is equally interested in the welfare of her subjects, and visits the women's and children's wards at Shanta Bhawan Hospital as well as those of government hospitals for inspection and for encouragement.

Along with the history of his country and the record of all King Mahendra has tried to accomplish for it, perhaps the most pertinent clue to his personality, his understanding of the need for both human wisdom and divine, may be found in the poem written by him and published under his family name of M. B. Shah:

The Quest

Thou art the object of my quest,
> None else is there to seek save Thee;
And none is there to hear me cry,
> "I haven't found Thee out."

Behold, upon my knees I pray,
   "Where should I go to seek?"
The eyes, of course, can't see Thy form
   So tell me how I am to see.

Tell me the place where Thou dost reside—
   In prayer or meditation;
In image or in living form;
   In woman or in man.

If I'm not worthy of vision of Thee,
   At least Thou shouldst keep me
In mind as one who helpless lies
   For lack of Thee, the Lord Divine.

Chapter Twelve

A Day with Bethel, Bob, and Sally Beth

Hospitality at the Fleming household is second only to prayer. A meal without guests would be a shock to Nucchi, their Nepali cook, in his immaculate white jacket, for he automatically adds at least four extra portions to whatever he is told to cook by Dr. Bethel: more oatmeal to the breakfast porridge, a cake for morning coffee, more sandwiches for tea. When he arrives at the Flemings' at seven A.M., he knows Dr. Bob and Dr. Bethel are over at the hospital for morning prayers, but that directly they get home, they will expect hot coffee, and before Dr. Bethel can finish her first cup, the chits will start to come.

"Hurry, hurry, hurry," Nucchi grumbles to himself. "All the time rush. Someday they'll all drop and what then?" But his face softens as he picks up a shawl Dr. Bethel has thrown into a chair, starts to take it to its place at the foot of the living-room davenport. But the davenport is occupied. A tall American boy is sleeping there, his blond head on a sofa pillow, a brown coat thrown over him, and on his stomach lies Sally Beth's Siamese cat, also asleep. It is David, Sally Beth's classmate, also a senior at Woodstock School, who has come up from India to visit her; there is another boy sleeping on the rug on the marble floor. He is a stranger. Does Dr. Bethel know he is here? Nucchi shrugs. David is a wise boy anyway; on a cold night a cat is warm on one's stomach. Nucchi begins to dust, walking carefully around the boy on the floor.

The Fleming's living room is large, filled with assorted furniture mostly shabby but comfortable; the only things of real value are the grand piano and Dr. Bethel's collection of little brass camels over the mantel: there are thirty camels ranging from half an inch tall to a six-inch camel, beautifully fashioned, given Dr. Bethel by a GP (grateful patient). A painted wooden partition separates the living room from the front hall of Salisbury Bungalow; someone is always stumbling over the high threshold. The floor is of marble, the walls cement; there are two great crystal chandeliers, and upon the walls the usual brightly painted pictures of Ranas hunting lions from elephant-back remind one that this was a former palace. The room is as frigid as Nucchi's icebox out in the kitchen, for no kerosene can be wasted this year on heating. But the boys on the davenport and on the floor do not seem to mind; they sleep on, though the cat opens one blue eye, winks at Nucchi, and goes back to sleep.

"Nucchi! Coffee!"

Dr. Bethel and Dr. Bob have come in by the dining-room door. Nucchi hurries toward the kitchen. He decides he will not tell Dr. Bethel about the strange boy for she is hungry, as are the two guests she has brought home for breakfast, a Nepali general whose wife is being operated on this morning so he needs to have his mind taken off his inevitable worry and a Japanese doctor with a beard who has just walked in from Tansen and looks dusty. They all hold hands around the breakfast table while Dr. Bob invites the Lord to bless this food, Amen. Nucchi has a chance to bring in the cereal, the marble-size oranges, the tiny bananas the thin length of a man's finger with black seeds that have to be spat out. But the coffee is hot, and there is plenty of it, although Dr. Bob sometimes complains, "Bethel, what is this stuff? What I'd give for a good cup of American coffee!"

Dr. Bethel picks up her cup. "Bob, what are your plans for this morning? I . . ."

Knock, knock, knock comes at the dining-room door. Bethel sets down her cup to read the chit the messenger has brought from the one telephone in the hospital which sits on the desk in the lobby. "The Embassy says one of the USAID workers has had a heart attack. They're sending him over." She tells the messenger, "Let me know quickly when the ambulance arrives." She picks up her cup, takes a couple of sips. . . .

Knock, knock, knock. This time the chit is for Dr. Bob. It's from Miss Franklin, head of Mahendra Bhawan, the boarding school for 200 girls run by the Nepal Mission, reminding Bob he is to speak to the senior class this morning at ten on flora and fauna of Nepal. "But I promised to meet that ornithologist from Switzerland this morning, to take him down to the river to hunt specimens. . . ."

Knock, knock, knock. Bethel sets down her coffeecup resignedly, reads the chit: "This would happen on my busiest clinic day! Isla Knight thinks there may be 400 clinic patients this Saturday. But I don't dare put them off; they might misunderstand, think we didn't want them. It's the Russians," she explains to the rest at the breakfast table. "Three of their doctors want to know if it would be convenient for me for them to look over Shanta Bhawan this morning. . . ." She sighs. "It's got to be convenient, I guess." She scribbles a cordial invitation to be phoned back to the new Russian fifty-bed hospital which is just getting started; after all, there is professional etiquette in any language.

"But they are not friends of your country," the Nepali general observes, his eyes narrowing. "Why do you put yourself out?"

"We are both guests here in your country; we do not talk politics but medicine," Dr. Bethel explains, trying to gulp a few mouthfuls of cereal before the ambulance comes with the sick American. It is like the time when the King had invited the Shanta Bhawan staff to a reception for Chou En-lai to which both she and Dr. Elizabeth Miller had gone, Bethel explains. None of the Embassy people could attend, of course, since the United States does not recognize China, but the doctors thought someone should accept the royal hospitality. The Chinese official had spotted the two lone Americans at once, and the foreign minister of Nepal had brought his important guest to meet them. Chou had beamed to Dr. Bethel and Dr. Elizabeth, "For you there is no bamboo curtain, ladies. Come visit Peking!"

"It was most embarrassing for us," Dr. Bethel admits to the

Nepalese general at her breakfast table. "All the reporters descended on us like vultures to ask what Chou had said to us and we to him. But we could hardly refuse to speak to the guest of honor at His Majesty's party! We just told Mr. Chou En-lai, 'Thank you, Your Excellency,' and let it go at that. . . . Good morning, darling!"

Sally Beth, seventeen and lovely in her long flowered dressing gown, her face under its smooth brown hair still childishly flushed with sleep, has come in from her bedroom and slips into her seat. The general and the Japanese nearly upset the table in their haste to leap to their feet but Sally Beth is undisturbed. She has been used to generals and chiefs of state, to titles and medaled coat fronts since she was tiny. Once, when she was only fourteen, Sally Beth had to act as hostess at a formal dinner party for Sir Edmund Hillary and ten of his Makalu Expedition when Dr. Bethel was called away to an emergency at the hospital. Sally Beth stifles a yawn politely, begins, "Mother, I meant to tell you last night but we came in too late . . ."

Knock, knock, knock. "The ambulance is here, Doctor. The nurse thinks the American sahib is dead."

Dr. Bethel gets up at once, snatches up her black doctor's bag. "Mother . . ." Sally Beth begs but the doctor is already gone. Sally Beth resignedly eats the cereal Nucchi has thrust in front of her.

"Is it always like this?" the general asks Dr. Bob, who says yes, usually. . . . Another knock. But this time it is to say that the general's wife has come down from the operating room; she is still under anesthesia but doing fine. If he wants to wait in her room till she comes round . . . The general exits hastily, followed by the Japanese doctor, and Sally Beth and her father are left alone. She tries again to get in a word with a busy parent.

"Daddy, David wants to see Bodenath. I know gas is scarce but if you happened to be going out that way, could we ride along? He has a friend, not a friend exactly, a boy we ran into last night. . . ."

This time the door opens without any knock and Dr. Bethel comes back in to finish her breakfast. Her face is grave and Dr.

Bob knows without asking that the nurse had been right: the American was dead upon arrival. "He's . . . was . . . a Catholic," Dr. Bethel explains, reaching for her coffeecup which Nucchi has refilled without being told. "Poor man, his wife is in the States; the Embassy's cabling. I sent the body over to Father Moran to lie in his chapel. I thought the Aid man's wife would like that."

"Mother," says Sally Beth desperately, hearing signs of movement beyond in the living room, "I've been trying to tell you . . ." Two disheveled, hungry American boys come through the dining-room door. "Good morning!" David says. Dr. Bethel has known him since he was teething. The other is a complete stranger.

"He's what I've been trying to tell you all morning," Sally Beth says plaintively. "Jim, this is my mother and father." She explains that she and David had met the other Peace Corps boy from India down the street last night; he'd just come over the Rajpath in a jeep and he didn't have any place to stay, so . . .

"Welcome home, Jim," Dr. Bethel beams. "Where did you sleep? The floor couldn't have been very comfortable. We'll have to find you a mattress for tonight. Sit down, boys, and have some breakfast. What is it, Sally Beth?"

"Mother, you simply must find time today to meet me at the bazaar to pick out the material for my new coat. David and I have to go back to school in two more days. I must have a new coat to graduate in; and I'll need it at College next year in the States." There is another knock at the door and Sally Beth murmurs helplessly, "Mother . . ."

She is leaving our home here in two days and then she'll graduate, take off for the States and college. Dr. Bethel smiles thoughtfully at her lovely daughter. She won't have a chance to do anything more for Sally Beth for four years, maybe longer if she marries, doesn't come back to Nepal. She isn't little any more; she's a grown-up with a beau. Dr. Bethel reads the new chit, sighs, and gets up again, reaching for her doctor's black bag. "All right, dear. I'll try to get off this afternoon after the clinic, but if I do that, I'll have to work right through the coffee hour. You'll have to pour out."

"But David and Jim and I wanted to go over to the Hotel Royal to see the American Expedition this morning. They have 900 porters. . . ."

David swallows his large mouthful of cereal to tell Dr. Bob, "There's a joke going around town. 'Why does the Expedition have to climb Everest at all? With so many porters, they could just pass the loads along to the top!' "

Dr. Bob smiles but Dr. Bethel is telling Nucchi, quietly, "There will be two extra at lunch. Those people from Philadelphia who gave the hospital bed: Bob, I hope you can get back? No, three extra. I forgot Chumbi."

"*Mother*! Not Chumbi. The last time he was here we couldn't get the room aired out for two days. He smells so."

"So would you, if it was too cold to bathe in anything but mustard oil. Anyway it's mostly his Tibetan shoes," Dr. Bob tells his offspring. "Remember that very important English physiologist we had to tea? His name was Pugh. . . . Dr. L.G.C.E. Pugh with a lot of honorary initials before and after his name. When he dropped in by helicopter that time, after three months in camp, his beard was a thicket and he smelled worse than Chumbi!"

"And there'll be eleven for dinner, Nucchi," Dr. Bethel is telling the cook over the babble of conversation. "I've invited some doctors from the American Expedition. Sally Beth, if you children go over to the Royal you might see if the Dyhrenfurths would like to come too. I couldn't get them on the phone; the head of the Expedition is pretty busy. Bob, could you spare a pint of blood? The bank's almost empty."

"Sure." Dr. Bob is getting up. He tells his daughter, "If the Swiss ornithologist comes early, tell him I'll be right back. And give him a cup of coffee."

"I'm late for the clinic." Dr. Bethel calmly but swiftly starts again for the door. "Sally Beth, if Chumbi comes early as he probably will, you can tell Nucchi to put the coffee table out on the lawn in the fresh air. It's a nice sunny day."

She goes quietly out the door in her soft rubber-soled black shoes. Dr. Bob rushes after her, hoping there is enough gas in the Volkswagen to get to Mahendra Bhawan and back, and that the

ornithologist he's had a date with for six months will be understanding. But whoever said the Orient moved slowly was talking
through his false teeth.

Sally Beth grins at the two boys. "Some family." Her voice is
soft and proud; she long ago accepted the fact that the hospital
was more important than she was. "So I pour coffee and you two
wait for me, hear?"

"Sure, who's Chumbi?" Jim, the boy new to Nepal asks. So
Sally Beth tells him the story of this Tiger of the Snows and of
Jungjean, his beautiful daughter, whom he gave to Dr. Bethel.

"Kunjo Chumbi's the Sherpa who went with Sir Edmund
Hillary to London, Paris, and New York for the experts to decide
if the 'yeti skin' were really that of the Abominable Snowman,"
she explains. "He's cute. He wears his hair in a braid around his
head tied with a red ribbon, a long black coat, and big soft Tibetan
boots that are comfortable if smelly. Chumbi and Sir Edmund
came here to dinner at Shanta Bhawan the night before they
flew to Europe. They showed Daddy the skin. He told them, 'It's
the skin of the serow (that's the wild goat-antelope that lives
high up in the mountains). I got one just like this on my last
bird-hunting expedition.' The experts abroad agreed with Daddy
but Chumbi wasn't convinced. To him, the Abominable Snowman was beyond argument but he was polite about it. He said that
no foreigner could be expected to understand another country's
magic! I guess he's right. Sir Edmund tells in his book *High in
the Thin, Cold Air**what a grand time Chumbi had, hopping
around the world; you'd never know he'd never been in a plane
before nor seen a train. Sir Edmund took him to call on Queen
Elizabeth at Buckingham Palace but unfortunately she was away,
so Chumbi left with an equerry the presents he'd brought for her
from Nepal, yak tails, barley flour, painted Buddhist thankas, and
bricks of tea, with a message saying he hoped to meet the Queen
in this life or the next. This amused the Queen so that a year later,
when she and Prince Philip made a state visit to Kathmandu and

* Douglas Doig and Sir Edmund Hillary, *High in the Thin, Cold Air*
(Garden City, N.Y.: Doubleday and Co., 1962).

she was asked if there was anyone special she wanted to meet, she said, yes, Mr. and Mrs. Kunjo Chumbi.

"Mrs. Chumbi was nine months pregnant but that didn't bother her; she and her husband set out at once for Kathmandu to meet the Queen. Kungjung where they live is nearly 200 miles from here, eight days' walk up and down mountains. Four days along the way, Mrs. Chumbi stopped by the side of the path to bear her fourth son. She named him Philip Tobgay, picked up the baby, and walked on. The family finally arrived at the Hotel Royal, where the Sherpas usually park in the yard out back, but the startled Russian proprietor phoned to Mother.

" 'Dr. Fleming, the Chumbis just arrived with a brand-new baby! We haven't any facilities for taking care of him. Will you take them in?'

" 'Of course, send them along to the hospital,' Mother said. 'I'll look the baby over.'

"Little Philip was fine, so Mother gave him and his mother beds in the ward at Surendra Bhawan. But Chumbi smelled so loud she had them put up a tent for him on the hospital lawn; he liked it better outdoors, anyway. Next day the Nepali nurses had a grand time bathing the baby and Mrs. Chumbi who was going to meet the Queen. They dressed Mrs. Chumbi all up in her best finery, her bright striped apron, her silver jewelry, and her charmbox with the great turquoise in the cover hung around her neck to show she was the wife of a man of consequence. So Kunjo Chumbi and his wife went off to see the Queen and Prince Philip, while the nurses baby-sat for little Philip Tobgay, his namesake, born by the mountain pathside.

"Chumbi, like all Sherpas, is very punctilious about returning hospitality, so the next time he walked in to Kathmandu he brought Mother a hostess gift—his sixteen-year-old daughter, Jungjean! She's awfully pretty, a strong big girl with long shining black braids and rosy cheeks. Her father took her hand, put it into Mother's, and said, 'Now she is your daughter, Doctor. Teach her something!'

"Mother didn't know just what to do with Jungjean. 'Can she read and write?'

" 'No. No school in Kungjung.'

" 'Then she can hardly train as a nurse.'

" 'Train her anyway you like. She is yours.' Chumbi shrugged and went away. But he left Mother another gift on the front lawn to pay for his daughter's keep, a donkey. Mother sent the donkey to the Kathmandu zoo but she kept Jungjean. She really is a doll. But we had no room for her in our apartment; the bedrooms hadn't been added on yet so my folks slept in the dining room and I had a cot behind the grand piano in the living room. Mother fixed a cot for Jungjean in the front hall with screens around it for a little privacy. As soon as she could, Mother gave Jungjean a bath in hot water, taught her how to take care of herself. Once she'd washed off the layers of dirt and sweat, she was lovelier than ever; she brushed her long braids till they shone, kept herself and her clothes immaculate. But she couldn't seem to learn to read or write; people interested her more than books. She helped out in the clinic, and finally she went to keep house for some friends of ours where there were two girls her own age. That suited her right down to the ground: our friend said you could eat off of Jungjean's floor. She wouldn't wear any jewelry because she couldn't afford any that was real turquoise. At least she'd learned a new set of standards.

"But when her father came down to Kathmandu to help with the American Expedition—he's head of the Sherpa porters for this year's Everest climb—the very sight of him and of her two sisters, whom her father had brought along to see the big city of Kathmandu, made Jungjean homesick. She has signed on as one of the women porters to carry a sixty-five-pound load back to the expedition base camp near her home.

" 'It will be nice to see a real mountain again,' Jungjean told Mother. 'These around Kathmandu are only 8,000 feet high'— mere hills to a Sherpa girl. Her two sisters came over here to see her, and Mother invited them yesterday to a sort of farewell luncheon for her Sherpa daughter. We had to wait and wait but finally Jungjean brought the two younger girls in, looking kind of wet and bedraggled. She'd had them both out back in the garden.

"'I've been giving them a bath,' Jungjean told Mother. 'My goodness, Doctor, those Sherpas were dirty!'"

While Sally Beth was regaling the boys with the story of her Sherpa sister, Dr. Bethel was immersed in a flood of patients in the clinic. There were five doctors on duty this morning, but the long line of patients sitting on wooden benches along the wall of the concrete corridor moved slowly. The place fairly seethed and bubbled with humanity of all ages, from tiny newborn babies to a grandmother so wispy that it seemed as if all that kept her together was her patuka, the wide belt she wore around her waist not only to keep her sari neatly closed but to hold groceries and her wedding charm box. There were old men, coughing and spitting, not onto the floor but into the paper handkerchiefs Miss Isla Knight, the nurse, had passed out; and there were young boys too scared to speak. Already over 200 patients were crowded into the long narrow corridor, with that many more waiting outside the door for space to come inside. Saturday was a big clinic day, since the government offices were closed.

Dr. Bethel's little office, about ten by ten feet, was already crowded with patients marshaled by her Nepali assistant, Janeki, an extremely pretty, efficient girl who today wore a white sari with pink flowers braided into her long pigtail of black hair; she permits no getting out of line by eager patients, sorts the big bunch of record cards, hands the doctor the right one, whisks the patient's sari open so that the stethoscope can get inside. The patients are mostly women either wanting or not wanting babies or suffering the consequences of their own efforts to treat themselves. They all looked worried. But who wouldn't when a woman who has no children can be divorced by her husband? Or a mother who has too many cannot afford to feed them?

"*Namaste*," Dr. Bethel greets each patient, folding her hands politely to put her at ease. She scans the patient's card. This poor girl, dark-eyed and frightened, has already had four six-months' miscarriages; if she loses this one it will be tragic. "Put her up on the examination table," Dr. Bethel orders. A few minutes later she is washing her hands at the basin, telling her assistant, "She'd better go over to the hospital for a few days in bed. We can't take any chances." The girl bursts into lamentations, "My husband will get him a concubine this time, Doctor. A second wife!" Dr. Bethel pats the girl's shoulder, soothing, "You're going to be all right. We're going to save this baby."

The next patient is a sullen-looking girl in a soiled green sari and uncombed hair. No wonder, Bethel thinks, looking at her thermometer which registers 103 degrees—probably from an induced abortion. She isn't married. "Give her a shot of penicillin. See if there's another bed empty in the women's ward. If not, put her out in the hospital corridor," Bethel orders. The girl is led away trembling. Shanta Bhawan must make room for her.

Into the tiny office the patients continue to push, as into the other four doctors' offices along the hall. There is no end to them: babies screaming and yelling in their mothers' arms; a small boy whose ears the rats have eaten off, terrified because he knows this means he is already a leper. Dr. Bethel orders laboratory tests, soothes the mother who begins to scream, "No, no, do not send a leper home to my house!" Dr. Bethel assures her that they can give the boy medicine so he will get no worse; so he cannot infect anyone else. Dr. Bethel tells her assistant patiently, "Send both of them over to Surendra Bhawan; maybe they can explain to his mother better than I can." It takes time to argue; with hundreds of patients still waiting in the clinic corridor there is no time . . . but Dr. Bethel lays her hand gently on the head of the small frightened boy with no ears and after a few moments he smiles back shyly.

All the patients need the touch of Bethel's hand; her smile of encouragement is as potent as medicine; yet they all take something from her. After three hours, the air in the tiny office is so thick with the smell of sickness, of unwashed bodies, that Dr. Bethel can hardly breathe. If only she could take a few moments out to go over to the house for a cup of coffee . . . but if she's to shop for Sally Beth's coat this afternoon she mustn't stop. She wonders how Sally Beth is making out with all her guests, as the office door bursts open.

"The Russians are here!" the wide-eyed messenger announces.

"I'll come at once." Bethel moves swiftly down the corridors among the murmuring patients, some of whom catch at her skirt, demanding: How much longer? Will she surely be back? Surely, surely. But she cannot stop because protocol decrees that the four Russian doctors be met by the medical head of Shanta Bhawan.

"*Namaste*, Doctor." The four Russians are big, friendly, but their smiles are wary, not reaching their eyes; they wish especially to see the laboratory and the kitchen to see how each is managed, if convenient, because they are equipping their own new hospital. Dr. Bethel has seventy more patients to see, but of course it is convenient. She takes them to the lab to show them how to coat the little Nepalese earthen pots with wax inside so they can be used to collect specimens from the patients—the native pots are cheaper than glass and can be thrown away, she explains, and the Russians say eagerly, yes, yes; it is a good idea. She takes them into the kitchen, which is a hive of activity getting ready for the staff's lunch; she offers them a brownie from the sheet that has just come out of the oven. Three of the Russians refuse hastily but the fourth gingerly takes a brownie, watching Dr. Bethel who takes a bite first to assure him the cake is not poisoned. She takes the Russians through the wards and finally they go away, thanking her effusively but obviously glad to shake capitalistic dust off their feet.

"Not that there is any dust in Shanta Bhawan," Dr. Bethel thinks jealously as she trudges back to the still-crowded clinic. "The Russian who ate the brownie was nice."

As Dr. Bethel comes back into her office the assistant reports, "Dr. Bethel, there's a Peace Corps boy out in the lobby. The nurse says he has a fever and dysentery."

"Did the Corps send him?"

"No. He says the office is closed on Saturday but he felt sick, so he just stopped by Shanta Bhawan."

Dr. Bethel sighs. "Well, put him to bed. I'll be over to see him when I finish here." That probably means she will not have time for lunch. Well, Bob and Sally Beth can manage the two guests from Philadelphia and Chumbi is an old friend. She washes her hands, again sits down at her consultation table. "Next patient, please."

While his wife is in the clinic, Dr. Bob has roared out in his Volkswagen to Mahendra Bhawan school. On his way he keeps a sharp eye out for birds and is rewarded by the sight of two Nepalese eagles, with a wingspread of ten feet, soaring and swooping above the road. He recalls that when he was the only foreigner on the committee to decide upon the Nepalese national bird, flower, and animal, he had suggested this great eagle but the Nepalese had preferred the impeyan pheasant. You couldn't blame them; the impeyan is such a beautiful bird with its wings of iridescent blue-green and purple, shading in the light, its mantle of green-gold and burnt orange, its head dark-green and gold— a magnificent bird, indeed. The committee had chosen red for their color and, of course, for the national animal, the sacred cow— sacred because its horns push open the gates of the Hindu paradise.

"Someone has piled too much wood outside the gates here," Dr. Bob notices as he drives up to the Mahendra Bhawan school which has a large central brick building for the boarders, with several smaller primary schools scattered around the grounds for the day pupils. Of these 200 girls, all but four are Hindus. They come from all over Nepal and beyond, from Darjeeling, Pokhara, Illam (the most distant provinces of Nepal), from Biratnagar, Theran, and Kathmandu. Some of the Rana girls have never even lifted a hand for themselves before, but Miss Elizabeth Franklin, the English woman who started and heads the school, insists upon every girl making her own bed, sweeping, and dusting. She says crisply, "This is neither a dormitory nor a hotel. It is our home. Each girl must do her share." Dr. Bob inspects the woodpile carefully; he does not see any cobras.

The senior class is assembled in the largest classroom, dressed in their school uniforms. Dr. Bob wishes vaguely they had been allowed to keep their bright saris; they looked so fresh and gay, like the bunch of sweet peas Nucchi put on the breakfast table. Dr. Bob greets the girls and they send back a loud "*Namaste.*" He tells them about a bird walk he has just had on the outskirts of Kathmandu where he has seen thirty-nine different birds. He holds up a bright orange-breasted chloropsis for the girls to see and a hiss of excitement ripples over the class. He gives them the Latin name, explains that the tiny tag on the bird's leg tells also where and when the bird was collected, whether or not this is mating-season plumage, and other facts. Their faces reflect the same bright wonder as his own. Queer, isn't it, how such a small creature can still give you a thrill after all these years? A green pigeon's feather is as beautiful in its way as the high black and white peak of Everest.

"How about singing me a song before I go?" Dr. Bob ends his nature talk. "What can you sing?"

They shout, "The Grandfather Clock!" "Carry Me Back to Old Virginy," and other American songs; they know the words from their English class. But Dr. Bob says he'd rather hear them sing in Nepali. How about their national anthem?

If he had thrown a match into tissue paper he couldn't have started a bigger fire of enthusiasm. The girls spring to their feet, throw back their heads proudly, and burst into full-throated song:

> Hail, the most puissant, gracious and noble King of the
> Nepalese! May Almighty God bless him with a long life
> and let his people flourish and prosper!

"These children know they are Nepalese, not only Gurkhas, Sherpas, Newaris, not Ranas nor untouchables," Dr. Bob thinks. "They are the hope and glory of Nepal!" He goes out of the classroom with a lump of pride for them in his own throat as he roars back in his little car to meet his Swiss fellow scientist. He will be only an hour late but Sally Beth can handle anyone; probably the Swiss has already asked her to come ski in the Alps. Dear Sally Beth—they're going to miss her terribly when she goes to college. But she'll visit your beloved boyhood Michigan, the lovely rolling country with its hills and forests, its bright summer days that make you feel good to be alive. Is it possible you're a little homesick?

Sally Beth has earned a little of her busy mother's time by presiding over the coffee hour and over lunch. At four that afternoon Dr. Bethel is washing her hands for the hundredth time that day, it seems, has taken time out for a sandwich and a cup of tea, and has herded the boys and Sally Beth into her car. If they can find the cloth for her coat at the bazaar without too much trouble, perhaps there will be time to show Jim and David the Buddhist shrine at Bodenath, Dr. Bethel promises. It is one of her favorite places in Kathmandu; but they'll have to hurry. Dr. Bethel puts her foot on the gas, Sally Beth screams as an awkward young heifer rushes out directly in front of the Volkswagen in the crowded street. Bethel slams on the brakes, but there is no chance of missing and the heifer drops down out of sight and Bethel's heart plummets, too. In no time at all a crowd gathers from nowhere, muttering and glowering through the windows of the little car. All foreigners in Kathmandu are warned by the police that if, by any misfortune, they do hit an animal to drive as fast as possible for the nearest police station where they can be protected from the angry mob while the police investigate. But already the little Volkswagen is hemmed in. Bethel, looking at her young people, goes white. It is safer in Hindu Nepal to run down a child than a sacred cow.

"Doctor!" The policeman who has been directing traffic comes running over, pushing through the menacing crowd pressing about the car with ugly murmurs. He bends down to set the heifer on its feet, brushes it off carefully, feels it all over to be sure it is uninjured. If only the children were not here, Dr. Bethel shivers.

"The sacred animal is not hurt, only scared," the traffic cop tells her. "Drive on fast, Doctor, when I clear the way." He smiles at her suddenly. "Don't you remember me? You set my leg at Shanta Bhawan." He yells "Back! Back!" waves his arms peremptorily. With a great surge of relief that no one is hurt, Dr. Bethel puts her foot on the gas, the car edges through the crowd, but only when the mob is safely behind them does she dare draw a deep breath. Near tragedy has brushed them with its wing. Thank the dear Lord for Shanta Bhawan . . . and that the heifer wasn't hurt.

The cloth they find in the bazaar comes from England, is a soft warm biscuit color which looks best with Sally Beth's dark hair. Tomorrow the tailor will cut it patterned on the old coat that Sally Beth likes; she'll have to remember to smooth out that wrinkle in the lining or the tailor will copy that, too. Dr. Bethel herds her young people back into the car. "We'll get to Bodenath just at candlelighting time in the monastery," she promises the boys. "That's the nicest hour of day there."

"Bodenath is one of the most famous shrines in Buddhism," Dr. Bethel tells the boys as the car sweeps under the tall arch on either side of which two ferocious lions glare, protecting the shrine from evil. "People have been worshipping here for 2,000 years. Lately the Tibetan refugees have taken over; hundreds of them live in that circle of apartments around the shrine, including the Chini Lama, the local representative of the Dalai Lama, who is a refugee in India. We had the Chini Lama's grandson at the hospital last month; he fell from a tree and ruptured his spleen but Dr. Berry fixed him up."

The boys stare at the great round dome surmounted by a tall four-sided tower, on each side of which is painted the great Eye of Buddha watching compassionately over his people, seeing both good and evil. Long lines flapping with prayer flags run to the circular mud-brick wall where, set in niches, a hundred prayer wheels click and whirl as the worshippers go round and round the shrine, praying by proxy. The hum of Tibetan voices, the click of the prayer wheels, the flapping of the prayer flags make strange gentle harmony. Dr. Bethel asks the American boys, "Do you know 'Om Mani Padme Hum,' the prayer on the wheels? 'O the jewel in the heart of the lotus'; this means of course Buddha himself."

(One of the best interpretations of this much-repeated prayer appeared recently in the *National Geographic Magazine*, by an unnamed translator:

OM—I invoke the path and experience of universality, so that
MANI—the jeweline luminosity of my immortal mind
PADME—be unfolded within the depths of the lotus-center of
awakened consciousness
HUM—and I be wafted by the ecstasy of breaking through all
bonds and horizons.)*

"The ecstasy of breaking through all bonds and horizons." Not
such a small desire, Dr. Bethel thinks.

She smiles at the crowd of Tibetans rushing out of the great
hive of buildings that encircle the shrine, in hope of making
a sale to her and her party. The refugees are very poor but smiling
in their rags; most of them have escaped from their Chinese over-
lords and have come here laboriously over the mountains with
little but the clothes they had on, except for the silver spoon each
Tibetan carries at his belt and a few family treasures to sell for
food. A rosy-faced, snotty-nosed small boy pulls at her skirt
whining, "The jewels of my ancestors brought from Lhasa,
Memsahib. Truly antique!"

"Don't give him anything or we'll be mobbed by the rest of
them," Dr. Bethel warns the boys. She gives the boy another warm
smile instead and he grins back; in spite of no money and a lost
country, the Tibetan refugees are a happy people—perhaps because those who have broken through to wide free horizons can
never be really far from home so long as there is Bodenath and the
compassionate Eye of Buddha watching over them.

"Look, Mother," Sally Beth cries, "they're lighting the butter
lamps up in the monastery!"

High up in the dusk, up a tall flight of orange steps, little lights
have begun to flower in the purple twilight. Dr. Bethel follows
more slowly the swift climb of her young people to the monastery
door. As the tiny yak-butter lamps flare up, the shadowy monks
take shape in their flowing robes and shaven heads; then the
Buddhas themselves begin to peer down out from the walls in the
brightening gloom. Is the fearful goddess Kali here with her necklace of human skulls that frighten little children? Kali is Hindu,

* *National Geographic Magazine* (May 1963), p. 686.

but they mix Hinduism and Buddhism here in Nepal so much
you never can tell which gods you'll find in what temple. When
they choose a new Living Goddess for Kathmandu the fearful
Kali is certainly there. They put several little girls, babies really,
into a dark room and try to scare them with leering human skulls,
with loud noises by beating bones and drums, by blowing great
ten-foot horns reputedly made from the thighbone of a virgin. The
baby girl who is not frightened is declared the new incarnation,
the Living Goddess to be worshipped and cherished. She is put
into a holy house which she never leaves except to ride in the two
great yearly religious processionals where the people bow like
frightened grain in the wind of her passing. The little goddess cannot run and play rough games like other children because the sight
of blood, even a scratch, would make her unclean; she can only
wave at her worshippers from an open window, accept their alms,
and, presumably, pray for them. When she comes to puberty, the
girl is dismissed at once, and a new Living Goddess is found. Poor
little adolescents, they have a hard time, in spite of their government pension, Dr. Bethel thinks. For who dares to marry an ex-
goddess? Better to be one of those stone Buddhas along the monastery wall, clad in mosquito netting and spangles that sparkle in
the flickering butter lamps. A beaming monk comes stumping up
to Dr. Bethel.

"Namaste, Doctor! Don't you remember me? I am the one who
stamped his sleeping leg to wake it and broke the bone! You found
the break by the magic light."

X-ray, Dr. Bethel translates, smiling at the toothless old monk
whose fantastic accident she has treated with a cast. Due to
malnutrition, of course, lack of calcium. "I light a lamp for you,
Doctor," the old monk beams. Christian and Buddhist smile at
each other as he adds graciously, "The gods smile down, too, from
the snows, at Shanta Bhawan."

The snows. "Goodness, we have to go! The American doctors
from the Expedition will be waiting for us for dinner." Dr. Bethel
gathers up her daughter and her boys, sweeps them back down to
the Volkswagen. The streets are not crowded now because every-

one except them seems to have already gone home; dim lights shine from the glassless windows of the little homes; torches flare, showing the little shops piled high with vegetables, lusciously green, red, and yellow but deadly to Western stomachs; here a Nepalese family squats beside its brass kitchen pots, waiting for the last stray rupee with which to end the day's custom. The peace of the night lies in the shadows, in the little lighted homes, in the magic memory of far-off unseen snowy peaks dreaming over the city. As they drive through the white gates of Shanta Bhawan, hurry across the grassy quadrangle, the Cross is already lighted, luminous and silent.

Dr. Bob and the Expedition doctors are waiting in the Fleming living room. One of them has put a package on the marble floor beside the davenport. He tells Dr. Bethel, "We couldn't get all our individual blood transfusion kits into the boxes for the Everest trek. So I brought you six, in case you could use them."

"Use them!" gasps Dr. Bethel. "They're a godsend, Doctor. How much was there left in the blood bank when you went there today, Bob?"

"Only my pint and one Dr. Edgar Miller gave," Bob admits.

"So you see . . ." Dr. Bethel smiles her thanks to the Expedition doctor, her brown eyes warm under her crown of white braids, for the Plan has not let them down.

"You mean, the staff is actually its own blood bank?" The Expedition doctor stares, horrified, at Dr. Bethel.

"If necessary."

Back home, the young doctor thinks, he never has to worry about a transfusion; he simply orders it. He promises, "If we have any kits left over when we get back from Everest, we'll leave them with you."

When they get back, never *if* . . . it's wonderful to be young. As the white-jacketed cook appears in the doorway, Dr. Bethel says, "Ready, Nucchi? Come on to dinner, my friends." She has been up since six this morning making ward rounds, treating clinic patients, soothing traffic policemen and monks, taxiing Sally Beth and her friends around the city, but as she sweeps through the door, takes her place at the foot of her hospitable table, she looks fresh, vital, restored by this good gift for her sick. Her young guest thinks, awed, she is not only a great doctor, she's beautiful with the candlelight on her face. No, the luminous brightness comes from within, quiet as the Cross shining silently all night out there in the hospital quadrangle. She reminds him of something his mother used to sing when he was a small boy scared of the dark.

> Keep me safe till the day breaks
> And the shadows flee away. . . .

Chapter Thirteen

How Beautiful upon the Mountains

How beautiful upon the mountains are the feet of him who bringeth good tidings, who publisheth peace. . . .

The Flemings often slip away from the hospital in their little car (the only place where they can be alone, where no chits, patients, or staff can reach them) to watch the sun set over the Kathmandu snows. These are not always visible, but when the mists clear away, there are two rows of mountains, ranging from 8,000 to 20,000 feet, a double string of jewels shining in the sun around the City of Glory. "A man needs a far look once in a while to bring into proportion the little things that trouble him," Dr. Bob says. "Great mountains bring out whatever is in a man, good or bad. At 18,000 feet up, there's a clarity of mind I never found in the valley. Man sees his own smallness in the greatness towering above him, in the majesty of God's world."

Something had been bothering Bethel all day, Dr. Bob realized one afternoon. To the casual eye her calm physician's face under its regal crown of white hair had been untroubled as usual, but to him who knew her so well, the lines of tension had tightened ominously around her mouth. Something was seriously wrong. Dr. Bob suggested, "Ganesh Himal is clear as a Japanese painting tonight; there'll be a wonderful sunset. Come along, Girl."

Dr. Bethel smiled, and the youth he had evoked came back into her eyes. There were patients to see, guests coming for dinner, but she and Bob needed this time together, this silent renewal of their closeness as Anteus had yearned to touch his foot to Mother Earth. Besides, she wanted to talk to Bob where they couldn't be overheard. She agreed, "I have to stop first by Surendra Bhawan to check on a baby brought in with pneumonia."

After she'd checked on her patient in the oxygen tent, they drove along the narrow street hemmed in by high orange walls until they found a widening in which to park, sat there in silence, waiting. Sunset is the moment when Kathmandu puts on its tender robe of beauty. The city lies dreaming in an opal glow, its sprawling white palaces and its humbler tawny little homes caressed and softened by the evening air. For an instant all hunger, strife, pain ceases to be important and the whole city seems to hold its breath before the beauty of the mountains, the lords of the sky; so deeply is this enchantment grown into the lives of its people that all this beauty belongs to the humblest child in the streets of Kathmandu, is a part of him. Behind the green and brown Mountains of the Moon stand the snowy peaks, majestic, immovable, waiting.

"Langtang, Gosainthan, Jugal Himal," Dr. Bob fingered over the rosary of names as he and Bethel sat there quietly together. "See how clearly they stand out, Bethel! There must have been a great wind up there; all day the banners of snow have been blowing, but now they are still. Look at the opalescent snows with the sun on them! Did you ever see anything more glorious?"

Like the shout of silent trumpets the last rays of the sun had blown the white peaks to fire, a blazing wonder almost too bright to be borne; then the glory softened into rose and gold leaving a faint glow on the little homes, embers of the dying day. Slowly, as the Flemings watched, the rose mist died away, and the white peaks towered naked against the darkening violet of the sky. "Did you ever think that the Himalayas, the tallest peaks on earth, have the loneliness of birth and death?" Dr. Bob murmured. "When man stands naked and alone . . ."

"Bob!" Dr. Bethel burst out, agonized into sharing her own naked fear. "We may have to close the hospital! We have only enough kerosene for the next twenty-four hours!" As Dr. Bob stared at her, appalled, she rushed on, "I've tried all over the city but there's no more to be bought. It's the war again; none has come up from India. What are we going to do?"

For once Dr. Bob was speechless. The sterilizer in the operating room ran by kerosene; they depended upon it to distill the water for intravenous injections, to heat water for hot packs, to warm patients in shock. . . . There had been no heat all winter in the hospital nor in the doctors' homes because of the kerosene shortage . . . but to close the hospital entirely was unthinkable! Where would the patients go? Many of them would die. . . .

Dr. Bob reached for the starter. "We'll go talk to Johshi, our friend who owns the gas station. He'll get us a little to tide us over."

"I already have been to see him," Dr. Bethel confessed. "He says he can't give us what he hasn't got. He may not get another shipment for a week, perhaps longer." She lifted her troubled eyes to the mountains, but the great peaks were now only chalky white warnings of disaster written large against the darkening sky. Bethel told Bob wearily, "I keep thinking about those men we saw off yesterday at Banepa."

The American Expedition, twenty-odd Americans and 900 Sherpa porters, had marched off gaily together to climb to the top of the world, leaving behind their families and friends waving and calling from Banepa where the road ends and the long trek to the waiting snows begins to Everest whose jagged black and white peak could toss off puny humans like bloody chaff. . . . How many of those eager laughing young men would come home? Dr. Bob wondered. If they did, they would all be changed a little. The chances were that some wouldn't make it back. Any day soon some of their broken or frozen bodies might came back to Shanta Bhawan to be patched up. What if the hospital doors were closed—for a little crazy thing like lack of kerosene? But an operating room that wasn't sterile . . .

"Hey, Doctor! Having car trouble?" A jeep from the American Embassy had stopped beside the Flemings to ask, "Need a tow?"

"No, thank you," Dr. Bob called back. "We're just watching the sun set."

The driver looked bewildered. Why take time out to watch what happened every day? As the jeep roared off Dr. Bethel said, "We'd better go too, Bob. I want to check on my pneumonia case again."

Dr. Bob sat there in the curving driveway of the hospital for women and children as Bethel went inside, trying to shake off the bleakness that had settled about him. Face the facts as real as those dark mountains. Nine years they had been working here in Nepal and there was still no real security, still not enough money, medicine, or nurses, not enough doctors. Shanta Bhawan had its own deep well now with plenty of water, but when the electricity went off, as it did frequently, they couldn't pump up what they needed. "We'll get our own emergency electrical system we need so desperately. Someone will give it to us. You'll see," Bethel had promised hopefully. But no one had. . . . Dear Bethel. She loved her babies so; yet she couldn't take time off from her executive job at Shanta Bhawan to build her well-child clinics she'd come to Nepal to start. Could it be that they had misread the Plan? They had only five more years before they would have to retire. Must they sow and someone else must reap? But Bethel had set her heart upon preventing the babies from getting sick. . . .

As Dr. Bethel came slowly, heavily, back down the steps, Dr. Bob didn't need to ask what had happened.

"My baby's gone. They brought him in too late," Dr. Bethel said wearily. "I delivered him myself six months ago; he was so plump and well and his parents were so happy with their first son. They said they didn't want to bother me yesterday when he first got to breathing heavily. But I *want* to be bothered!" She was as close to tears as Bethel ever came, but when they drew up at the white door of Shanta Bhawan she was the calm physician again. "I'll make my rounds and be over. Tell Nucchi we'll have an early tea."

As Dr. Bethel climbed the steep hospital stairs at Shanta Bhawan she heard laughter and then a soft chord of music. It was Samson and his harmonium in the men's ward. "Sing, Samson!

Just one more song before the nurse throws you out." Bethel hung
on to the balustrade listening to the fresh young voice singing the
song he had composed in Nepalese:

> "Away in a stable
> There lay a sweet Babe.
> High in the sky
> Shone a Star. . . ."

As Dr. Bethel rustled in her white uniform into the ward, followed by the attending nurse, Samson put away his instrument
and the Grand Old One, as the nurses called him, got up from his
armchair and bowed. He was imposing, regal, this big old man
with, unlike most Nepalis, a thick gray beard and long flowing
robes; he sat up all day and many nights because his heart
wouldn't let him lie down. But he always managed to get up to
bow to Dr. Bethel. *"Namaste!"*

As they saluted each other gravely, with their hands folded
under their chins, the Grand Old One told Dr. Bethel, "Tomorrow
I leave you. I have learned much. I had heard of Christians but
I did not know what they were till I lived here with you at Shanta
Bhawan. You give more than medicines; you give yourselves."

Warmth grew about Dr. Bethel's heart and the cold hand of
fear about tomorrow eased as she said, *"Namaste.* Go in peace."

Samson was right in his song: that extra something Shanta
Bhawan had to offer was a Star. God's Plan could not fail: yours
might but not His. You must pray a little harder, hold hard to your
faith.

People had often asked her, "Why do you missionaries bother?
Why not leave medicine to the government aids? The Russians
are here. And the Swiss. The English. The World Health Organization. All the American Aid. Why not leave relief to them?" The
Star and the Baby were why; it was not so much what you gave
that mattered as the humble spirit in which you gave it. How had
Jonathan Lindell put it? "I have the same sins, the same inade-
quacies as the farmer I'm trying to teach. I fail as he does. The
difference is, I have a high aim to come back to, to set my sights

by. . . ." Bethel lifted the white crown of her head higher and moved to the next bed. You could not fail these people. Somehow you had to manage to keep the hospital open. Could you possibly convert the sterilizer to burn charcoal? There was plenty of cow-dung fuel but it was hardly sterile. You'd think of some way because you had to.

But that night neither of the Flemings could sleep. Bethel lay rigid on her side of the big bed trying not to wake Bob and then she realized his body was too still beside her: he was trying not to wake her, also. She jerked off the crumpled sheet. "Let's get up." She snapped on the light and surprisingly it worked the first time. She reached for a long paper folded on the bedside table. "Did you see this petition from Lapsebot? It was signed by 900 villagers, mostly fingerprints of course, because they can't write."

Lapsebot was a mountain village in a remote section of Gorkha, but Bob had walked there on one of his birding trips. He knew the narrow dirt street, the thatched houses empty of everything except a few brass cooking pots, the thin woven pallets on the mud floor. Yet even here they had heard of the new kind of healing; the new furniture of these homes was hope. He read:

To the minister of health, Singha Durbar, Kathmandu:
Sir: In the densely populated northern sector of W. No. 2 there is no hospital or dispensary where we can purchase medicine or have treatment for fractures, cuts, sores, burns, digestive disorders, fevers, worms, T.B., cholera, etc. For ordinary or serious diseases we cannot have any kind of treatment and to this day we must call in the witch doctor and sacrifice fowl, goats, etc. Treatment would cost at a dispensary Rupees 1 but by the above method people spend Rupees 50 to 100 and if fortunate may recover but most die an untimely death. For want of a dose of worm medicine those who believe in witchcraft as a remedy are continually causing the worms to grow and multiply resulting in pain and even death. In the south of Gorkha District at Amp Pipal Bhanjyang, be-cause of the School and Dispensary under the auspices of the United Mission, twenty thousand patients annually receive good

treatment without fees and medicine at a simple price. We have requested the leader of this Mission, Mr. Howard H. Barclay, to put such a Dispensary in this area. He has seen the condition of this district and encouraged us in the possibility of putting a Dispensary in this area if permission is obtained from our Government. Therefore we request that His Majesty's Government would give the necessary conditions of agreement to the United Mission to place a Dispensary at Lapsebot. In getting treatment and medicine the lives of many men, women, and children of this place will be saved. We await your pleasure.

Dr. Bob laid the petition back on the bedside table. "This thing is too big for us to carry, Bethel. Let's offer it up again to the Lord." So they finally went to sleep.

"Are you going to the Sundarijal clinic as usual today?" Dr. Bob asked Dr. Bethel at breakfast next morning. Thursdays were her day there but with all these war shortages . . .

"I don't know how much gas is in the ambulance tank," Dr. Bethel said. "But I have to go if I can. I'm taking two patients back to the village, the poor old man whose legs I had to amputate and the girl with the bad heart who's been here six months. I had to tell her we couldn't help her any more, that we needed her bed. If I'm not home by dark, don't worry. I can stay with Victor and Ananadkumari."

Victor and Ananadkumari, his wife, were two nurses whom Dr. Bethel had trained herself and of whom she was very proud. When they had gone to the village of Sundarijal to live so that they could treat minor ailments between the doctor's visits, they had steadily refused any help in fixing up their village home. "We want to do it ourselves. We want to use materials available to any other villager if he's willing to work," Victor explained. "A clean Christian home that is lived in like any other speaks louder than many words."

They had whitewashed the mud walls of their home themselves, built cabinets out of discarded wooden packing boxes that still said on the sides GLASS—HANDLE WITH CARE. HORLICK'S MALTED

MILK. The medicines were kept safe by heavy wired netting and padlocks they had to buy; they had also bought screens for the big downstairs windows and for the door to keep out the flies. But the clinic floor was of mud pounded as smooth as glass and Victor even made his own sink of cement. To be sure, the water ran directly down a drain into the backyard, but it was the only sink in the village. Anyone who wished could make one like it instead of dumping dirty water out onto the mud kitchen floor.

Victor also had his own ideas about building up self-respect. "A man values only what he pays for," he told Dr. Bethel. "We shouldn't give away all our medicines; we should charge what little a man can pay. Only if he has no money at all, we can give."

"But we promised to give our medicines," Dr. Bethel protested. "The government wants it that way."

"I will talk to the headman in the village," Victor said stubbornly. "He *is* the government in Sundarijal, the head of the local panchayat."

The headman sat cross-legged on a rug covering the mud floor of his house when Victor arrived. The headman could not read or write on paper but he could read life; he knew that the workings of a man's mind, the texture of his courage were as important as that his body be strong. Farmers needed muscles to swing the heavy hoe by which they broke up the clods of earth hardened almost into rock by the hot sun, so that the ground could be pulverized to plant maize or wheat. They needed strength to harrow and then to harvest, to store the grain in great circular bins surrounded by tightly wedged rustling corncobs so that no rat could gnaw its way in unheard. There was pride in the wisdom that garnered food for themselves, stored it safely for the winter. Whatever weakened that pride, that independence of spirit, was not good.

"I will think it over: I will advise you truly," the headman of the panchayat told Victor when he asked if the villagers could pay anything at all for the medicine they got at the clinic. Naturally, the nurse agreed, on an income of two rupees a day (twenty-six cents American) the farmer could hardly pay for a pill of chloromycetin that would cost a day's work. But perhaps he could make a token payment of a few pice (less than a penny)? "Give each patient a chit and leave the matter to me," the headman said firmly. "I will handle it."

Victor nodded, went out leaving the headman sitting quietly cross-legged, still meditating on what was best for his village. He had not long to wait to put his theories into practice. That very next day after Dr. Bethel's clinic, an incensed villager rushed to the headman to complain, "That clinic should be run out of here! They're making money, hand over fist. They had the nerve to charge me for this medicine!"

"Let me see your chit," the headman said, reaching out his hand. He read it gravely, looked up at the irate farmer.

"Fifty pice!" the farmer protested, shaking the twist of newspaper that held the medicine. "Two hours of hard work in the fields for ten little white pills! It is an outrage!"

"I paid ten rupees for the same medicine in the Kathmandu bazaar," the headman told the farmer quietly. "But it pleased me to pay. Because once I had paid, I owed no man anything at all. I was no man's servant, but my own master."

The farmer stared, his eyes widening. He, too, was a proud Nepali. *Now he owed no man anything, either.* He folded the twist of paper slowly about the pills, tucked them safely into his wide belt. "Perhaps," he agreed, "fifty pice is not too much to pay, after all. *Namaste.*" He folded his hands and went in peace.

"From then on, each has paid what he can and it is good, for there is more for everyone," Dr. Bethel thought as she bumped in the ambulance along over the eight miles of unpaved road to Sundarijal that morning, but the road was easier than that to Chapagaon, perhaps because it went out to the King's forest where the tall trees arched, lacy-leaved, over His Majesty's modest summer palace. The village must be prospering under the wise headman, she saw, for there was new paint, bright red, blue, and yellow, on the clothes of the gods at the Hindu shrine by the river. The engine gave a little cough, and she asked the driver anxiously, "Is the gas gone?"

"No. I think perhaps we get water in the gas these days." The driver shrugged. What he could not remedy did not bother him; what was to be, was.

"Are you two all right back there?" Dr. Bethel turned to look at her two patients. The old man with no legs was too tightly propped up in pillows to fall and the girl with the bad heart which could not be cured smiled back at Bethel. "Yes, Doctor. I am fine." But she was not fine; she would never be, Bethel thought. What brave people these were, these Nepalese whom she loved. A bed hardly got cool before a new patient came; Shanta Bhawan *had* to stay open. Perhaps by the time she got home this afternoon, the good news of a new shipment of kerosene from India would have come. If not . . . Dr. Berry had scheduled all the operations he could manage into this morning and afternoon, just in case the sterilizer could not be used tomorrow. Each day gained was something.

As the ambulance drew up at the front door of Victor and Ananadkumari's, Dr. Bethel looked down the long line of patients already squatting along the roadside, waiting. Men, women, little children . . . She counted sixty as far as she could see and there were more beyond. The yard was full of patients too, the bare mud yard where no grass grew: a baby whose eyes were swollen shut with pus was sucking from his mother's bare breast; old men who had never in their lives had enough to eat were shivering in spite of the thick scarves wound round and round their heads—they looked sixty or seventy but probably they were in their forties. Those she could help a little, but it was the babies who were important. If only she could teach the mothers how to care for them before they got the pus in their eyes, went blind. . . .

"*Namaste!* Good morning!" Dr. Bethel climbed down from the high front seat of the ambulance. "I see we have many patients, Victor."

"*Namaste*, Doctor!" Victor was bowing and smiling at his low front door which was also that of the clinic. "Yes, over eighty. They began to come at daybreak but I have arranged them all in line. Ananadkumari has put the medicines on your table; we can begin."

The tiny front room they used as a clinic was indeed ready, with a chair drawn up in front of the scrubbed wooden table where Dr. Bethel sat, the curtain drawn in front of the examining table in case she wanted to diagnose a patient more thoroughly. On the wall were Victor's two prized pictures someone had given him, an English calendar with on the top an impossibly bright-blue-robed Madonna and Child and a Currier and Ives print with (of all things) a New England picture of a "one-hoss open sleigh"! Usually this made Bethel smile inwardly but today Victor's reaching out for a wider world, his bustling importance as he ushered in the first patients, seemed somehow pathetic. He was a big frog kicking his legs in a little puddle; and so, Bethel reflected grimly, was she. What had she really accomplished in Nepal? She was only one doctor and there were still millions of patients. What was the matter with her today? With an effort she threw off her sense of foreboding, smiled at the little Nepalese family squatting on the mud floor in front of her, the old father, a man and his wife holding a baby sucking on an empty bottle. Bethel put out her arms for the baby and the mother smiled and handed him over.

"He's a fine boy," Dr. Bethel said in Hindi. But the red in the baby's dark hair indicated a serious vitamin deficiency. Dr. Bethel gently eased the bottle from the baby's fingers and he set up a loud howl. But bottles were too expensive for playthings; no bottle, no vitamins. The doctor handed the bottle to Ananadkumari to be filled, rubbed gentian violet on the ugly rash upon the baby's fat little neck, gave him a swift kiss on the cheek, and handed him back to his mother, who opened her dress to comfort him.

"The old fellow's eyes need a surgeon, but we do not yet have an eye specialist at Shanta Bhawan. Perhaps the Lord will send us one soon," Dr. Bethel remarked to Victor in English. "The husband has T.B. I think. Give him a pink card for Shanta Bhawan; tell him to go for a lab test."

He would have to walk the eight miles to the city, for there was no bus and he wouldn't have had the fare if there had been. His clothes were patches upon patches until it was hard to tell which was the original cloth. Then he would walk across Kathmandu another five miles to suburban Patan to the hospital—if it was not closed by then. As the little family went out with their vitamins and the pink card, Bethel saw the old fellow furtively trace a Hindu good-luck sign on his forehead; he was taking no chances with Christian medicine.

"Next patient, Victor."

The next patient had such a large tumor she looked pregnant; she must go to Shanta Bhawan for an operation, Bethel explained. The following patient had a thickening of the skin on her cheek; she was terrified of leprosy but Bethel thought it was only too much sun in the fields, but how could she stop work when the rice was ready? On and on they came, these worried people to whom Bethel's smile spoke reassurance; surely if the doctor could smile, there was no need to despair, even if pain like a tiger tore at one's belly.

On and on they came, twenty, thirty, forty . . . The air in the small room grew thick, almost unbreathable, and still they pushed inside the door, so many of them the screen door never shut so that the flies were terrible today on Bethel's face, on her hands using the stethoscope, even flies tangled in her hair. . . .

"It is time for lunch, Doctor," Victor said firmly. "My wife has made it ready." He raised his voice to shout, "The rest must wait!"

With a deep breath of relief Dr. Bethel climbed the two ladders that led to the long cool dim room on the top floor that was Victor's living room-kitchen-dining room. There were no screens at the small windows at each end but the breeeze blowing through kept the flies away and ruffled Ananadkumari's immaculate white flowing skirts. She was a strong robust woman with shining smooth dark hair and everything about her was immaculately clean: the baby on her arm with his bright eyes and rosy cheeks, the bright brass pots and pans shining in a basket under the eves, the towels drying on a line across the room. Dr. Bethel settled down on the wooden bench in front of the long home-made table, beside Victor.

"That curry looks wonderful. You're a good cook, Ananadkumari."

The food was hot, strong, and sweet and there was delicious whey to spread on the thick bread and hot, hot tea. "What on earth is that peeping noise?" Bethel demanded. Victor sprang up to lift a tall basket in the corner of the living-room floor and out stepped a proud hen with eight tiny yellow chicks. "She knows it is time for her lunch too," Victor said with a laugh as he threw them some grain. "Those are the baby's playmates."

Laughter, that was what made this family different, Bethel thought; as you went along the streets of Kathmandu, people might smile but you seldom heard anyone laugh aloud. She pushed back her plate. "That was a real treat, Ananadkumari. Well, I suppose we must get back downstairs. I want to take a look at the builders before I leave."

She had finally inveigled the money from the mission budget to renovate two village houses here for the well-child clinics she wanted so badly. The sick patients could still be treated here at Victor's but two resident nurses were just waiting for the other clinic to be finished, to come there to live, a German midwife and Nurse Isla Knight. She was the wise experienced pioneer who had scrubbed the floors of the old cholera hospital, and now ran the Shanta Bhawan clinics. She would be missed there but her heart, like Dr. Bethel's, was with the children who must not only be cured but be taught how to keep well. Already Nurse Knight was saving seeds to plant, to turn the mud yard into a garden around the houses. She would give some seeds to the mothers who came to see the midwife and soon the whole village would be in bloom.

Four hours and fifty patients later Bethel was free to inspect the new well-child clinic and the house where the nurses would live. The pounding of the carpenters grew louder and the cloud of dust coming out the doorless opening looked industrious as she approached down the village street. The living room would be the big room in front, with two bedrooms upstairs, while downstairs would be the bathroom, native style with a hole in the cement floor and a cold-water tap, and the goat shed was being turned into a guest room for the doctor if she had to stay the night with a sick patient. Or perhaps sometime there would be a resident pediatrician. . . .

"*Namaste*, Doctor!"

A well-dressed young Nepali man who had braked his bicycle beside her in the village street got off his machine to greet Dr. Bethel with a low bow. She wished she could recall his name; he was a graduate student she'd met at the University; she knew so many it was hard to keep them straight. Dr. Bob had said jokingly that Bethel could go into the bushes anywhere in Nepal and come out with a Rana on one arm and an untouchable on the other, and she the link between them. "Nonsense!" she'd sputtered, but his nonsense lightened the heavy load of other people's pain. She wished suddenly he were here.

"It is good to see you," she told the student. "Why are you not at your examinations? I read in the paper they had begun."

"I am just back from Lhasa. I was one of the committee to settle the border dispute between Tibet and Nepal," he explained. A small young man but strong, he wore his Nepali cap with an air. "I came fast, for the new road from Lhasa is a fine one right to the Nepal border." So now when the Chinese finished the road that connected with the Rajpath, the way to India across Nepal would be open. Would this be good or evil? Would they get more food and kerosene? Or would the Chinese guns roar through to India? Who could tell? "I had hoped to take my exams this time, to get my degree as Doctor of Education, but tomorrow I must go north again to inspect some schools." The student sighed and then smiled. "I suppose to have good village schools is more important than my being called 'Doctor.' Anyway it is ordered, so I go."

"*Namaste*, peace go with you," Bethel said.

"The most encouraging thing in a long time is the way these university students are accepting national responsibility," Dr. Bethel told Dr. Bob when she got back to Shanta Bhawan in time for the late tea which Nucchi brought in. Dr. Bethel, weary to her bones, noticed that the cook had put a newly picked fragrant bunch of sweet peas in the center of the table and he had made the sandwich filling Dr. Bob liked best, little sardines with lemon. He must have opened the last can from home. What was the special occasion? Nucchi always had a reason. She glanced at him but the little Nepalese did not meet her eyes, so she went on telling Bob, "Too many students think only of getting themselves a better job with more pay. It is encouraging to find a young Nepali who knows all wisdom is not in books, that one who gives, gets. . . . Yes, Nucchi, what is it?" He was still standing there in his red corduroy coat cut down from one of Dr. Bob's old ones for a uniform; he must have some problem on his mind.

"No dinner I cook," Nucchi reported. "Is no more kerosenes."

So that was why he'd given them this special tea. Before Dr. Bethel could answer, there came a knock on the living-room door which Nucchi went to open. A strong, sturdy woman in nurse's uniform and a white cap stood there, Lena Graber, the Menonite who was the head of the nurses' training school, who knew as much as most doctors. She still had her black bag in her hand from the case she'd been out on all night and she looked as tired as Dr. Bethel felt.

"Come in, Lena. You're just in time for a cup of tea." Dr. Bethel reached to fill a fresh cup and the nurse sank gratefully into the Flemings' easy chair under the marching brass camels. "Did the Rana baby come all right?"

"I'm just back. It's a lovely little girl." Lena Graber reached hungrily for a sandwich. "It was quite a night. I had to sit beside the mother, hold the baby still attached for half an hour till the auspicious moment arrived when we could cut the cord and the baby be born officially!"

"That's one reason why I never make a home delivery any more," Dr. Bethel reminded the nurse. "I want them to come to the hospital."

"These young people wanted to but the head of the family said 'No!' It was a very special case. The young husband had just spent a year studying at Oxford where his wife had learned to keep house; she'd never even boiled rice before. But they're both modern in their ideas. When she found she was pregnant they planned to come to Shanta Bhawan to have the baby delivered. But Grandpa and Grandma were traveling in Europe; when they heard what was happening, they rushed to England, made the son promise to have his first child at home, in the ancient Rana custom."

"I know. They came to me, begging, 'You've got to help us!

You never know what'll go wrong with a first baby, Doctor!' That's why I sent you. Was it a difficult delivery, Lena?"

"Not too difficult, just prolonged labor—fortunately," Lena Graber reported. "When the prospective mother's pains started, they sent for me and I found the whole palace in a terrible flutter. They have their own priests, of course, like all wealthy Ranas, who had just told the frightened family that there couldn't possibly be any more inauspicious time for a baby to be born!"

"Goodness, what was wrong?"

"The priests said that if the baby was born now, the father couldn't see it for twelve years," Lena Graber told the Flemings. "That would be kind of tough, wouldn't it? I pointed out not much could be done to delay the birth once it started. The four sisters-in-law who were fluttering around—you never saw such lovely saris as they had on, silver tissue, with rose-red bands—they said I didn't understand. A baby wasn't born actually till you cut the cord! I started to say things moved pretty fast about that time, to delay might be dangerous for both mother and baby, then I shut up. No need to cross that bridge until we came to it. First babies usually take longer anyway.

"The hours went by; the mother was in hard labor but the baby hadn't come. The priests kept running in and out making announcements. The time seemed to be getting more and more auspicious. Now it would be only twelve months the father would have to wait to see the newborn baby; then they got it down to twelve days, then twelve hours. If baby held off until two this afternoon, everything would be fine, everybody happy and auspicious." Lena Graber chuckled, took a sip of hot tea, and admitted, "You know I got to counting the minutes too? I couldn't help myself. When the hands of the clock passed two, I could have cheered. The baby was born twenty minutes later. I was as happy as the family! I just sat there, beaming, holding her in my lap till the oldest sister-in-law finished the Hindu rites, and I could cut the cord."

"Did you remember to sterilize them . . . the old button, the piece of string, the knife, and the piece of gold money?" Dr. Bethel asked.

"Of course. Was I relieved when the ceremony of bathing the new baby began! Her aunt poured water over her out of a silver pitcher with a lip of gold, the only fit metal to touch a Rana baby. The women of the household sat outside the open door singing a gay chant, 'Unto us a child is born, a beautiful little girl.' It was lovely, really . . . after the suspense was over."

"Think what such a delivery would have meant in an untouchable home where the family lives up over a stable, where the doctor has to stumble over chickens, pigs, maybe nudge aside a water buffalo before she can climb the ladder with all her equipment to get upstairs to the patient! No, I want the mothers to come here to the hospital where they'll be safe. It isn't enough for a baby to be born; he's got to live." Dr. Bethel pushed back the tea table. "Well, I have to make my ward rounds. Nucchi, you still here? What is it now?"

"No dinner, no kerosenes," Nucchi insisted anxiously.

"I know. I'll talk to you later when I get back."

No kerosene. The nurse's eyes opened wider; she knew what that meant. That was what was worrying Dr. Bethel; if the Flemings' kerosene was gone, maybe the hospital tank was empty too. "I'll make rounds with you," she offered.

Dr. Bethel straightened her shoulders under her white coat with the stethoscope in the pocket. "Thank you, but no."

There were some things you had to face alone. Her feet felt heavy as she went down the veranda steps, across the grass of the lawn, climbed up the cement steps to the hospital's screen door. She stood for a moment just inside the lobby, drawing strength to herself to do what she must, to tell the hospital staff. She'd trusted so hard in the Lord's Plan for Nepal; it had never let her down before. When they'd needed a resident surgeon so badly, Dr. Bob Berry had come; she couldn't think how they'd managed without him. When the blood bank ran out, the American Expedition doctors had given them some transfusion kits. Then an ordinary thing like kerosene could defeat you. Well, you'd prayed and you'd worked and you'd trusted and now you'd come to the end of the road. You'd have to tell the staff that tomorrow there'd be no operations and maybe the next day you'd have to close the wards. . . .

"Telephone for you, Doctor!" the desk man called across the lobby to where Bethel stood, irresolute. "It's the Embassy. The ambassador's been trying to reach you all afternoon."

"I've come to show you the laughing thrush that I named for Bethel." Dr. Bob came bouncing cheerfully into the hospital Memorial Room, laying upon my bed a small bird with blue wings. It was beautiful like the woman he loved. "I just finished stuffing it. Feel how soft it is." The feathers of the blue wings were like satin under my fingers; the bird had a throat and underbody as softly white as Dr. Bethel's own lovely crown of hair. "Garrulous Affinis Bethelai," Dr. Bob intoned its Latin name. His eyes twinkled. "Garrulous because she's a lady . . . why, Bethel!"

"Bob! *Bobby!*" The wise, calm doctor of medicine had burst into the room as excited as a child. "The ambassador's sending us three barrels of kerosene! We won't have to close Shanta Bhawan!"

Stars sang in her voice, her face was radiant as she rushed on. "Some government jeeps just came over the Rajpath with kerosene; he says we can buy what we need from them till the war emergency is over! *The Lord's Plan didn't fail us, after all!*" Was it perhaps she herself who had failed? The light drained out of Dr. Bethel's face; she began to tremble. Her eyes were suddenly wet as she asked him who knew intimately even her weakness, "What was wrong with me? How could I possibly have doubted that we'd be taken care of?"

"Without doubt, there would be no need of mercy," he comforted her gently. "No real faith. You're human, darling, like me."

He smoothed the soft feathers of the garrulous affinus Bethelai as if it were her own hand he was caressing, Dr. Bethel's wise hand which had comforted so many. "Aye, aye, aye, aye!" The room was suddenly filled with the sound of music, the soft minor strumming on a harmonium, the gay sound of a boy's voice singing in Nepali. Dr. Bob's smile widened. "Listen, Bethel. Do you hear what he's saying? Samson has made a new song!"

> "I don't know about tomorrow
> I don't worry what will come.
> For I know Who walks beside me
> And I know Who holds my hand. . . ."

They stood there, comforted and together, listening to the hospital messenger boy singing his own story of what he had learned at Shanta Bhawan. If the two Doctor Flemings had come to Nepal on the wings of a bird, Samson had learned how to fly, too. Could it be their very humanness had taught him how?

> "There's an ending to the rainbow
> Where the mountains touch the sky
> So his presence is a brightness
> On earth and in the sky.
> Many things about tomorrow
> I don't seem to understand;
> But I know Who holds tomorrow
> In the hollow of His hand."